Lincolnshire
COUNTY COUNCIL

COMMUNITIES, CULTURAL SERVICES
and ADULT EDUCATION
**This book should be returned on or before
the last** ~~d~~

LINCOLN CENTRAL
TEL: 01522 782010

D1375903

GRANTHAM LIBRARY

1 3 MAY 2009

0 4 MAR 2011

01522 782010

~11 DEC 2009

WITHDRAWN
FOR SALE

renew or order library books please telephone 01522 782010
or visit www.lincolnshire.gov.uk
You will require a Personal Identification Number.
Ask any member of staff for this.

EC. 199 (LIBS): RS/L5/19

1 3 MAY 20□□   □□ MAR 20□□   □□ MAY 20□□

The **Rough Guide** to

Walks in London &
Southeast England

written and researched by

Helena Smith

with additional contributions by

Judith Bamber

NEW YORK • LONDON

www.roughguides.

AD 04448165

Lincolnshire
County Council

AD 04448165

Askews

914.21

Contents

Introduction 4

1 London.......................... 13
Regent's Canal........................ 15
The Parkland Walk 20
Hampstead Heath 25
The Thames Towpath 31
Richmond Park 37
The Grand Union Canal 42
Downe and around................. 46
Limehouse Basin 51
Walthamstow Marshes 56
Epping Forest 63

2 The North Downs 69
Box Hill 71
Guildford to Compton 76
Gomshall and the North
  Downs 82
The Pilgrims' Way 86

3 The Weald 99
The Eden Valley..................... 101
The Greensand Way............... 107
The High Weald Walk 112
Bayham Abbey....................... 119

4 The South Downs........ 127
Along the Arun 129
Cissbury Ring........................ 135
Mount Caburn and the South
  Downs 141
The South Downs Way 147

5 The Saxon Shore 159
The Saxon Shore Way........... 161
The 1066 Country Walk......... 168
Chichester Harbour............... 178

**6 The North Wessex Downs
  to the New Forest** 183
The Ridgeway 185
The North Wessex Downs 195
Stonehenge........................... 199
The New Forest..................... 206

7 The Thames Valley...... 211
Windsor Great Park............... 213
The Thames Towpath and the
  Chiltern Way....................... 219
Roman Silchester.................. 224

**8 The Chilterns and
  Blenheim**...................... 229
The Misbourne Valley........... 231
The Northern Chilterns 236
Ivinghoe Beacon 243
Around Blenheim Palace....... 250

**9 St Albans to
  Bedfordshire**................ 257
The Lea Valley Way 259
St Albans and around........... 265
Woburn Estate 273

**10 Essex, Cambridge and
  the Fens** 279
Along the River Stort............. 281
Uttlesford 286
Along the Cam 292
The Fens 298

Index 305

Introduction to

Walks in London & Southeast England

Few cities can rival London's distinctive mix of the urban and the pastoral. Despite being the largest city in Western Europe, home to a staggering 7.5 million people, the capital preserves surprisingly extensive stretches of green space.

In fact, over a third of it is made up of greenery, not only in the famous parks and gardens, but also in less obvious places – canalside paths, disused railway tracks and reclaimed industrial land – as well as along the banks of the Thames as it winds through the city. These hidden footpaths are thoroughly enjoyable in themselves, and also offer a fascinating insight into the social, architectural and industrial history that went into the making of one of the world's most vibrant cities.

Despite the sprawl of suburbs that girdles the city, many parts of **southeast England** remain almost miraculously unspoilt. Fast train services make it very easy to reach open countryside from just about anywhere in London – indeed, it's surprising just how far from the capital you can get in a single day and still have time for a rewarding walk and a great pub lunch.

To the south and west of the capital there's sweeping **downland**: the lush North Downs and the barer and more open North Wessex and South Downs. You'll find spectacular stretches of **coast** – from the towering sandstone cliffs at Hastings to the wavy chalk formations further west – as well as areas of dense ancient **woodland**, which are at their most extensive in the New Forest. The **Thames** cuts a green swathe west of the capital, linking a chain of attractive towns and villages, while to the north are the pristine wooded **hills** of the Chilterns and the limitless flatlands of the **Fens** around Ely. The striking variety of landscapes around the city is part of the attraction – from the prettily manicured landscapes of the Kent Weald to the hauntingly bleak chalk uplands of the Wessex Downs.

As with London itself, the southeast has always been a densely inhabited area, and the impact of human activity on the land, while more diffuse, is no less profound, visible in Iron Age forts, medieval field terraces and grand country-house estates. All the landscapes described in this guide, even the bogs of the New Forest and the windswept crests of the South Downs, bear the marks of cultivation: a vast testament to the people who cleared, drained, shaped and even – in the case of the prehistoric chalk figures that dot the region – drew upon the land for millennia.

How to use this book

▲ SILCHESTER

The walks in this book have been designed to be accessible from the capital as **day-trips** using public transport; we've also included some two-day **weekend walks** (although these can also be broken down and done as separate day-trips). Each walk includes a map, route details, background historical information and a recommended lunch stop, often in one of the fine old pubs that dot the region.

The walks are geared to **public transport**, either starting from one train station and finishing at another, or circling back to the station where you started. At the beginning of each account we've given details of the relevant train services; we haven't recommended specific trains, partly because timetables are subject to change, and also to avoid being prescriptive. Most walks outside London are within an hour's train journey of the city, although we've stretched this criterion where we think a really great walk justifies a longer journey. For all but the very longest routes, starting your train journey at around 10am will ensure that you can get to the specified pub for lunch and do the walk in good time.

There's at least one circular walk in each chapter, convenient if you're **driving**, although virtually all the non-circular walks can also be done by drivers, who need only make a short train trip back to the beginning of the walk to pick up their cars.

....

For information on train times, journey durations and costs call
℡ 08457/484950 or see ⓦ www.nationalrail.co.uk. For travel in the
capital, go to ⓦ www.tfl.gov.uk.

....

Five of the best: buildings

Blenheim Palace Vanbrugh's magisterial monument to the victory of the Duke of Marlborough over the French – part stately home, part mausoleum. See p.254

Ely Cathedral The "ship of the Fens", whose mighty bulk is adorned with delicate stone tracery, dominates the surrounding country from its clay island. See p.302

Hampton Court One of the most spectacular sights along the Thames, this Tudor masterpiece was home to Henry VIII and Oliver Cromwell, amongst others. See p.35

Ightham Mote Half-timbered, moated and packed with fascinating artefacts: the quintessential English manor house. See p.109

Watts Chapel A Byzantine-style chapel in the Surrey countryside, whose interior features a lyrical and lovely decorative scheme. See p.79

▲ HAMPTON COURT

Five of the best: pubs

The Garden Gate A cheerful, buzzy place with a big garden, on the edge of Hampstead Heath. Generous portions of food and farm cider on tap. See p.30

The Harrow Inn An archetypal Kentish village pub, which serves award-winning grub. See p.109

The Ram Spectacularly located at the foot of the South Downs, with good lunches, local ales and a ghost upstairs. See p.144

The Stag & Huntsman A cheery and busy place, located in the attractive brick and flint village of Hambleden in the Chilterns. See p.222

The Swan Tasty organic food is the draw at the seventeenth-century *Swan*, on the edge of the North Wessex Downs. See p.197

Ticket prices can be surprisingly high, even for shortish journeys, so it's worth investigating the range of discount **railcards** on offer, which give discounts of up to a third. **Young persons** (aged 16–25; ⓦwww.16-25railcard.co.uk) and **senior** (60 years and over; ⓦwww .senior-railcard.co.uk) railcards are accepted on all train lines; both cost £24 per year. **Network Railcards** (ⓦwww.railcard.co.uk; £20 per year) give the holder and three other adults savings of a third on off-peak journeys. Other types of travelcard, from one-day two-zone cards to annual all-zone ones, should get you some discount on the price of your train ticket – it's always worth asking about this, as you're unlikely to be told. It's best to **buy your train ticket** be-

fore getting on board; on many lines, you aren't permitted to buy a cheap-day return from the conductor and you can get stung for a ticket that costs almost twice as much.

In the interest of making every walk a great day out, we've recommended the very best **pubs** and cafés along the way.

These are often housed in exceptional old buildings, and we've also tried to uncover places that dish up especially good but reasonably priced food – mains average £7–9. Phone numbers are given for all the pubs listed – most stop serving **lunch** at 2pm, but if you think you're going to arrive later it's worth phoning ahead to say you're on your way. They will generally put aside cold food – a Ploughman's or a sarnie – for you.

The **distance** of each walk is flagged at the top of each account, and the level of **difficulty** is indicated alongside. The grading system we've used – "easy", "moderate", and "strenuous" – assumes average fitness. At the start of each walk we calculate how long it will take, but this doesn't factor in any stops and is based on a fairly steady 4km per hour. Metres and kilometres are used throughout the guide – to figure out the distances in miles, multiply the number of kilometres by 0.62.

The **maps** in this book are sourced from Ordnance Survey originals, with the route and the places you

What to take

To avoid forgetting something crucial for your walk, here's a **checklist**, in rough order of importance. Some of the items on this list are optional, some are seasonal and most are obvious. It goes without saying that you should wear a decent pair of waterproof walking shoes or boots; muddiness can be a feature of these walks even in summer, and trudging along with wet feet is a real misery.

Water bottle

Waterproof jacket/cagoule and trousers

Spare layer – jumper or fleece

Sun cream

Antihistamine

Plasters

Camera

pass along the way picked out in colour. Our maps also show contours and the surrounding roads and paths, so, combined with the route details in the text, they should keep you on the right track. However, to view the walks in a fuller context, you may want to take the relevant **Ordnance Survey Landranger** (1:50,000) or **Explorer** (1:25,000) maps – we've listed these at the start of each account. For sights, EH denotes English Heritage and NT National Trust: take the relevant membership card with you.

The first chapter of this guide covers **London** itself, its canal, river and woodland walks. Subsequent chapters move clockwise round the capital, starting with the green ridges of the **North Downs** and the bountiful **Weald**, followed by the undulating **South Downs**. The **Saxon Shore** chapter explores a stretch of Sussex coast, much of it reclaimed from the sea over the last thousand years; next comes the chalky **North Wessex Downs**, dotted with prehistoric remains, and then the **New Forest**, which comprises great tracts of ancient forest and heathland. **The Thames Valley** chapter describes a prosperous, attractive corner of the southeast, while to the north

Five of the best: wildlife spotting

The Arun The Arun River near Arundel sees a multitude of geese and ducks, as well as rare migratory birds. See p.133

The Fens The watery fens provide a home for many wetland birds, including widgeons and redshanks. See p.298

The New Forest Timid otters, dainty sika deer and small shaggy ponies. See p.206

The Pett Levels Crisscrossed by water channels, the Levels attract a mass of birdlife, especially herons and swans. See p.164

Woburn Huge herds of deer plus a safari park full of elephants, zebras and other African wildlife. See p.273

NEW FOREST PONIES

Five of the best: Roman remains

Anderida A still formidable ring of Roman walls, built to keep Saxon pirates at bay. See p.168

Calleva This major Roman settlement escaped subsequent development, and the town walls and amphitheatre remain remarkably intact. See p.227

Fishbourne Palace Features the finest in-situ mosaic floors in the country. See p.179

North Leigh Roman Villa The scant but evocative remnants of a Roman villa, set in a green valley. See p.256

Verulamium Dotted around a spacious park in St Albans, these are the remains of a major Roman trading post. See p.268

FISHBOURNE PALACE

lies the chalky escarpment of **the Chilterns**. **Hertfordshire** and **Bedfordshire** are home to a string of attractive market towns surrounded by plentiful Roman and Celtic remains. To the north of London, gentle riverside walks in **Essex** give way to the flat, watery farmlands and wide open skies of the bleak **Fenlands**.

There are three **two-day walks** in this guide which cover sections of established routes: the Pilgrims' Way leads through hop gardens, orchards and forests to Canterbury (see p.86); the South Downs Way provides a stretching hike along the downs and the white cliffs (see p.147); and the Ridgeway, the oldest road in the country, takes you to Neolithic tombs, Iron Age forts and the famous White Horse (see p.185). For these routes we give suggestions for **accommodation** as well as eating and, as with the recommended pubs, we've tried to suggest places that are out of the ordinary, from B&Bs in historic houses to a stunningly located youth hostel.

Five of the best: afternoon teas

Fir Tree House Tearooms Loose-leaf tea, home-made cakes and a lovely Kent garden – what more could you ask for? See p.105

Orchard House Tearooms Make like Rupert Brooke and enjoy tea and scones on a deckchair in this paradisal Cambridgeshire orchard. See p.294

Peacocks Tearoom Ely boasts this deliciously inviting and homey tearoom, which has been voted the best in the country. See p.302

Petersham Nurseries An elegant option for a secluded afternoon cuppa, with abundant greenery, exotic antiques scattered about and excellent food. See p.39

Watts Gallery Tearoom Unhinge your jaws to make way for the giant cakes on offer at this eccentric former pottery at the Watts Gallery near Guildford. See p.78

Where appropriate, we've suggested when might be a good **time of year** for a particular walk: Windsor Great Park, for example, is at its best in late spring with the rhododendrons and azaleas in full bloom, while the orchards of Kent dazzle with blossom in spring and have a more mellow allure in autumn, when the trees are heavy with fruit. But, in general, any time of year is a good time to do these walks and, in the temperate climate of southern England, you're unlikely to encounter truly wild weather. There are, of course, fewer hours of daylight for winter walks, but the austere beauty of wintry landscapes can hold as much appeal as more verdant summer ones.

EPPING FOREST

1

London

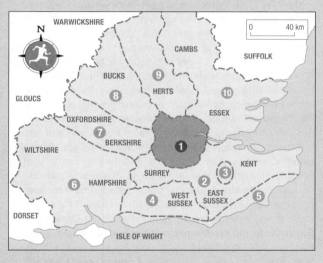

Regent's Canal

Camden Lock to Little Venice 15

The Parkland Walk

Finsbury Park to Alexandra
Palace 20

Hampstead Heath

Across the heath to Kenwood 25

The Thames Towpath

Richmond to Hampton Court 31

Richmond Park

Petersham and the park 37

The Grand Union Canal

Horsenden Hill and around 42

Downe and around

Chelsfield to Down House 46

Limehouse Basin

Bethnal Green to Wapping 51

Walthamstow Marshes

Hackney to Walthamstow 56

Epping Forest

Queen Elizabeth's Lodge to Connaught
Water 63

Greater London doesn't immediately spring to mind as a place for a quiet, off-road walk, though even the most urban of the capital's landscapes can conceal surprisingly sylvan patches of greenery. Paradoxically, it's the remnants of the capital's Victorian industrial age – the nineteenth-century **canals** and **railways** which did so much to shape London – that now provide some of its best walks. There are also surviving pockets of ancient **woodland**, notably at Highgate and Epping, and some glorious stretches of towpath along the **Thames**. All the walks in this chapter are within the girdle of the M25, and within **travel zones** 1–6.

The first route follows an elegant, willow-lined stretch of the **Regent's Canal** as it heads west from Camden through Regent's Park to bohemian Little Venice; the second is the unusual **Parkland Walk**, a verdant corridor that follows the course of a former railway to Highgate Wood and Alexandra Palace; while the third takes in the celebrated beauty of **Hampstead Heath**. In leafy west London, water is the connecting thread: two enchanting walks lead along the **Thames Towpath**, from Richmond to Hampton Court, and from Richmond along the river to Petersham and into the heart of massive **Richmond Park**, while the **Grand Union Canal** snakes below the less known territory of wooded Horsenden Hill. In the south of the city, the rustic walk to **Downe** takes you from city suburbs into deep countryside, with a stop-off at Darwin's House. To the east, you can explore the watery landscape of the **Limehouse Basin**, while the **Walthamstow Marshes** route links urban Hackney with Walthamstow, via canals and open marshland. North from here, expansive **Epping Forest** offers a surprisingly rural landscape.

REGENT'S CANAL

Camden Lock to Little Venice

Distance and difficulty 5km; easy.
Duration 1hr 15min.
Trains Northern Line to Camden Town (zone 2); return on the
Bakerloo Line from Warwick Avenue (zone 2).
Map OS Landranger 176: *West London*; OS Explorer 173: *London
North*.

The **Regent's Canal**, completed in 1820, was constructed as part
of a direct link from Birmingham to the newly built London
docks. This enticing and secluded stretch along the canal's
towpath starts off at **Camden Market**, but soon leaves the city
streets behind to follow the canal through leafy **Primrose Hill**
and around the northern edge of **Regent's Park** and **London
Zoo**, passing right by Lord Snowdon's colossal tetrahedral aviary. The walk ends at the canal basin of **Little Venice**, with

Building the Regent's Canal

The **Regent's Canal** was designed to link the Grand Union Canal,
which terminated at Paddington, with the docks on the Thames at
Limehouse. A company to oversee the construction and running
of the canal was established in 1812; one of its directors was the
celebrated architect **John Nash** – it was Nash who secured the
patronage of the Prince Regent (later George IV), after whom the
canal is named. Despite royal approval, the project suffered from
a couple of significant early reverses. In 1815, one of the canal
company's directors, Thomas Homer, was convicted of embezzling
canal funds and sentenced to transportation, while in 1818 an
experimental new lock at Hampstead had to be scrapped at great
cost in favour of a conventional system. In all, the project came
in at twice its original budget and four years behind schedule.
The canal was finally opened in 1820, though its problems didn't
end there. By 1835, it was running short of water and the River
Brent had to be dammed and diverted to fill it – and the resultant
reservoir had to be extended in 1837, and again in 1854. The
most dramatic event in the canal's history, however, occurred in
1874, when a barge carrying gunpowder exploded at Macclesfield
Bridge – or "Blow Up Bridge", as it subsequently became known.
Despite such mishaps, it was continuously used as a commercial
route until the mid-twentieth century; it's now used exclusively for
recreational purposes.

its narrow boats cheerfully decorated with flowers and painted pots. From here, you can head back to Camden Market by canal boat or home from Warwick Avenue **tube**, just a few hundred metres north of Little Venice.

With two excellent **cafés** along the way and a **pub** at the end, you won't go hungry or thirsty on this route.

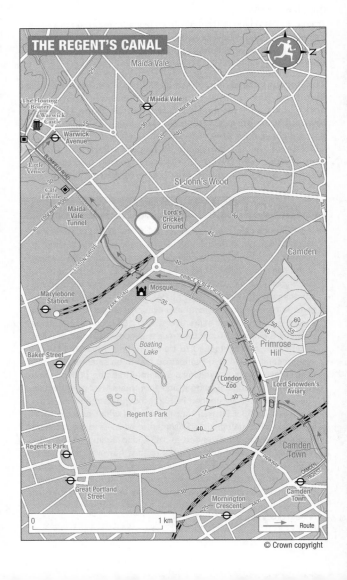

© Crown copyright

Getting started

0.5km

Take the right-hand exit out of **Camden tube**, turn right and head up Camden High Street for 200m to **Camden Lock**. Turn left just before the bridge over the canal, joining the canal-side path on its south side right by the lock. A few metres ahead, a wrought-iron bridge crosses the canal at the boundary wall of the market court-yard. Cross this bridge and turn left along the northern bank of the canal, or turn into the market.

The arrival of the canal in Camden led to a period of rapid devel-opment as the city sprawled north, and by the end of the Victorian era Camden Town had become one of the capital's most notorious slums. Camden is now best known for its **market**, centred on a cobbled courtyard amidst disused timber wharves and warehouses.

Primrose Hill to Regent's Park

3km

The towpath continues past slick new apartment buildings and under three crumbling Victorian bridges as you walk through affluent **Primrose Hill**. The attractive gardens of Georgian town houses tumble down the opposite bank, while the spire of Victorian **St Mark's Church** pokes up above the willows ahead.

At St Mark's the canal turns west, passing under two more Victorian wrought-iron footbridges and running on through the northern edges of **London Zoo**. Most of the zoo lies to the south of the canal, but the northern reaches – most notably the tent-like, aluminium-framed **aviary** designed by Lord Snowdon in the 1960s, which looms right above the towpath to your right – run beyond the canal and right up to Prince Albert Road, at the perimeter of Regent's Park. There are good views into the enclosures from the canal, but if you'd like to see more of the zoo consider getting the combined **boat and zoo ticket** from the Waterbus Company at Little Venice (see p.18).

Beyond the zoo, the canal continues around the northern edge of **Regent's Park**, passing under Macclesfield Bridge and past several grandiose Victorian mansions, built in a rather crass Palladian style, while behind rises the minaret of **Regent's Park Mosque**. A few metres beyond the last of the mansions, the canal reaches the western boundary of the park.

Maida Hill Tunnel and Edgware Road

1km

Beyond the park, you become aware of the city streets again as you pass through the lower reaches of **St John's Wood**. About

750m beyond Regent's Park, the canal disappears into **Maida Hill Tunnel**, a 250-metre-long tunnel under Edgware Road, too narrow and low for a towpath (it's so small, in fact, that traffic lights have to be used to control the movements of barges through the tunnel). The path heads up the steep flight of steps just to the right of the tunnel, bringing you out onto **Aberdeen Place**, which leads to Edgware Road, on the far side of which the canal emerges from the Maida Hill Tunnel.

Swanky *Café Laville* (Mon–Sat 10am–10.30pm, Sun 10am–1pm; ☏020/7706 2620) straddles the west end of Maida Hill Tunnel, on Edgware Road. Superbly located, with views from its picture window along the leafy Blomfield Road Moorings, it serves brunches, pasta dishes, salads and cakes.

Blomfield Road Moorings and Little Venice

0.5km

Cross Edgware Road and head on down **Blomfield Road**, which flanks the north bank of the canal where it emerges from Maida Hill Tunnel. The wrought-iron railings between the road and the canal mark the boundary of the private **Blomfield Road Moorings**, home to dozens of colourful houseboats festooned with potted flower tubs, painted metal jugs, quirky furniture, topiary figures and other unusual bric-a-brac. The towpath forms part of the moorings, so you'll have to follow Blomfield Road for the first few hundred metres before rejoining the towpath just before Warwick Avenue.

A few metres ahead the path heads under a road bridge and comes out at the canal basin of **Little Venice**. A pool formed by the junction of the Paddington Branch and the Regent's Canal, this spot was formerly known as **Browning's Pool**, after the poet Robert Browning, who once lived in a house overlooking it and is credited with giving the basin its Italianate name. Today, the canal is still home to an artistic community, with three barge-based businesses – a puppet theatre, art gallery and café – adding to the bohemian atmosphere.

Moored on the southern side of the canal, *The Floating Boater* (daily 9am–5pm; ☏020/7266 1066) barge serves inexpensive toasted sandwiches, jacket potatoes, tea and coffee on board and at canal-side tables.

Head over the wrought-iron bridge to the left bank of the canal for a boat back to Camden: the **Waterbus Company** (☏020/7482 2660; £6 or £16.50 including entrance to the zoo) runs year round between Little Venice and Camden Lock, making a couple of stops along the way. Alternatively, double back along the northern bank of the canal for **Warwick Avenue tube** (zone 2), 200m north along Warwick Avenue itself. Before you reach the tube, a left turn down Warwick Place brings you to the attractive *Warwick Castle* **pub**, a snug place with wood panelling and Victorian stained glass.

THE PARKLAND WALK

Finsbury Park to Alexandra Palace

Distance and difficulty 9.5km; easy.
Duration 2hr.
Trains Victoria Line tube or overground train from King's Cross to
Finsbury Park (zone 2); return by overground train from Alexandra
Palace (zone 3) to King's Cross.
Map OS Landranger 176: *West London*; OS Explorer 173:
London North.

The **Parkland Walk** follows the course of the former **Great
Northern Railway**, which was dismantled and transformed into
a footpath in the mid-1980s. Starting in Finsbury Park, the walk
follows the leafy corridor of the former railway through cuttings
and across embankments to **Highgate**, then continues through
Queen's Wood and **Highgate Wood**, two remnants of the Forest
of Middlesex, the once-great tract of woodland that covered the
whole of the north London area. Beyond the woods, the walk
resumes along the course of a former branch line of the railway to
the sprawling Victorian **Alexandra Palace**. For **lunch**, secluded
Queen's Wood Café is a great option.

Getting started

0.5km

Head out of the main exit at **Finsbury Park tube station** (follow
signs for Station Place) and turn left across Stroud Green Road.
Just to the left of Rowan's tenpin bowling alley, go through the
metal gate by the cycle park and follow the gravel path to the left
signed "**Capital Ring**". Beyond the tennis courts you come to a
T-junction; turn left here, following the sign to Highgate. You
cross a small footbridge over the railway, then turn sharp right to
join the course of the former Great Northern railway.

Finsbury Park to Crouch End station

2.5km

The disused railway soon climbs to higher ground, widening out
and cutting a broad swathe through the city sprawl. It starts to
feel positively rural, with the wooded hilltops of Highgate and
Hampstead ahead of you, and the suburban development on either
side obscured by trees and bushes.

After about 1.5km, the path dips under **Crouch Hill** road by way
of a Victorian arched bridge. A few hundred metres beyond you

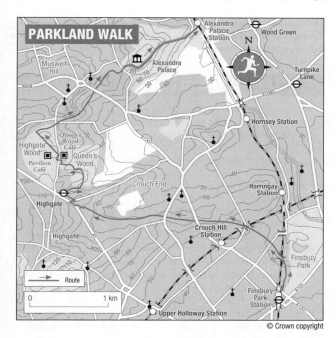

© Crown copyright

come to the ghostly ruins of **Crouch End station**, whose weed-strewn platforms and arches constitute the most intact railway remains along the entire route. Don't miss the sculpted **Green Man** (see box, p.22), climbing out of the fifth arch from the right. Crowned with oak leaves, this impish figure – the work of local artist Marilyn Collins – represents the pagan spirit of renewal, his arms clasping the arch as he pulls himself out from the undergrowth. Incorporated in the modern bridge at the far end of the station platform is all that is left of the old station building; overgrown steps to the right lead down from the old ticket office.

Highgate terminus

1.5km

Beyond the old station, the route continues for another 1.5km through a dell-like cutting up to **Highgate**. The first part of the Parkland Walk ends here, a couple of hundred metres before the cavernous tunnels just south of Highgate Station. The old rail line continued through these tunnels, calling at Highgate Station before reaching Alexandra Palace, but the tunnels have long since become overgrown and the path that leads up to them is now fenced off. Instead, follow the side path that forks left and up onto

Holmesdale Road. Turn right here and then right again at the T-junction with busy Archway Road and head up to the traffic lights, opposite the entrance to **Highgate tube**.

The Green Man

The precise origins of the **Green Man** remain obscure. Images of a human head surrounded by a mass of leaves have been found on memorials across Europe, some dating from as early as the second century AD. Within a few generations, similar images had begun to appear on Christian tombstones, and figures growing out of – or even made from – leaves became a common decorative feature of many European churches and cathedrals right through to the nine-teenth century.

It's usually thought that the Green Man was a pagan symbol embodying the natural cycle of birth, death, decay and regeneration, being subsequently incorporated (like so many other such sym-bols) into Christian mythology. The Green Man is also linked with **Spriggan**, a mischievous but essentially benevolent creature who is fond of stealing children from cruel parents or money from greedy men and keeping both safe in the woods.

It was for the Green Man's association with renewal that Victorian romantics adopted him as **Jack in the Green**, who heralded in the spring in their May Day celebrations, part of the nostalgic search for a "Merrie England" that included the revival of morris dancing. Spriggan has also entered the popular conscience through such quintessentially English figures as the **Green Knight**, from the Arthurian legend of Sir Gawain, and **Robin Hood**, who acquired many Spriggan-like features during his evolution into the character we think of today.

▼ The Green Man, Crouch End Station

Queen's Wood

1.25km

At the traffic lights, turn right onto **Shepherd's Hill** and then left down the track just before the library on the far side of the road. This leads down to **Priory Gardens** road. Turn right here and head uphill; just before the road bends and makes its final steep ascent back to Shepherd's Hill, turn left, following the path as it descends steeply between the houses into **Queen's Wood**.

Along with neighbouring Highgate Wood, Queen's Wood is a pocket of undisturbed woodland that comprises an atmospheric tangle of hornbeams and oaks – though less well known, less visited and less landscaped than its neighbour.

Follow the Capital Ring signs, taking the broad stepped path ahead of you. The route crosses **Queen's Wood Road**; continue to follow the Capital Ring signs through the wood. The path emerges, 250m after crossing the road, at the ramshackle *Queen's Wood Café*, a timbered chalet-style building surrounded by trees.

Hippyish vegetarian *Queen's Wood Café* (Mon–Fri 10am–5pm, Sat & Sun 10am–6pm; ☏ 020/8444 2604) is open daily, serving good salads, pizzas and falafel for around £5, as well as all-day breakfast and home-made cakes.

Into Highgate Wood

1km

Exiting the café, turn right up the tarred path and cross the road at the pedestrian crossing, heading into the hornbeam and oak trees of **Highgate Wood**, through the New Gate entrance. Turn right into the wood, again following the Capital Ring signs. Continue for 300m to a T-junction marked by a tall wooden signpost. If you want some refreshment here, turn left and head down towards the playing fields, on the edge of which you'll find the wisteria-covered **Pavilion Café**, which dishes up mezze and an array of cakes. Just beyond the café there's a small **information hut** with leaflets and displays about local conservation work and guided tours, such as the popular night-time bat walk.

To continue the walk from the signpost, turn right at the T-junction and carry straight on to reach a marble **water fountain**, carved with an excerpt from Samuel Taylor Coleridge's *Inscription for a Fountain on a Heath*: "Drink, pilgrim, here; Here rest!" (though the fountain's sorry trickle of water doesn't now provide much sustenance). From the fountain, take the main fork left to the edge of the wood and turn right in front of Bridge Gate. Carry on for 250m to leave the woods by the Cranley Gate exit.

Back on the Parkland Walk

1.25km

Passing through Cranley Gate, turn left onto **Muswell Hill Road** and take the path under the road a few metres ahead to regain the Parkland Walk, which here runs on higher ground than before, with the land dropping away sharply to the right and affording sweeping views south across London. Even on a cloudy day you can pick out the City and the towers at Canary Wharf, while on a clear day the views stretch south to the Crystal Palace radio transmitter and beyond. The panoramic views are short-lived, however. After around 750m you reach an underpass beneath **Muswell Hill Park Road**, on the far side of which the path leads round to the right, up a plastic-covered ramp, and deposits you in a sheltered park beyond. Either loop around the park will take you to the exit on the east side onto **Alexandra Palace Way**, with the western facade of the palace itself standing proud on the hill above.

Alexandra Palace

1.5km

Alexandra Palace, or "Ally Pally" as it's affectionately known, was built in 1873 as a People's Palace to rival Crystal Palace in south London and remains an enduring monument to the self-assurance of the Victorian era, stretching for over 300m along the brow of the hill and dominating the local skyline. As a commercial enterprise, however, it never really took off, largely thanks to a fire that devastated the palace just days after it opened. In 1936, the BBC leased part of it to make the world's first public television transmission, and it continued to be used for television broadcasts until after World War II (during which time it was used to house German POWs) – a massive radio transmitter stands at the east end of the building, a legacy of the BBC years. Left empty and semi-derelict for many years, however, the palace fell victim to another disastrous fire in 1980, after which it was again rebuilt. It's now used as a conference and exhibition space, and is a lively weekend venue for antiques and craft fairs. Around the palace, **Alexandra Park** tumbles down to the northern reaches of Hornsey, giving fine views across the city – from Telecom Tower in the west, through the high rises of the City over to the towers of Canary Wharf in the east.

You can take the regular **W3 bus** back to Finsbury Park from any one of several stops along wide Alexandra Way, or continue 750m east along this road to **Alexandra Palace station**, from where there are frequent services (every 10–30min) to King's Cross. Just beyond the theme-park style boundary – a hefty wooden banner supported by totem-pole-style posts that marks the eastern edge of the Alexandra Palace estate – a footbridge (slightly hidden in the trees) leads off to the right across the rail tracks to Alexandra Palace station.

HAMPSTEAD HEATH

Across the heath to Kenwood

Distance and difficulty 5.25km; easy.
Duration 1hr 20min.
Trains Overground train to Hampstead Heath station from stations
between Richmond and Stratford.
Map OS Landranger 176: *West London*; OS Explorer 173:
London North.

Eight-hundred acre **Hampstead Heath** is London's most beautiful open space, with its sweeping grassland, jaw-dropping urban
vistas, ancient woodland and artfully designed eighteenth-century
parkland. To the north is **Kenwood House**, which boasts a wonderful collection of paintings and an enticing café. This circular
walk takes you from Hampstead Heath station to the house via
the bathing ponds (take your swimming things in case the murky
waters appeal), and back to the station via Keats's House. Back at
the station, the *Garden Gate* **pub** is well worth a visit.

Getting started

0.5km

Coming out of **Hampstead Heath station**, turn right to head up
South Hill. After a few metres, bear right onto Parliament Hill
road, passing tall red-brick gabled houses on either side. After
250m, Parliament Hill ends quite abruptly and you're on the
heath. Go straight ahead on the path.

Parliament Hill to the bathing ponds

0.75km

At the first crossroads in the path, after 50m, make the short detour
up **Parliament Hill**, much loved by kite-flyers. From an elevation
of 97m you get a panoramic view of the city, from the Dome and
Canary Wharf in the east via St Paul's, St Pancras Station and the
terracotta British Library to the NatWest Tower and Regent's Park.
Crystal Palace is visible in the far distance. The hill is supposed to
have earned its name because Guy Fawkes's co-conspirators gathered here to watch parliament in flames – if their plans had come
to fruition they would certainly have had a spectacular view.

To rejoin the walk, go back down to the path you were on before
and turn right. The path leads through the gently undulating park,
with its tall grasses and clumps of mature beech and oak trees; it's
a playground for north Londoners on a sunny day, with people

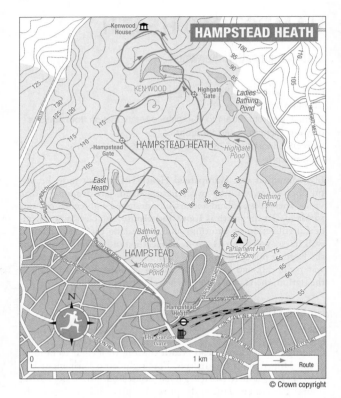

© Crown copyright

picnicking and playing football. Smaller paths lead off to either side, but stay on the major tarred path. Some 300m beyond Parliament Hill you'll see a line of trees ahead of you and a wooden fence, behind which are the **bathing ponds**. The ponds are natural – the heath is the source of several of London's "lost rivers", including the Fleet.

The path slopes down towards the line of trees, with a fence and a path running alongside it; when the path you're on joins the one along the bathing ponds, go straight ahead. To your right, sheltered by trees, is the men's pond, a well-known spot for London's gay community, and vividly described in Alan Hollinghurst's *The Line of Beauty*; beyond this is a more open pond, ringed by park benches. At the far end of this pond, turn left up the hill, away from the water.

Towards Kenwood House

1km

Around 250m further on the path splits into three – take the right-hand fork which, after just 100m, crosses a small bridge over what is usually no more than a trickle of water. After 200m you join a tarred path – go straight ahead here for around 10m until you come to a crossroads with a mature oak to your right. Go straight ahead, through **Highgate Gate** into **Ken Wood**.

The dirt path heads slightly to the right into secluded woodland, through holly bushes, rhododendrons and azaleas. You'll soon see a lake through the trees to your left. The path, now tarred, emerges into open picturesque parkland. As you ascend the hill in front of you, **Kenwood House** is revealed in all its wedding-cake white, Neoclassical magnificence.

The *Brew House* (daily: April–Sept 9am–6pm; Oct–March 9am–dusk; ☎ 020/8341 5384), located in the "service wing" of Kenwood House, is a perfect place to stop for lunch or afternoon tea. The lofty interior features *trompe l'oeil* decoration, while outside there's a terraced cottage-style garden. Food, including their hot breakfasts, is free-range and locally sourced, with scones and jam, mini pavlovas and cakes at teatime.

Kenwood House and grounds

0.75km

The house dates from the seventeenth century, but owes its current appearance to Robert Adam, who remodelled it for Lord Mansfield in the 1760s and 70s. The graceful proportions, gilded

▼ Kenwood House

friezes, glittering library and stucco ceilings are stunning, but what really distinguishes it is the Iveagh Bequest made in 1927, the then owner gifting the house with a superb collection of paintings by Vermeer, Hals, Romney, Gainsborough, Reynolds and Turner. For many the highlight is a sombre late self-portrait by Rembrandt, craggy and impressionistic.

Kenwood House is open April–Oct daily 11am–5pm; Nov–March daily 11am–4pm; free.

To continue, walk past the house, on the side facing the lake. Continue along the wide gravelled tree-lined avenue just beyond – look out for the Barbara Hepworth figurative sculpture on the lawn to your right.

Dido Belle at Kenwood

One of the most celebrated and unusual portraits to emanate from Kenwood, though it now hangs in Scone Palace in Scotland, is that of **Dido Belle** and her cousin Lady Elizabeth Murray. The two young women are dressed in sumptuous clothes with a fashionably sylvan scene behind them: the picture, attributed to Zoffany, resonates with their charm and affection for each other, expressed by the hand that Elizabeth tucks under Dido's elbow. What makes the painting unusual is that Dido is black, and that she is not presented in a subservient role, but as a genteel, lively and marriageable woman.

Dido's father is thought to have been John Lindsay, a naval captain, and her mother Maria Bell, a slave in the West Indies. Dido was brought up by Lindsay's uncle, **Lord Mansfield**, the owner of Kenwood house and a high-powered judge; in 1772 he made a significant ruling on the legality of slavery that was a stepping stone on the way to abolition. Lord and Lady Mansfield had no children of their own, but also raised another great-niece, Lady Elizabeth. Dido was well educated: she could play music and read and write, and oversaw the dairy and poultry at Kenwood, a task that was well within the remit of a refined young woman. Mansfield's social prominence and the elegance of the house meant that she would have moved in the most fashionable society. A startled-sounding Thomas Hutchinson, governor of Massachusetts, dined at Kenwood in 1779 and wrote, "a Black came in after dinner and sat with the ladies, and after coffee, walked with the company in the gardens, one of the young ladies having her arm within the other". He also remarked on Mansfield's affection for Dido.

The year Lord Mansfield died, 1793, Dido married John Davinier, a gentleman's steward. They had three sons and lived in Pimlico, in comfortable circumstances, though not in the splendour provided by Kenwood.

Just beyond here the path forks – take the left-hand fork with the **Henry Moore sculpture** on the left. The path curves down the hill, with trees on the right and open parkland to the left. Continue on the gravel path towards the lake.

The path splits at the bottom of the hill; bear left instead of crossing the little wooden bridge to the right. Skirt the **lake**, keeping it on your right-hand side, and then head uphill to rejoin the tarred path on which you approached the house.

Through Ken Wood and back to the heath

1.5km

Return to **Highgate Gate**, on the edge of Ken Wood, but instead of exiting the wood, turn right and stay within the boundary, delineated by iron railings. Carry on for a meandering 500m along the edge of Ken Wood, with picket fences on either side. Eventually you come to a sign that marks **Hampstead Gate**, where you exit the wood.

Follow the path that curves round to the left for a few metres, ignoring the two roads to the right. At the crossroads, go straight ahead. The wide dirt path leads through woods, soon following a gentle descent. After 250m you come to another junction in the path in more open parkland: to the left you can see the spire of a Highgate church. Turn right here, to descend the hill.

Go straight ahead and you eventually come to a wide avenue of limes, planted to replace trees lost in the great storm of 1987. After 300m you come to the edge of the park at **East Heath Road**, which is lined by red-brick mansions.

Back to the station

0.75km

Turn left down East Heath Road and continue downhill for 600m. **Keats Grove**, to your right, is a quintessential leafy Hampstead street, with graceful Regency villas and Victorian mansions with lush gardens. On the left of the road is the house where the poet **John Keats** lived from 1818 until he departed for Rome, where he died in 1821 at the appallingly young age of 24. It was in the garden here that Keats wrote the *Ode to a Nightingale*, and in the four-poster bed that he first coughed blood; as a medic he was in no doubt that consumption was the cause, describing the blood as his "death warrant". Although the house is now in one of the most desirable and wealthy parts of London, at that time the handsome villa was divided in two and made quite a humble dwelling; next door lived Fanny Brawne, with whom Keats fell deeply in love.

Back on East Heath Road, now called **South End Road**, cross
the road to reach the station. If you want a pint before you
go back to the station, the *Garden Gate* **pub** is a great nearby
option. Just continue on South End Road, past the turn-off to
the station; you'll see the looming monolith of the Royal Free
Hospital ahead of you and the pub on the left-hand side behind
a long brick wall.

. . . .

The *Garden Gate* (Mon–Thurs noon–11pm, Fri noon–midnight, Sat
10am–midnight, Sun 10am–10.30pm; ☎ 020/7435 4938) serves up
strong organic farm cider on tap and has a good wine list. The
spacious paved garden is circled by a sheltered terrace, while
inside there's wood panelling and colourful Victorian glass. The
menu features cottage pie, sausage and mash, and steak and
chips (mains from £7), as well as sarnies and good snacks.

. . . .

THE THAMES TOWPATH

Richmond to Hampton Court Palace

Distance and difficulty 13–15km; easy–moderate.
Duration 3hr 15min–3hr 45min.
Trains District Line tube or overground train from Waterloo to
Richmond (zone 4); return by overground train from Hampton Court
or Teddington (both zone 6) to Waterloo.
Map OS Landranger 176: *West London*; OS Explorer 161:
London South.

This riverside walk begins in urbane **Richmond** and then heads
upriver along the **Thames Towpath**, through some of Greater
London's most bucolic landscapes. Passing meadows and woodland,
you come to two fine country estates: creamy-white **Marble Hill**,
on the far bank of the river, and red-brick **Ham House**, on the
river's near side. The *Orangery* tearoom at Ham House is a good spot
for **lunch**. Beyond Ham, the route passes **Eel Pie Island** and more
meadows before reaching **Kingston upon Thames**, where you cross
the river to reach the northern boundary of **Hampton Court Park**.
There are great views into the park from the towpath, which flanks
the eastern boundary of the estate. The walk ends in the attractive
village of **Molesey**, at the main entrance to **Hampton Court Palace**.

Getting started

1km

From **Richmond station**, turn left onto Richmond's main street,
The Quadrant. Follow the road (which subsequently changes its
name to George Street) for roughly 400m. Turn right just past
Topshop down tiny Brewer's Lane, crammed with small shops,
onto Richmond Green. Cross the green on the path ahead of you,
to the top left-hand corner. Joining the road at the crenellated villa
ahead of you, turn right and go straight ahead down Old Palace
Lane, which curves left and takes you down to the river. Turn left
onto the towpath to reach **Richmond Riverside**. The riverside was
pedestrianized and terraced in the late 1980s, which, along with the
Georgian buildings that flank it, makes the whole place feel a bit
like a stage set. It's a busy spot, especially on sunny summer days.

To Ham House

2km

Head under **Richmond Bridge** – built in 1777, this elegant five-
arch span of Purbeck stone is London's oldest extant bridge – and

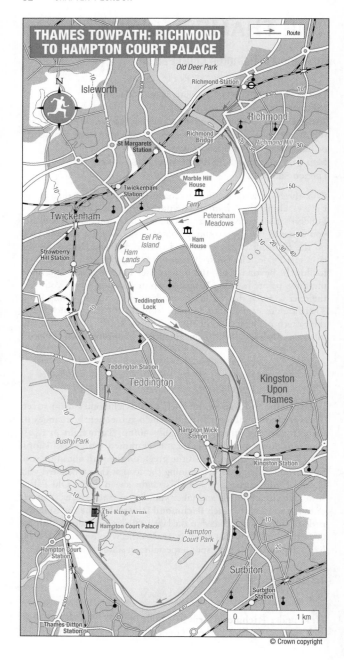

THAMES TOWPATH: RICHMOND TO HAMPTON COURT PALACE

→ Route

N

Old Deer Park

Isleworth

Richmond Station

Richmond

St Margarets Station

Richmond Bridge

Richmond Hill

Twickenham Station

Marble Hill House

Twickenham

Ferry

Petersham Meadows

Eel Pie Island

Ham House

Strawberry Hill Station

Ham Lands

Teddington Lock

Teddington Station

Teddington

Kingston Upon Thames

Bushy Park

Hampton Wick Station

Kingston Station

The Kings Arms

Hampton Court Palace

Hampton Court Park

Hampton Court Station

Surbiton

Hampton Court Park

Surbiton Station

Thames Ditton Station

0   1 km

© Crown copyright

follow the path as it hugs the river bend. Beyond, to the left of the towpath, cows graze placidly in Petersham Meadows.

Peeking through the trees on the far bank of the river, 200m beyond Petersham Meadows, is the splendid facade of **Marble Hill House**, a creamy Italianate confection built in 1729 for **Henrietta Howard**, the Countess of Suffolk, who was George II's mistress and lady-in-waiting to his wife, Queen Caroline. The *ménage à trois* was no secret and the two women were said to have "hated one another very civilly". Howard enjoyed a lavish lifestyle here, entertaining the likes of Alexander Pope and Horace Walpole in the extravagantly gilded reception rooms. These rooms are now ornately furnished with some fine period furniture.

If you fancy visiting the house you can catch **Hammerton's Ferry** (Feb–Oct daily 10am–6pm, Nov–Jan Sat & Sun 10am–6.30pm; £1) across the river. The ferry runs from a well-marked spot on the riverbank by the path to Ham House, crossing on demand between Marble Hill and Ham House (see below). Marble Hill doesn't really compete with the attractions of Ham House and Hampton Court, however, and is probably best visited on a separate occasion.

Ham House

A hundred metres beyond Hammerton's Ferry, a grassy avenue flanked by lime trees runs up from the towpath to the main entrance of **Ham House** (March 15 to Nov 2 Mon–Wed, Sat & Sun noon–4pm; gardens same days 11am–6pm; £9.90, garden only £3.30; NT). Built in 1610 for the first Earl of Dysart, the house was greatly expanded and lavishly decorated by Dysart's daughter, Elizabeth, and her second husband, the Earl of Lauderdale. The building works left the family heavily in debt, however, and little was changed over the following three hundred years by the cash-strapped Lauderdales, with the result that the house now survives as an unusually well-preserved period piece. In 1948, the National Trust acquired the house and began restoration, while the **gardens** have also recently been returned to their seventeenth-century glory. Features include a cherry garden, a "Wildernesse" (actually a maze-like area of hornbeam hedges concealing four circular summerhouses), a kitchen garden and an orangery, which now serves as a tearoom and makes a good place for **lunch**.

The Orangery (Mon–Wed, Sat & Sun 11am–5.30pm) serves soups, veg tarts and salads made using ingredients from the kitchen garden. Outside seats survey the formal gardens, which date back to the seventeenth century. If you don't want to visit the house, you'll have to pay the small entrance fee to get into the grounds, but the food itself is reasonably priced.

Eel Pie Island

0.5km

A couple of hundred metres beyond the grounds of Ham House you'll come to one of the largest islands on the Thames: **Eel Pie Island**. Pies and ale were sold on the island in the sixteenth century (Henry VIII is said to have stopped off once en route between Whitehall and Hampton Court to sample the local fare), though the island didn't acquire its present name until the nineteenth century. It had a reputation for revelry and entertainment into the twentieth century, with steamers bringing day-trippers down the river from London – the Rolling Stones played here in the Sixties. Today, the island is home to a bohemian community of artists and inventors, each house having steps or ladders leading to a boat. The surrounding waters are surprisingly clear and you may even catch sight of the eponymous eels.

The Ham Lands

2km

Beyond Eel Pie Island, the river meanders on, past gently sloping banks where small shingle beaches make ideal sites for a **picnic**. Inland, meadows stretch off to the horizon. There's a sense that the city hasn't yet encroached here, even though you're just a few hundred metres away from the northern reaches of Kingston upon Thames, while the suburbs of Twickenham and Teddington lie on the opposite bank, obscured by mixed woodland and weeping willows.

Surprisingly, this apparently rural landscape is very much a product of its urban surroundings. Prior to World War II, the **Ham Lands** – the stretch of meadow flanking the Richmond side of the river between Ham House and Teddington Lock – was an ugly, industrial landscape, scarred with gravel pits. Land reclamation began here in the late 1940s, using rubble from bomb-damaged sites in central London to fill in the gravel pits. The made-up ground has been carefully managed ever since: looking at it today, it's hard to imagine that there was ever anything here but unspoilt countryside.

Teddington Lock to Kingston Bridge

3km

Roughly 2.5km beyond Ham House you come to **Teddington Lock**, the collective name for the series of locks and weirs that mark the end of the tidal river. Some 1km beyond this, you join a paved road which heads past attractive Edwardian houses and, eventually, into the centre of Kingston. Stay alongside the river, following the cycle route through **Canbury Gardens**, where the terraced garden at the riverside *Boater's Inn* is a nice stop for a drink. From the inn, an avenue of plane trees brings you to the far edge of Canbury Gardens. Coming out of the gardens onto the road, go straight ahead past the white clapperboard building and take the raised path past the back of John Lewis. Go through the tunnel under the **Kingston Bridge** and then take an immediate left turn up the slope and then left again at the top and onto the bridge.

Hampton Court Park and Palace

4.5km

Head over Kingston Bridge and, before reaching the roundabout, turn left to follow signs for the Thames Cycle Route. You're now at the northeastern tip of **Hampton Court Park**, though there's little to see for a while apart from the suburban sprawl on the opposite bank. A few hundred metres on, the views open up to reveal the park, with the chimneys of the palace itself rising above the trees in the distance. This corner of the grounds is given over to a golf course, but the deer, which roam freely here as elsewhere in the park, appear unperturbed by the golf balls and plus-fours. Across the river, boathouses nestle by the suburban apartments and villas of Surbiton.

The vista opens up with the final bend of the river on the approach to Hampton Court: the palace lies just ahead, with the village green at **Molesey** on the opposite bank. In summer this is a quintessentially English scene, with cricketers playing on the green, people by the river, and pleasure boats trawling the Thames.

Hampton Court Palace was built for Cardinal Wolsey in 1516 and purloined by Henry VIII thirteen years later. Cromwell moved in during the Commonwealth (he died here in 1658) and some of the most ambitious building work was carried out in the late seventeenth century, during the reign of William and Mary, who hired Sir Christopher Wren to remodel the palace. Wren had planned to demolish the Tudor structure and rebuild it in the style of Versailles, though his ambitious plans were brought to a halt by the death of Mary in 1684. The Classical additions that he was able to make to the palace, including the king and queen's own apartments, form a contrast with the original red-brick structure. The palace was opened to the public by Queen Victoria in 1838.

Hampton Court Palace is open daily April–Oct 10am–6pm;
Nov–March 10am–4.30pm; Royal Apartments £13.50.

Entrance to the grounds is free, but to see the Royal Apartments you'll need a ticket – expensive, but well worth it. You can stroll around at your own pace, or take one of the excellent guided **tours** (price included in entry fee), although these only cover Henry VIII's State Rooms and the King's (William III's) Apartments. It's also worth having a look at the **Tudor Kitchens** and **Wine Cellar**: the workaday underbelly of the palace, these offer a stark contrast to the opulent interiors upstairs. Henry VIII had the kitchens quadrupled to their current size and they are kitted out as they would have been to cater for the massive banquets for which he was famous.

....

Hampton Court Palace has a café and a restaurant, though both are a bit pricey and overcrowded, and there are plenty of great spots for picnics in the grounds. If you want a drink, go for the *Kings Arms* on Hampton Court Road, by the Lion Gate.

....

The palace's **grounds** cover almost seven hundred acres, but the main attraction, the famous **maze** (covered by the ticket to the Royal Apartments; otherwise £2.10), lies close to the palace itself near the Lion Gate to the north of the complex. The maze is quite tricky – leave yourself plenty of time for getting lost if you plan on giving it a go.

Bushy Park

2km

From the palace, you can either catch a train back from **Hampton Court station** (just across the river by Hampton Court Bridge) or head through **Bushy Park** – the entrance is opposite the Lion Gate at the northern boundary to the park – to Teddington station, 1.5km to the north. Bushy Park was Hampton Court's royal hunting park, and today is still home to abundant red and fallow deer, though with more than a thousand acres to lose themselves in, you may see surprisingly few. The route to Teddington takes you along **Chestnut Avenue**, designed by Sir Christopher Wren and lined with 300-year-old horse chestnuts. Exiting on the far side of the park, head straight ahead down Avenue Gardens. At the T-junction at the end of Avenue Gardens bear right then take the first left down Victoria Road; **Teddington station** is in front of you.

RICHMOND PARK

Petersham and the park

Distance and difficulty 10km; easy.
Duration 2hr 15min.
Trains District Line tube or overground train from Waterloo to Richmond (zone 4).
Map OS Landranger 176: *West London*; OS Explorer 161: *London South*.

This circular walk explores **Richmond Park**, London's largest green space, with its great herds of deer, sweeping grassland and venerable oak trees. This is no manicured city park, but a real chunk of pristine green within easy reach of the centre of town. While it's hugely popular with dog-walkers, cyclists, horse-riders and walkers, its vast 2500-acre extent means that you can get a real sense of open space and solitude; lack of signage adds to the wilderness feel, and the complex tracery of tracks and horse rides can make finding your bearings a bit tricky. This route takes you from Richmond station across **Richmond Green**, a jousting ground in the Tudor period, and along the **Thames** for a stretch. From the riverside you cut across meadows to Petersham, where the **Petersham Nurseries** café serves up award-winning lunches and cakes in irresistibly pretty surroundings. The route then runs into the park, and loops via the **Isabella Plantation** through grassland and woodland to land you at **Pembroke Lodge**. From here you descend spectacular **Richmond Hill** to return to the station.

May and June are the best months to see the azaleas and rhododendrons of Isabella Plantation, and you may also see baby deer at this time. Alternatively, check out some stag-rutting action in the autumn – three hundred red and three hundred and fifty fallow deer roam free in the park.

Getting started

2km

From **Richmond station**, turn left onto Richmond's main street, The Quadrant. Follow the road (which subsequently changes its name to George Street) for roughly 400m. Turn right down tiny Brewer's Lane just after Topshop onto Richmond Green and cross the green on the path ahead of you, to the top left-hand corner. At the crenellated villa ahead of you, turn right and head down Old Palace Lane, which curves left and takes you down to the river. Turn left onto the towpath to reach **Richmond Riverside**. Follow

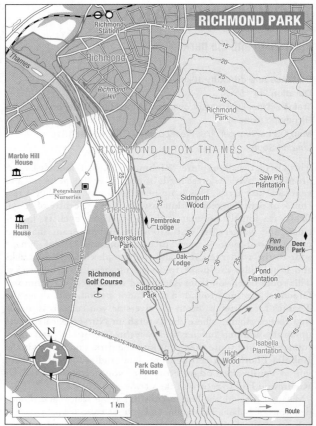

© Crown copyright

the towpath for **a kilometre**, till you reach the public loos and the fingerposts. Go through the metal kissing gate, following signs for Petersham.

Petersham

0.5km

The tarred path leads across the meadow for 300m, till you reach another metal kissing gate – carry on up the tarred path between the hedgerows. You come out onto a lane with the church ahead of you; turn right to reach **Petersham Nurseries**. On the left after 200m, a gap in the fence leads to the nursery buildings.

Tucked amongst the bedding plants at Petersham Nurseries
is a tempting, leafy **café**, which sells cafetières of excellent
coffee, loose-leaf teas, soup and home-made cakes,
from Chelsea buns to sticky beetroot cake; it's open Tues–Sat
10am–4.30pm & Sun 11am–4.30pm; ⓦwww
.petershamnurseries.com, Ⓣ020/8605 3627.

Coming out of Petersham Nurseries, turn right to go back
towards the lane to the church. Turn right on this lane and just
before you reach the church follow the **Capital Ring** sign to the
left, down the narrow path along the graveyard. You come out
onto Petersham Road – cross over it and go straight ahead, into
the park.

Across the path to Ham Gate

1.5km

Follow the wide track straight ahead of you, with the playground
to your right. Up to the left are the icing-white Georgian buildings
at the top of Richmond Hill while down to your right after 400m,
behind a fence, is Sudbrook Park and Richmond Golf Course.
Beyond the golf course, the park opens out again, with some fine
solitary oaks up to the left, and a swathe of grassland to the right.
You emerge onto a road that runs through the park – down to the
right is **Ham Gate**.

The park was a **royal hunting ground** from the thirteenth
century, but was enclosed by Charles I in 1637 – he raised a
ten-mile brick wall around the purloined land, causing immense
controversy. It wasn't until 1758 that public access to the park
was secured by local brewer John Lewis, who waged a fierce battle
that resulted in his own bankruptcy.

Isabella Plantation

1km

Cross the road and turn left after 10m, taking the path that initially
runs parallel to the road and then veers to the right, up the hill. Go
up the steepish hill for 200m and at the tarred road cross over and
turn left, following the road. At the junction you'll see a white sign
to Ham Gate – take the path immediately opposite this, heading
right, away from the road. Just 50m beyond this you reach a wide
horse ride, where you turn right, heading gently uphill towards
High Wood. After 250m, at the edge of the wood, take the path
that leads left, along the outer edge of the treeline. The path runs
straight ahead for 250m along the trees, until you come to a gate
that leads into **Isabella Plantation**.

Richmond's parakeets

Keep an eye out in this section of the park for the colony of ring-necked **parakeets** that are breeding here with great success – there may be up to a hundred pairs. One urban myth suggests they escaped from a container at Heathrow, another that they were let loose by Jimi Hendrix, though it's more likely that they are descended from pets who fled the cage and that recent mild winters have allowed their numbers to flourish. The parakeets' startling lime-green feathers, rosy-red beaks and harsh squawk make them pretty easy to pick out.

Go through the gate, taking the path that leads left into the plantation, soon coming to a heather garden. From here you can detour to explore the plantation: enclosed in 1831, it is a showcase for acid-loving plants such as rhododendrons, camellias and azaleas, and is also thick with bluebells in May. Otherwise, bear left at the heather garden, keeping the little stream to your right. You come out at **Peg's Pond**; circle the pond, keeping it to your right, and exit the plantation, via the wrought-iron gate, into the car park.

To Pembroke Lodge

3km

From the car park, take the gravel path straight ahead away from the plantation towards the road. Turn right at the road, and continue alongside it for 400m. To the left you come to **Pond Plantation**, a dense cluster of rhododendrons and woodland, enclosed by a fence. Just before you reach this, turn left off the road, up the horse ride. After 100m you cross a little stream; follow the broad track as it curves right from here. Down to your right you'll see expansive Pen Pond. The path continues its gentle climb up the hill – close at hand to the right is little Leg of Mutton Pond while to the left is the birch and beech woodland of Queen Elizabeth's Plantation. The path leaves the edge of the plantation, and comes to a junction with a much broader dirt track, marked with the **Capital Ring** sign. Turn left up this track and up the hill for 150m. After around 100m, a post in the middle of the track marked with the Capital Ring sign points left into the woods. Follow this and, after 200m, bear right at the junction, continuing to follow the Capital Ring sign. This section runs for 500m alongside the woodland to reach **Oak Lodge**.

Beyond the lodge, the paved track reaches a wide road through the park. Cross the road to the viewpoint, which looks west towards Twickenham. You can continue to follow the Capital Ring signs here to get back to Petersham. For a more varied return to Richmond however, go through the metal gate on the right, into **Pembroke Lodge gardens**, which feature dense drifts of snowdrops and banks of daffodils in spring. Walk straight through the pretty parkland towards the pristine white Georgian building itself, which was the childhood home of philosopher Bertrand Russell. Keeping the building to your right, carry on through the parkland – you might want to stop for a cuppa at the **cafeteria** here, which you can enjoy on the terrace in front of the lodge.

Richmond Gate to the station

2km

The route continues through the lodge gardens, running parallel with the road, past a thatched gingerbread-style cottage to your right. Eventually it emerges at a gate, with a memorial to an eighteenth-century poet to the left, on to the road. Carry on through the park along the road, till you reach **Richmond Gate**. Go straight ahead down **Richmond Hill**, past the Star and Garter home (built for disabled sailors, soldiers and airmen in 1924) on the left, and a 1720s terrace, with its tall porticoes and wrought-iron verandas, to the right.

Head straight down, past Richmond Hill's enticing shops and cafés, to reach Richmond Bridge. Go straight ahead on **Hill Street**, and follow the curve to the right on its continuation, George Street, to get back to **Richmond Station**.

THE GRAND UNION CANAL

Horsenden Hill and around

Distance and difficulty 6km; easy.
Duration 1hr 30min.
Trains Piccadilly Line to Alperton (zone 4); return on the Central Line from Greenford (zone 4).
Map OS Landranger 176: *West London*; OS Explorer 173: *London North*.

This walk follows the quiet and leafy course of the **Grand Union Canal** as it winds through west London. Built in 1801, the canal linked London to the rest of the country's canal system, which began in Birmingham and terminated at the Paddington basin. The canal brought new industries to the area, and within three generations this formerly agricultural community had been subsumed by the city's western sprawl. Nearby **Perivale**, a hamlet when the canal arrived, still retains a village-like feel.

Following the towpath west from **Alperton**, this walk leads out past Horsenden Farm to **Horsenden Hill**, from whose summit there are superb views across the city and out to the countryside north and west of London. The summit was visited by nomadic Stone Age people 7000 years ago, and settled 2500 years ago by Iron Age farmers. Beyond here, the walk continues west along the canal, past **Perivale Wood** and around the bird-rich wetlands of **Paradise Fields** to finish in nearby **Greenford**.

With the enticement of the adventure trail at Horsenden Farm, this relatively short walk is a good option for **kids**. There's nowhere to eat along the route, so it's best done as a morning's or afternoon's stroll, or planned around a **picnic** on the hill.

Getting started

0.3km

From **Alperton tube station**, turn right onto the A4089 (Ealing Road). Cross over the road at the pedestrian crossing, just beyond the station forecourt, then turn right and head straight down to the T-junction with Bridgewater Road. Turn left here and cross the road bridge over the **Grand Union Canal**, on the far side of which steps lead down to the canal. At the bottom of the steps, turn left and then left again onto the towpath and head under the road bridge.

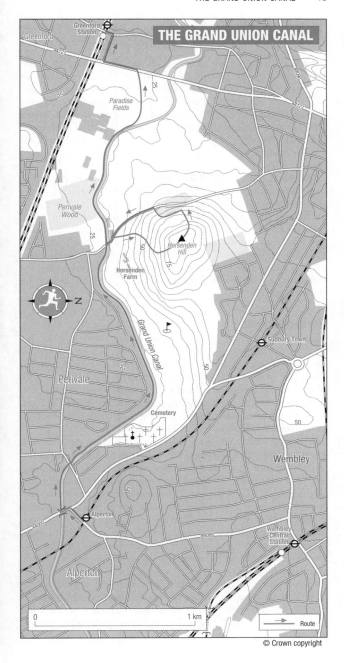

THE GRAND UNION CANAL

Greenford
Greenford Station
Paradise Fields
Perivale Wood
Horsenden Hill
Horsenden Farm
Grand Union Canal
Perivale
Sudbury Town
Cemetery
Wembley
Alperton
Alperton
Wembley Central Station

N

0   1 km

Route

© Crown copyright

Along the Grand Union Canal

1.7km

Dotted with colourful narrow boats and frequented by swans and moorhens, the canal makes a surprisingly tranquil contrast to the road above. After 500m the views begin to open up ahead as you skirt the southern side of Alperton's **cemetery**, opened during World War I and maintained in part by the War Graves Commission (though all you can see from here is the attractive red-brick chapel and a few gravestones), and hilly **Sudbury Golf Course** beyond, with Horsenden Hill rising steeply at its western reaches.

Beneath the hill nestles **Horsenden Farm**. The farm was here long before the canal, but took full advantage of the waterway, becoming a major supplier of hay to the capital (which it exchanged for a pungent mixture of manure, refuse and offal from the city's streets). The farm is now given over to a canoe club and a kids' adventure trail – you can see the wooden sculptures, including a giant heron, a galleon and flying fish, across the canal – and is a particularly pleasant spot, with willows overhanging the waterside and herons, moorhens and ducks splashing around on the canal itself.

Horsenden Hill

2km

Continue along the towpath to the western end of Horsenden Farm, just beyond a metal kissing gate, where you reach a narrow Victorian road bridge and, flanking it, a modern pedestrian bridge. Cross the pedestrian bridge, passing the gated entrance to the farm, and follow the pavement round the bend to the left to reach an information board at the foot of **Horsenden Hill**.

Here, a dirt track heads off the pavement and up onto the hill. Heading up a series of rough dirt steps, the track emerges in less than 100m onto heath and grass land, rich with wild flowers and butterflies in summer. A solitary oak tree stands just to your right; the track leads right a few metres before it, heading on up the hillside, back into the trees and up a series of dirt steps to emerge after 300m on the grassy summit. This is a popular spot for kite-flying, and it has rough-hewn benches, plenty of grassy banks to settle down on to catch the sun, and sweeping views north to Harrow-on-the-Hill, southeast to central London and west out of London to as far as the Chilterns.

To continue the walk, turn left down the field and follow the Capital Ring sign just before the information boards, descending the wooden steps. Ignore the second Capital Ring sign and carry on down the hill. Bear left on the tarred path signed towards the visitor centre and head downhill to return to the bridge you crossed earlier, over the canal just before Horsenden Farm.

On to Greenford
2km

Turn left at the towpath, head under the bridge and continue west, past **Perivale Wood**. This 27-acre nature reserve protects a patch of ancient oak woodland and is closed to the public except on the first Sunday of May, when the carpets of bluebells for which the woods are renowned are in full bloom.

To your right, there are good views back to Horsenden Hill. Some 300m beyond Perivale Wood you'll come to a wooden footbridge over the canal. Turn off the towpath here at the public footpath sign and take the path that leads south, away from the canal and the footbridge and around the edge of **Paradise Fields** wetlands. Occupying two man-made lagoons on former industrial land, the wetlands were established in the late 1990s; they already look well established and attract water birds, including sandpipers and lapwings. The path skirts Paradise Fields for about 500m before reaching steps up to the A4127 (Greenford Road).

Head up here and cross to the far side of the road, following the signs for Greenford underground station: go left and down to the traffic lights just before the bridge under the railway, then right along Rockware Avenue. At the T-junction, 200m further on, turn left onto Oldfield Lane and head under the rail bridge, on the opposite side of which is **Greenford station**.

DOWNE AND AROUND

Chelsfield to Down House via Cuckoo Wood

Distance and difficulty 14.75km; moderate.
Duration 3hr 40min.
Trains Charing Cross via London Bridge to Chelsfield (hourly;
30min); return from Chelsfield to Charing Cross (hourly; 30min).
Map OS Landranger 177: *East London*; OS Explorer 147: *Sevenoaks
and Tonbridge*.

This walk covers the territory where the London suburbs end and,
magically, the Kent countryside begins. From Chelsfield, the route
runs up to **Cuckoo Wood**, which contains some ancient woodland
as well as orchids, bluebells, violets and primroses. Emerging from
the wood you come to a country lane that leads to **Downe**, which
was Charles Darwin's home for forty years. There are a couple
of **pubs** in the village, or you can eat at the tearoom in **Darwin's
house** itself. The route then follows an intricate network of tiny
paths that cuts through fields and woodland to the venerable
church at **Cudham**. From here you begin to circle back towards
Cuckoo Wood, with Canary Wharf shimmering on the horizon.

Getting started

1.5km

Exiting Chelsfield **station** on the platform 2 side, walk up the
long sloping path to the road. Turn left down the hill. Where the
road forks, go left down Windsor Drive and carry on up the wide
suburban street. From Woodlands Road onwards, the road heads
downhill, with a curve of countryside ahead of you.

Passing Woodland Road on the left, cross Glentrammon Road
and carry on, straight downhill on Vine Road. Turn left at the
red-brick Baptist church. Around 200m further on there's a roundabout – go anti-clockwise here, passing the *Rose & Crown*. Take a
right off the roundabout down Cudham Lane North. After just
10m the road forks at a red post box – turn right up Old Hill. After
20m turn left, follow the public footpath sign that leads round the
back of no. 17 **Old Hill**, and up the slope. The path leads through
a wooden kissing gate by a pylon, and out into open countryside.

Cuckoo Wood

2km

The path runs up the field for 400m towards **Cuckoo
Wood** and then into the wood and gently uphill through

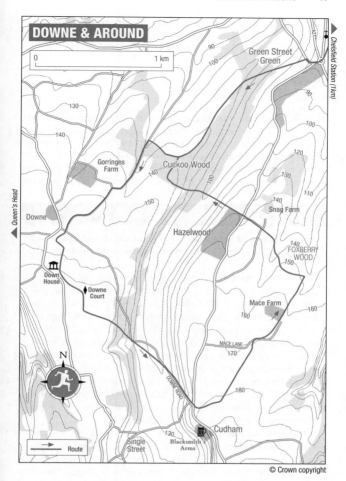

DOWNE & AROUND

0   1 km

Green Street Green

Chelsfield Station (1km)

Gorringes Farm

Cuckoo Wood

Snag Farm

Downe

Hazelwood

Queen's Head

Down House

FOXBERRY WOOD

Downe Court

Mace Farm

MACE LANE

N

DOWNE ROAD

Cudham

Single Street

Blacksmith's Arms

→ Route

© Crown copyright

a corridor of greenery; you're now in High Elms Country
Park.

Go past a crossroads with a bench and after 250m you reach a fork
in the path. Go left. At a second fork a bit further on, go right and
follow the edge of the golf course. After another 250m you come
to another crossroads, with the golf course immediately on the
right, a path leading downhill to the left signed Green St Green
Circular Walk (which you'll come back up on the return trip) and
one straight ahead marked **Cudham Circular Walk** – follow this
one, still edging the golf course. This eventually leads downhill to a
small car park with some information panels. Leave the car park and
turn left onto the narrow country road heading towards Downe.

Watch out for traffic and use the parallel path to the road where available. You'll come to a brown sign pointing left for Down House, follow it on the signed bridleway that parallels the road.

Downe

1.75km

After a kilometre you come to characterful **Downe** village, composed of a scattering of pretty cottages and grander houses, a thirteenth-century church and a couple of pubs. Just past the primary school on the right a narrow passageway leads down to the back of the *Queen's Head*, a good real-ale **pub** that was apparently frequented by Darwin. Otherwise, head on into

Darwin in Downe

At last gleams of light have come and I am almost convinced that species are not (it is like confessing murder) immutable.

So wrote **Charles Darwin** to Sir Joseph Hooker in 1844, from his rural sanctuary in Downe. Darwin, his wife Emma and their children lived here from 1842 until his death in 1882, and it was in this Kent retreat that he crystallized the research and learning from his extraordinary five-year journey on HMS *Beagle* into *On the Origin of Species*, published in 1859. Darwin's theory of **natural selection** took twenty meticulous years to develop, the same theory flashing upon the naturalist Alfred Russel Wallace in 1858 when he lay in a fever – Wallace developed the theory in two hours, and wrote it up over the course of three evenings. Wallace sent his ideas to Darwin, who was then propelled to publish his own work, though the two men translated their rivalry into friendly support.

Down House was a haven for the invalid Darwin, who avoided the rigours of a more public life for a contemplative and studious existence, supported and protected by Emma. At the large former farmhouse where they made their home, he alternated his studies of barnacles, orchids and bees with walks, copious letter-writing, and a daily hour dedicated to smoking.

The ground floor of the house is much as it was in Darwin's time, while the first floor features an interactive **exhibition** on his life and work. In the garden there's an observation beehive and a **greenhouse** containing orchids and carnivorous plants. Darwin's studies of less exotic plant and animal life in the surrounding fields were essential to his work – as well as making close observations on grasses and soils, he set his children the task of monitoring the flight path of bumble bees, and studied the seed content of bird droppings, using this as evidence of dispersal in *On the Origin of Species*.

the village, past the church. Turn right onto the High Street, following the signs for Down House. Beyond the church, turn left towards Down House, passing some brick and flint cottages and a Baptist church.

After 150m, take the **public footpath** to Cudham, which leads down to the left. The path runs up the edge of a field, through a hedge into another field where you should turn right (a red English Heritage sign points the way). Go through the metal kissing gate and over the road to reach the house.

....

Down House is open Wed–Sun: March 11am–4pm; April–Oct 11am–5pm; Nov to mid-Dec 11am–4pm; £7.20 (EH).

....

Down House to Cudham
2km

From Darwin's house, cross the road and go through the gate back onto the footpath, but turn right instead of coming back the way you came. The path takes you round the buildings of Down Court – for the moment you're on **Circular Leaves Green** route, which you follow as it zigzags round the farm buildings and fields.

You come to a **crossroads** of public footpaths on the edge of the field – go left here down the edge of another field. Follow the path right, steeply downhill through the woodland for 250m. The path descends some wooden steps to come out at a narrow country road; join the lane for just 50m, and then turn right again over the stile, following the yellow arrow towards Cudham on the permissive footpath. This section of path cuts across a field to come out at a path alongside a lane; the path runs steeply uphill for 500m to Cudham.

The path emerges onto a road – just keep heading uphill into the village. You soon come to **Cudham**'s eleventh-century flint **church**; take the footpath that leads through the churchyard to the right of the church. Turn left here beyond the church to continue the walk, or, if you want a **pub** stop, turn right along the playing field to get to the main part of the village. Turning right at the lane at the end of this path brings you to the Cudham's *Blacksmith's Arms*, a nondescript but friendly village inn.

Cudham to Cuckoo Wood
3.5km

Continuing the walk **from the churchyard**, head left round the playing field and go through the black kissing gate. Cross the lane and go up the public footpath, following the **Cudham Circular Walk** signs. You're now walking across open countryside – the views open out and suddenly you can see London to the north beyond the trees, with Canary Wharf glittering like the Emerald City in *The Wizard of Oz*.

The path cuts through a thin strip of woodland, then joins a narrow lane where you need to turn right. You pass Mace Farm and carry on up the lane; beyond **Mace Farm**, the tarmac peters out and you're on a path, which you follow for 500m downhill into Foxberry Wood. Ignore the yellow waymarker that leads off to the right and go straight ahead.

Some 150m further on, follow the **public bridleway** sign with the yellow arrow that leads left out of the wood and uphill between two fields. The path winds between tall hedgerows and light woodland until eventually you come out at a country lane. Go straight ahead here for 200m. At the T-junction cross over the road and take the permissive path that leads down the edge of the field parallel to the road. After 150m, turn left up through the fields, following the sign towards High Elms.

Back to Chelsfield

4km

The path goes alongside a field and climbs uphill back into **Cuckoo Wood**, dipping and then running diagonally up through the wood. At the top you cross a path with "no cycling" signs to either side – carry on straight ahead, past a line of tall beech trees. Another 250m further on, you come to the edge of the golf course at the crossroads you encountered earlier in the walk. Turn right to head along the edge of the woodland, the way you came earlier. Just retrace your steps through the wood and at the edge of the woodland head back down the field to rejoin **Old Hill**.

At the roundabout at the bottom of Old Hill, go back the way you came, following the road to Orpington. At the Baptist Church, turn right onto World's End Lane. Go up Vine Street and carry on straight ahead to reach the **station**.

LIMEHOUSE BASIN

Bethnal Green to Wapping

Distance and difficulty 5.5km; easy.
Duration 1hr 20min.
Trains Central Line to Cambridge Heath (zone 2); return on the
Docklands Light Railway from Limehouse.
Map OS Landranger 177: *East London*; OS Explorer 173:
London North.

This straightforward route runs down the **Regent's Canal** to
the watery landscape and gleaming developments at **Limehouse
Basin**, a once mighty dock that degenerated in the late Victorian
period into one of London's most notorious slums. Here the canal
joins the Thames, and you can go west on the **Thames Towpath**
to **Wapping** and enjoy a pint at the characterful *Prospect of Whitby*
pub, established in the reign of Henry VIII.

For an invaluable insight into the social history of the area, it's
worth timing your visit to coincide with the limited opening
hours of the terrific canalside **Ragged School Museum**, a moving
memorial to the charity and energy of Dr Thomas Barnardo.

The route makes for a good Sunday stroll – foodies could punc-
tuate it with **Sunday lunch** at Gordon Ramsay's gastropub *The
Narrow*, on the edge of Limehouse Basin. It's also a great option
for cyclists, who can continue up the Thames Path to the Tower of
London and beyond, unhampered by gates or stiles.

Getting started

0.75km

Exiting **Bethnal Green** station, turn right up busy Cambridge Heath
Road – keeping the Museum of Childhood to your right – and carry
on for 750m. Just beyond Vyner Street, to your right, is a bridge over
the **Regent's Canal**; cross the bridge and descend the steps on the
right to join the towpath. Go left here, heading east along the canal.

You can also begin this walk from **Hackney**, following the route
described on p.56 until you reach Victoria Park.

Victoria Park to the Ragged School Museum

2.5km

Pass the entrance to **Victoria Park** and keep going along the canal.
Underneath a bridge, distinguished by a VR and a crown sculpted

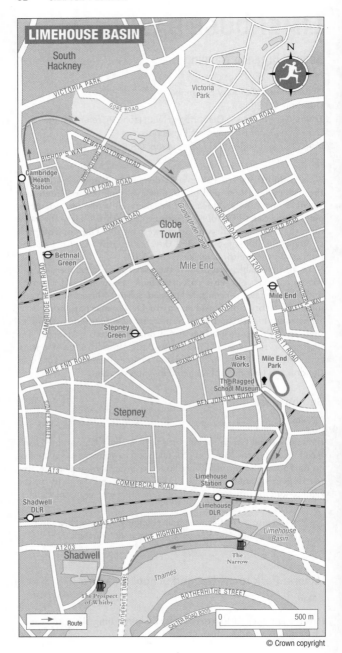

LIMEHOUSE BASIN

South Hackney

Victoria Park

N

VICTORIA PARK

GORE ROAD

OLD FORD ROAD

BISHOP'S WAY

SEWARDSTONE ROAD

Cambridge Heath Station

OLD FORD ROAD

ROMAN ROAD

Globe Town

Grand Union Canal

GROVE ROAD

A1205

LICHFIELD ROAD

Bethnal Green

Mile End

BANCROFT STREET

Mile End

SOUTHERN GROVE

CAMBRIDGE HEATH ROAD

Stepney Green

MILE END ROAD

HAMLETS WAY

BURDETT ROAD

ERNEST STREET

SHANDY STREET

Gas Works

Mile End Park

MILE END ROAD

The Ragged School Museum

BEN JONSON ROAD

Stepney

SIDNEY STREET

A13

COMMERCIAL ROAD

Limehouse Station

Shadwell DLR

CABLE STREET

Limehouse DLR

Limehouse Basin

A1203

THE HIGHWAY

Shadwell

ROTHERHITHE TUNNEL

The Narrow

Thames

The Prospect of Whitby

ROTHERHITHE STREET

SALTER ROAD B205

0   500 m

→ Route

© Crown copyright

in stone, you come to a section of the water that's overhung with trees and lined with canal boats, with a picturesque lock keeper's cottage to the left, at Old Ford Lock.

Passing under Roman Road Bridge, you come to the edge of **Mile End Park**. This is one of London's newest parks, in what was once a heavily industrialized area, crammed with wharves, warehouses, shirtmakers and factories. The park, attractively landscaped but not overly manicured, features play areas, an eco park and an indoor climbing wall.

Head straight along the towpath, with warehouses to the right and Canary Wharf rearing up ahead of you. At **Mile End Lock** the path dips and goes under Mile End Road bridge; some 500m further on is the Ragged School Museum which you can access from the canalside by taking Ben Johnson Road.

The Ragged School Museum

The **Ragged School Museum** (Wed, Thurs & 1st Sun of the month: 2–5pm; free), housed in Dr Barnardo's second ragged school, is a gem of a place, offering both an insight into enlightened education for the Victorian poor and into the social history of Tower Hamlets, from the matchworkers' rebellion at the Bryant & May factory to the dark days of the Blitz. The first floor has a classroom done out in the colours Barnardo specified, while the top floor is dedicated to domestic life in the East End, with a re-creation of a tiny kitchen.

At the canalside entrance of the museum you'll find a small and basic **café**.

Dr Barnardo

Dr Thomas Barnardo was born in 1845 to an Irish father and a Jewish mother, and came to London from Dublin at the age of twenty to train as a missionary at the Bow headquarters of the China Inland Mission. Profoundly affected by the sight of children begging and sleeping outdoors, he began preaching in the streets and teaching at a ragged school. Increasingly absorbed by this new mission, he gave up his plans for China. In 1876, he converted some nearby warehouses and began schooling the children of the local poor, alongside helping them gain employment.

What marked Barnardo amongst other benefactors was that he helped all children, regardless of race or disability. The Ragged School Museum traces the stories of young West Indians who worked on ships and, becoming destitute, were taken under Barnado's wing. Remarkably, he is thought to have saved more than sixty thousand kids, including those whose parents worked at the nearby gasworks, from extreme poverty.

Towards Limehouse Basin

0.75km

Back on the towpath beyond the Ragged School, go along the stretch of scrappy parkland with a tall brick chimney at the far end. Head under the railway bridge, onwards up the towpath to **Salmon Lane Lock**, where you go under a little metal bridge and past a derelict lockhouse. Around 300m further on you emerge at the shimmering marina of **Limehouse Basin**, where the Regent's Canal meets the Thames.

Here you pass under a long brick railway viaduct built in 1840 – the second oldest in the world and now traversed by DLR trains.

The rise and fall (and rise) of Limehouse Basin

The glossy developments of the marina and its rather sanitized air convey little of the fact that **Limehouse Basin** was once a powerhouse of London's economy. The area was named for the fourteenth-century lime kilns that once sat by the river, and it was a significant port from Tudor times. It was in 1820 though, with its inauguration as the Regent's Canal Dock, that Limehouse Basin became truly significant. The basin was a crucial conduit between central London, the River Lee Navigation, the Thames and the world's oceans – it was a busy, vital place where coal from Northumberland and ice and timber from Scandinavia were loaded onto barges and carried up the canal. Much larger in extent than today's marina, the dock was once so busy with ships from all over the world that you could walk right across it, hopping from one vessel to the next.

With crews often discharged at the end of a voyage, it became an area where **immigrants**, including African and Chinese sailors, settled. The Chinese of Limehouse gained notoriety for supposed vice and the association with the opium trade, though in reality theirs was a generally law-abiding, if closed, community. In fact, the image of the debauched, iniquitous Chinaman owes much to the fiction of the period: Sherlock Holmes visited the fog-swathed streets of Limehouse to gather information on suspects; Sax Rohmer cooked up master criminal Fu Manchu – "the yellow peril incarnate in one man"; and Wilde's Dorian Gray visited the area's opium dens to "buy oblivion".

Eventually, as maritime activity declined and canals were superseded by the railway, the area declined too and became an overcrowded slum. When it was shattered by bombing during World War II, the Chinese community relocated to Soho. In 1969, the basin closed to commercial traffic, to be reborn and redeveloped in its current incarnation in the 1980s.

The Thames Towpath

1.5km

Continuing to the Thames Towpath, go down the western side of the basin, following the path round the water's edge. Looming over the basin on the opposite side is Hawksmoor's church of **St Anne's**, which alludes to the former importance of the area. The highest church clock in London, it was an important landmark for shipping.

Continuing along the path, you pass the freestanding Limehouse Lock office with its octagonal roof. Just beyond, cross the thin metal bridge over the lock, turning right after to come to the **Thames Towpath**. Turn right again and cross the road bridge over the basin, where you can absorb the magnificent view west along the Thames. At the edge of the basin you'll find *The Narrow* **gastro-pub.**

- -

The Narrow (Mon–Fri 11.30am–11pm, Sat noon–11pm, Sun noon–10pm; ☎ 020/7592 7950) is a Gordon Ramsay-owned gastro pub with a great riverside setting. The food is fairly pricey but hearty and good, with mains such as steak and chips and Cumberland bangers for £10–15. The interior, plain and attractive with flagstone floors and an open fire, has expansive river views.

- -

For more of a traditional boozer experience, keep going along the Thames Towpath towards Prospect Wharf. This stretch of the towpath initially follows Narrow Street, an atmospheric run of looming converted warehouse buildings. After 250m at the end of the street the Thames Towpath continues, becoming an actual path. The path joins the river, which is spectacularly wide at this point, with fine views back to Canary Wharf. Another 500m further on you reach King Edward Memorial Park (dawn–dusk). Carry on through the park, past its little bandstand – at the edge of the park the path detours from the river's edge for a 100m stretch. You pass some tennis courts, and at end of the path turn left onto the road, and over a red metal bridge to the *Prospect of Whitby* at **Wapping Wall.**

- -

The *Prospect of Whitby* (Mon–Wed & Sun noon–11pm, Thurs–Sat noon–midnight; ☎ 020/7481 1095), built in 1520, is the oldest riverside inn in London. It's an atmospheric old place, with a higgledy piggledy dark interior, flagstone floors, varnished wood, river views and a small terraced garden. They serve reasonable food: burgers, fish and chips and so on for around £8.

- -

From here you can retrace your steps to the basin and **Limehouse station** or go back up the canal to return to Bethnal Green station. Another option is to carry on along the Thames Towpath to Tower Bridge (2km). Otherwise, take the D3 bus, which stops just in front of the pub, and runs between Crossharbour and Bethnal Green.

WALTHAMSTOW MARSHES

Hackney to Walthamstow

Distance and difficulty 13.75km; easy–moderate.
Duration 3hr 15min.
Trains and buses Overground train to Hackney Central from stations between Richmond and Stratford, or buses #38, #55, #106, #242 from central London.
Map OS Landranger 177: *East London*; OS Explorer 173: *London North*.

Hackney and **Walthamstow** are on the edgier side of east London: crowded, multi-cultural boroughs with a vibrant and sometimes volatile street life. But if you think these two areas are all grit and no green spaces, you're in for a big surprise. This route cuts a green slice from Hackney Central to the heart of Walthamstow, linking three **waterways** – the Regent's Canal, Hertford Union Canal and River Lee Navigation – and taking you along the site of the 2012 Olympics and through the sweeping open spaces of the Hackney and Walthamstow **marshes**. The walk is bookended by two hugely contrasting **markets**: genteel "farmers' style" Broadway Market, on Saturdays, where you can grab a cappuccino and compose an excellent picnic for the walk, and the sensory overload that is Walthamstow Market (Tues–Sat 8am–6pm), Europe's longest, with a continuous colourful kilometre of stalls piled high with cheap clothes and homeware. Walthamstow village even provides a secluded **pub** for a post-walk pint: the inviting *Nag's Head*.

With flat terrain and no stiles, this is a good option for bikes and prams, though it's not recommended at dusk or for lone female walkers.

Getting started
0.25km

From the eastbound platform of Hackney Central, exit the station down the long sloping path. At the bottom of the slope you come out onto Amhurst Road – bear right under the railway bridge to emerge onto buzzing Mare Street. Go straight down Mare Street, past Woolworths and the **Hackney Empire**, a flamboyant Victorian variety theatre. Cross Wilton Way and the piazza in front of the imposing Art Deco Town Hall. Ahead of you is the library and Hackney Museum. Cross the road in front of the library and head down Hackney Grove, the narrow **cycle and walking route** to the right of the museum.

London Fields and Broadway Market
1km

The cycle route leads you alongside the museum for 200m; at the end, cross the road to head down narrow Martello Street, underneath the wide railway bridge. You pass the *Pub on the Park* with its attractive outdoor terrace – carry on down the road for 200m with the metal railings of **London Fields** to your right. The entrance to London Fields is flagged by two metal poles with balls on top – turn into the entrance then bear left, down the long straight cycle route.

The cycle route leads through the park for 250m; at the end, cross the road at the pedestrian crossing and head straight on into **Broadway Market**, a perfect example of urban regeneration, where local traders and residents work passionately to keep developers at bay. For centuries Broadway Market was used by drovers from Epping Forest, who took their cattle along here, via the grazing at London Fields, for slaughter at Smithfield.

During the week Broadway Market (Sat 9am–5pm) is a quiet enclave of laptop-wielding media types, who congregate in *Climpson & Sons* at no. 67 for excellent cappuccino. On Saturdays the street leaps into life for the weekly market, a foodie's paradise: try the Sporeboys stall near *Climpson & Sons* for freshly fried mushroom sandwiches. You can also pick up great picnic goods: quality cheeses, quiches and pies, sumptuous cakes and tarts and fresh fruit. F. Cooke at no. 9 is an atmospheric old pie and mash shop.

After 300m you come to the end of Broadway Market – cross the road and go through the metal gate onto the Regent's Canal: turn left and head along the canal towards the giant gas tower.

Regent's Canal and Victoria Park
2.5km

This section of the **Regent's Canal** has a different feel to that described on p.15: it's semi industrial with somewhat dilapidated red-brick wharf buildings, but on a sunny day, with birds bobbing along, it has a definite charm of its own. Part of a network of London waterways, the canal is an important migratory route for cormorants, coots, moorhens and mallards.

After 400m you pass under a rail bridge and then a bridge labelled Mare Street – beware of bikes that often shoot through these bridges at high speed. Pass the entrance to Victoria Park and keep going along the canal. Underneath another bridge, distinguished by a VR and a crown sculpted in stone, you come to

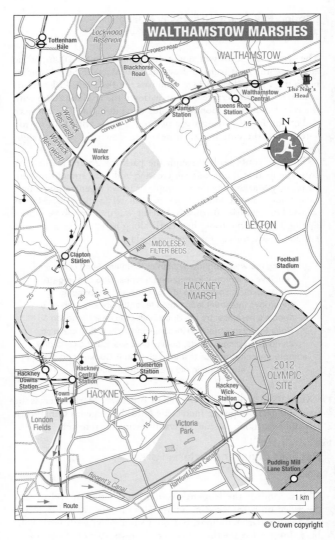

WALTHAMSTOW MARSHES

© Crown copyright

a section of the water that's overhung with trees and lined with canal boats.

Just before the canal lock, turn left into **Victoria Park**, bearing right onto the wide pavement that borders the lake. Head towards the domed Lakeside Pavilion and the loos; keep these to your left and exit the path via the grand wrought-iron blue gate. Take a left out of the gates with the roundabout in front of you. A zebra crossing takes you across Grove Road; go through the second set of blue gates, which leads you to the next section of the park.

Turn right, following the cycle sign, up a wide avenue of plane trees. After 500m you'll see to your right a wrought-iron **pedestrian bridge** over the Hertford Union Canal. Don't cross the bridge but go through the ornate gate and head down the brick path to your right. At the bottom, turn left along the canal, passing under the pedestrian footbridge.

The Hertford Union Canal and the River Lee Navigation

2.25km

The **Hertford Union Canal** initially runs along the eastern edge of Victoria Park, where it is lined with tall grasses and overhung with weeping willows and tall plane trees. You soon pass a lock with an attractive lock-keeper's cottage; at the second lock you come to the prettily landscaped **Growing Concerns Garden Centre**, where they'll sell you a cuppa and a slice of home-made cake or an ice cream.

Some 250m beyond the garden centre you go under a wide road bridge, towards another lock. The canal is wider and feels more industrial at this point, without the seclusion of the earlier section. The path dips under a thin metal pedestrian bridge, with a lofty glass and wood development on the opposite bank.

Just beyond the flats you bear round to the left and the Hertford Union Canal meets the **River Lee Navigation**. Just 50m beyond this bend, at the metal road bridge, you need to cross to the opposite bank of the canal. Continue in the same direction, following the wooden sign to Hackney Marsh. After 600m you pass under two adjoining road bridges. Beyond this to your right is a stately avenue of plane trees and you'll see the Lesney Matchbox Toys factory on the opposite side.

Hackney Marsh

2km

Just beyond another road bridge and opposite the factory, you come to the edge of the **Hackney Marsh**.

Instead of following the canalside path here, take the tarred path, signed with a blue **National Cycle Network** marker. After 600m you approach a pedestrian bridge; follow the blue arrow marker on the bollard, which curves round to the right, away from the canal towards the base of the bridge. Beyond the bridge the wide spaces of the playing fields (see box, p.61) of the Hackney Marshes appear to your right, and there's a line of iron railings to your left. At a clump of trees, head away from the riverside path, once again following the blue cycle sign towards a low brick building.

Continue along the edge of the playing fields for 500m until you reach a metal **footbridge**. Cross the footbridge, following the sign towards the Walthamstow Marsh Nature Reserve. On the other side, follow the blue cycle signs straight ahead through the metal gate. Take the tarred path that curves around the **Middlesex Filter Beds** until you come to a junction; continue straight ahead, following the sign towards the nature reserve – the path dips under a road bridge and heads uphill.

Walthamstow Marsh

2km

Coming up the slope from the road bridge the views open out and you are on the edge of **Walthamstow Marsh**. This, one of the last of London's marshlands, was managed under the system known as **lammas** from Anglo Saxon times to the early twentieth century. The land was enclosed in spring so that grass could grow, and opened for grazing in August on Lammas Day. In an echo of this ancient tradition, cattle are still brought onto the marsh in the summer for grazing.

Go straight ahead, following the long path ahead of you, ignoring the wooden cycle path sign to the right. This is the most open part of the walk, with meadows to the left, a line of pylons ahead and, to the right, horses grazing in their paddocks and a line of low industrial buildings beyond.

Follow the path for 750m, approaching the twin-arched railway bridge. Don't go under the bridge; just before you reach it, bear right onto the concrete path that dips down under a metal bridge. Go under this bridge then head up the path; for this stretch the banks of the path are bordered by elderflower and wild rose bushes.

Around 750m beyond the railway bridge you come to a little car park. Go through it and turn right, following the bike sign towards Walthamstow.

Towards Walthamstow

3km

From here you follow a leafy lane, lined with cow parsley, wild roses, elderflower and willows, towards **Walthamstow**. After 500m you come to the extensive Thames Water treatments works and after another 750m to a pair of metal gates with leaf shapes imprinted in them.

You are now on Coppermill Road; go straight ahead up the road, passing the *Coppermill* pub on your right. After 300m, turn right on to Leucha Road, following the cycle-route sign towards Walthamstow. To either side you'll see the distinctive **Warner**

Olympic development

At the time of writing, the 88 football pitches on Hackney Marsh were still extant. To the great concern of locals and **football fans**, this historic resource is to be redeveloped in preparation for the 2012 Olympics. It's hard to escape the irony that the pitches, a haven of Sunday league football and once a training ground for the young David Beckham and other stars, are to be destroyed in the name of sport. The plan is to restore the land post 2012, but whether the diverse community of Sunday leaguers returns remains to be seen.

Houses, built by the Warner family at the beginning of the twentieth century to provide quality affordable accommodation for ordinary people. They are in fact purpose-built flats or "half houses", their arched recessed porches sheltering two doors – one leads to the upper flat and one to the ground floor. Other features to look out for are terracotta heads and other ornaments, and the swirly "W" device denoting Warner.

Tranquil Leucha Road leads, after 300m, to a T-junction, where you'll suddenly be greeted by a very urban racket and a line of kebab shops, Turkish bakeries and pizza joints. Turn left here, then almost immediately right up the High Street, the site of **Walthamstow Market** (see below).

After 750m, you'll see a wide square to the right – cut through this to get to the **train and bus stations**. The bus station is to the left, the train and tube lie across busy Selbourne Road.

Walthamstow Market (Mon–Sat) is proud to advertise itself as Europe's longest, its stalls piled with pound-a-bowl fruit and veg, synthetic lingerie, peacock feathers, lurid kids' toys, cut-price electrical goods, harness-style pitbull collars, Ghanaian fabrics and football memorabilia. Carts sell jellied eels and Jamaican patties, while to either side of the street are pound shops and discount clothes stores. Look out for Manzi's at no. 76, a tiled pie and mash shop that's an intriguing survivor of the old East End.

Walthamstow Village
0.75km

This worthwhile detour allows you to explore the surprisingly verdant **village** heart of Walthamstow, taking you to the *Nag's Head* pub. Pass the bus station to your left and head up Selbourne Road. At the junction at the top of Selbourne Road, go straight ahead at the pedestrian crossing onto St Mary Road. Follow

St Mary Road for 250m; at the end of the road head up Church Path, with a row of terraced cottages to the left and the Vestry House Museum to your right.

Continue straight ahead, passing the eighteenth-century Squire's Almshouses and St Mary's Church to your left. To your right is the wattle and daub **Ancient House**, a restored fifteenth-century hall house. Cross the road here and turn right on to Orford Road. On the left you'll see the *Nag's Head*.

The *Nag's Head* (Mon–Thurs 4–11pm, Fri 2–11pm, Sat & Sun noon–11pm; ⊙020/8520 9709) serves up Belgian fruit beers and has an extensive wine list; head for the pretty terraced garden at the back or curl up on one of the battered sofas inside. There's live jazz on Sundays. (There's no food on offer, but don't follow the advice to go to their sister pub to eat, as it's mediocre.)

EPPING FOREST

Queen Elizabeth's Lodge to Connaught Water

Distance and difficulty 11km; shorter walk 5.5km; easy–moderate.
Duration 2hr 45min; shorter walk 1hr 20min.
Trains Liverpool Street to Chingford (every 20–30min; 30min); return
from Chingford to Liverpool Street (every 20–30min; 30min).
Map OS Landranger 177: *East London*; OS Explorer 174: *Epping
Forest & Lee Valley*.

Starting in the northeast fringes of London, the ancient deciduous
woodland of **Epping Forest** stretches along a high gravel ridge for
almost twenty kilometres into the Essex countryside. Originally
a royal hunting ground, Epping Forest was opened to the public
in 1878, since when it has been managed by the Corporation of
London. Covering some six thousand acres, the forest is London's
largest public open space, and its sheer scale comes as a surprise
to the first-time visitor, not least because of its proximity to the
urban sprawl. It remains a popular spot, and at any time of year
you can expect to share the forest with plenty of horse-riders and
cyclists, as well as many fellow walkers.

This circular walk heads from **Chingford station** up to **Queen
Elizabeth's Hunting Lodge** before heading north into the heart
of the forest. The midway point is the woodland village of **High
Beach** – the *King's Oak* here makes a good **lunch** stop. The second half of the walk takes you further east, past the Iron Age
earthworks of **Loughton Camp** and on to **Connaught Water**,
the largest of the 150 ponds that dot the forest. The route follows
clear trails throughout, though few of them are waymarked and
the public footpaths marked on the Ordnance Survey maps can
be misleading (we've indicated below any instances where there is
likely to be confusion). You can **shorten the walk** from 11km to
5.5km by deviating off the main route at the top of Long Hills and
rejoining it at Fairmead Road.

Getting started

0.4km

From **Chingford station**, turn right onto Station Road (the
A1069). Almost immediately, **Chingford Plain** – the grassy
expanse on the forest's edge where royalty once hunted – opens
up before you, with the forest beyond. Follow the main road as it
heads uphill, keeping the plain on your left and the large houses of
Forest Avenue to your right.

Queen Elizabeth's Lodge and Butler's Retreat

0.1km

At the brow of the hill, just beyond the mock-Tudor *Royal Forest* pub, **Queen Elizabeth's Hunting Lodge** comes into view. Built for Henry VIII in 1543, and renovated for Elizabeth I in 1589, the timber-framed lodge served as a grandstand from which hunts on the plain below could be watched – as such, it would originally have been open to the elements, though its timber frame was later enclosed with plaster. There's no evidence that either monarch ever actually used the building, but the association with Elizabeth stuck, and by the seventeenth century the lodge had acquired its present name. Used variously as a law court, tearooms and a family home, it now houses a small **museum** (March–Sept Wed–Sun 12.30–5.30pm; Oct–Feb Sat & Sun 11am–4pm; free), with low-key exhibits on the history of the building; as you'd expect, there are great views from the gallery across the plain, where hunts would have taken place.

Next door to the lodge lies **Butler's Retreat**, a traditional white-washed and red-tiled Essex barn which was subsequently converted into a "forest retreat" (see box, p.66) to cater for the crowds of urban pleasure-seekers who frequented the forest during the late nineteenth century.

....

Butler's Retreat (☏ 020/8524 2976) restaurant and snack bar serves inexpensive snacks and hot drinks (from the kiosk on the north side of the building) and more substantial meals, including filling breakfasts (served inside). There's also a fancier evening menu at weekends if you want an after-walk dinner.

....

Into the forest

3km

Turn left on the far side of *Butler's Retreat* and follow the path down between the retreat and the small Butler's Retreat Pond, across Chingford Plain towards the forest. The path here, along with many of the tracks through the forest, is classified as a bridleway, so can become a bit churned up by the many horses that use it.

After some 500m you reach the edge of the forest and the ground becomes firmer underfoot. Follow the path as it runs dead ahead into the trees, which form an impressive avenue known as **Green Ride**. Head straight on for around 1.5km, passing straight over a crossroads after 500m and then making the gentle ascent up **Long Hills** to reach the summit of the ridge on which the bulk of the forest sits.

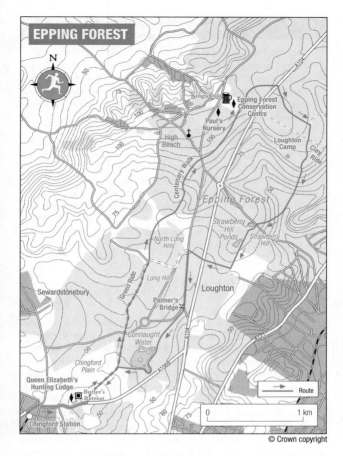

© Crown copyright

At the top of the hill, just beyond a left-hand turn, the main path bears off to the right; follow this for the **shorter loop** described below. To continue on the main route, take the second track, which carries straight on from this bend, over a small "crossroads" and up along the right-hand side of a small clearing, up **North Long Hills** and out of the trees to the edge of **Whitehouse Plain** – cows are often let out to graze here, reflecting the forest's status as common land. The path snakes its way north for 750m, up along the left-hand edge of the plain and then back into the trees to climb steeply uphill to a minor road.

If you want to **cut the walk short** here, continue along Green Ride as it bears around to the right before the clearing described in the main route. In a few minutes you'll reach a north–south trail; turn left (north) onto this to head round to Fairmead Road (see p.67).

The forest retreats

On May 6, 1882, Queen Victoria officially opened Epping Forest as "an open space for the recreation and enjoyment of the public" as outlined in the Epping Forest Act of 1878 – an act that made the London Corporation responsible for the forest's conservation and effectively prevented landowners from enclosing land or selling it off for development.

Dubbed the **"Cockney Paradise"**, Epping Forest soon began to attract visitors in their tens of thousands. Both Chingford Plain and High Beach became crowded with day-trippers, who were entertained with donkey rides and other fairground attractions, while giant refreshment rooms – or **"forest retreats"**, as they were popularly known – were also set up to cater to the crowds. The larger retreats could seat up to two thousand people at a time, though only one of these survives, **Butler's Retreat** (see p.64), which opened in 1891 and is still going strong today, although its capacity has fallen from six hundred people to just forty.

Up and Down Ride to High Beach

1km

Cross the road and pick up the trail on its far side, which runs parallel to the busy A104, whose traffic can mar the forest's tranquility here, especially during the summer. The distant roar of cars is more than compensated for, however, by the dramatic landscape here, as the trail – the aptly named **Up and Down Ride** – begins to rollercoaster through ancient coppiced and pollarded woodland.

A few metres beyond the final rise out of Up and Down Ride you pass the site of a former forest nursery, **Paul's Nursery**, over to your left. The nursery was reincorporated into the forest in 1920, though it's still home to exotic plant life found nowhere else in the forest, including foreign maples – spectacular in autumn – lilies of the valley, azaleas and rhododendrons.

Some 750m beyond Paul's Nursery, and a couple of hundred metres beyond a right-hand turn (to which we will return later), the track comes out on the road into High Beach village. Take the track to your left just before the road, on the near side of Oak Plain Pond, to reach the **Epping Forest Information Centre** (Easter–Oct Mon–Sat 10am–5pm; Nov–Easter Mon–Fri 11am–3pm, Sat & Sun 11am–5pm; ☎020/8508 0028). The centre has good displays on the forest's history, flora and fauna, and past and present management techniques. Behind the information centre lies the village of **High Beach**, little more than a clutch of houses, a green and a **pub**, the *King's Oak*, which offers filling bar meals; the attached kiosk serves takeaway tea, coffee and inexpensive hot and cold snacks.

Towards Loughton Camp

1.5km

From High Beach, go back the way you came along the trail towards Up and Down Ride. Ignore all the wheelchair-access trails close to the information centre; after a few hundred metres, turn left at the first proper fork, just before Paul's Nursery. This track takes you in around 400m to the busy **A104**, the main road through the forest.

Cross the road to the small car park opposite, then take the main track leading out of it, southeast into the forest. About 750m further on, this trail joins another heading south. Turn right onto this, passing the wide, grassy avenue of **Clay Ride** a few metres further on to your left (Centenary Walk, marked here on Ordnance Survey maps, is very overgrown, which can make map-reading confusing).

A hundred metres or so south of Clay Ride, to the right of the trail, you should be able to make out the earthworks of the Iron Age settlement of **Loughton Camp**, a twelve-acre site that is now somewhat obscured by pollarded trees inside and around it. This is one of two earthworks in the forest (the other is Ambresbury Banks, in the northern reaches of the forest): it's thought that these sites were bolt holes for local people and their livestock during periods of tribal warfare, rather than permanently settled places.

Loughton Brook to Palmer's Bridge

2km

Past the camp's southern reaches the trail descends sharply down to tiny **Loughton Brook**, then rises steeply again towards the road into nearby Loughton. To the left of the trail you can see the brook twisting and turning as it meanders along the valley floor, carving out a surreal landscape of exposed tree roots and muddy flats.

Cross the Loughton Road and continue along the trail to the left of the man-made **Strawberry Hill Ponds**, created as fishponds in the nineteenth century and still used for fishing today. Follow the track as it leads downhill, past fields and the greenhouses of Loughton nurseries to your left, to reach a trail where you turn to the right, 750m or so from the road and just after the second of the two ponds. Continue for another 750m to arrive back at the A104.

Cross the road, then take the trail to the right, which leads across heathland, skirting the northern side of the nearest trees before joining the old **Fairmead Road** (now closed to through traffic) a few hundred metres further on. Where you meet the road, a path leads off into the woods; this is where you'll come out if you took the short cut described earlier (see p.65).

Turn left onto Fairmead Road and head south for just under a kilometre to reach **Palmer's Bridge** to your right – a grand name

for a couple of planks over a little ditch. Continue along Fairmead Road for another 10m or so and then take the path that bears right off it, by the edge of the trees.

On to Connaught Water

3km

Continue along the path, which follows the left bank of a tiny stream to **Connaught Water**, 750m beyond Palmer's Bridge, an attractive man-made lake which was created in 1893 by damming tiny Ching Brook and digging out the adjacent marshy area. The lake is very popular with day-trippers, even on the bleakest of winter days, and is also home to a rich variety of **wildfowl**, including the striking multi-coloured mandarin ducks that breed here over winter and which are easily spotted from early October through to spring.

Follow the circular path around the lake to the opposite side of the water, where a sluice marks the exit point of the tiny brook that feeds Connaught Water. Take the path down to follow the brook for a few metres before crossing it by way of a little wooden bridge. Head straight over the grassy clearing through the trees, across a gravelled path and back uphill to *Butler's Retreat* (see p.64), which can be seen through the trees ahead. From here, retrace your steps back up to the main road, turn right and head downhill, past Queen Elizabeth's Hunting Lodge and Chingford Plain, to reach **Chingford station**.

2

The North Downs

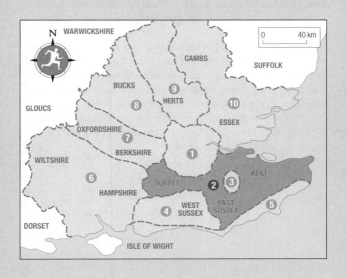

Box Hill

Westhumble to Mickleham Downs and

Box Hill 71

Guildford and the North Downs

Guildford to Compton and back 76

Gomshall and the North Downs

Gomshall to Shere and back........... 82

The Pilgrims' Way

Charing to Chilham and

Canterbury...................................... 86

The chalk escarpment of the **North Downs** stretches from Surrey to the cliffs between Dover and Folkestone. At their western extent, the wooded downs provide unexpectedly dense greenery in an otherwise over-developed corner of the southeast, while to the east they are characterized by profuse orchards and farmland, and by almost untouched, prototypically English villages. The first walk in this section takes you up on to the steep slopes of **Box Hill**, which inspired writers such as Keats and Jane Austen; the second leads from handsome **Guildford** to the secluded village of **Compton**, where the Watts Gallery and Chapel are compelling and unusual sights. The shortest walk here, **Gomshall and the North Downs**, links a couple of medieval Surrey villages and provides a leg-stretching climb up and along the downs. The final walk, the two-day **Pilgrims' Way**, climbs up onto the North Downs, leading from Charing to Canterbury. You can easily treat this as two separate one-day walks, although spending a weekend walking the route does give a satisfying sense of the original pilgrimage.

Trains are frequent throughout the area and journey times short (around 1hr), while the price of tickets is relatively low. For Gomshall you depart from **Waterloo**, with stops at Vauxhall, Queenstown Road and Clapham Junction en route (you can also get slower trains to Gomshall from Victoria; 1hr 25min). The departure point for the other destinations is **Victoria**. Except for the Pilgrims' Way these walks are circular, so convenient if you're driving.

BOX HILL

Westhumble to Mickleham Downs and Box Hill

Distance and difficulty 8.5km; easy–strenuous.
Duration 2hr 30min.
Trains London Victoria to Box Hill & Westhumble (hourly; 50min);
return from Box Hill & Westhumble to London Victoria (hourly;
50min).
Map OS Landranger 187: *Dorking & Reigate*; OS Explorer 145:
Guildford & Farnham.

Box Hill has long been one the famous beauty spots of the south,
its popularity soaring with the arrival of the railway here in 1867;
Box Hill & Westhumble is a lovely little station, built in ginger-
bread/Gothic style. The steep folds of the chalk hills round about
are unusually spectacular for southeast England, Box Hill itself
soaring to 193m. The area supports varied woodland – oak, beech,
ash and yew – as well as the celebrated evergreen **box trees**: more
familiar cut into novelty shapes in gardens, they grow wild here.
The walk leads across a valley to the village of **Mickleham**, which
enjoys a lovely leafy situation in the lee of the downs. You ascend,
via an excellent **pub** that makes a good lunch or pint stop (though
it gets very busy at weekends), into the woodland of **Mickleham
Downs**. From here, the path plunges down to valley level, then
up onto Box Hill, where the National Trust servery at the summit,
housed in a nineteenth-century **fort**, dishes out tea and cakes.

There are some ear-popping altitudes on this walk so, though the
distances are short, it is strenuous in parts.

Getting started

1.5km

Exit the station from platform two of **Box Hill & Westhumble
Station**. Turn left out of the station, cross over the railway bridge
and, opposite the "Chapel Lane" sign, take the public footpath that
leads alongside the **railway**. The path emerges into a field; walking
along the field you'll see stately white Norbury Park House on the
hill ahead, while to the right is the dramatic escarpment of Box Hill,
which you come to later in the walk. At the arched brick railway
bridge, take the path across the metal pedestrian bridge alongside.
Some 30m beyond the railway bridge, turn right to take the path
underneath the railway and up the hill. Cross the busy **A24** and turn
left up the wide tarred path for 300m. This section is a bit of a slog,
with traffic hurtling past, until you come to a **public footpath** to
Mickleham, signed with a yellow arrow, leading off to the right.

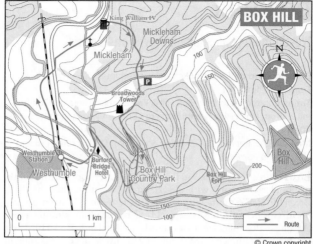

© Crown copyright

To Mickleham

1.5km

The path leads along the edge of a field – ahead you'll see the spire of **Mickleham**'s church. Where the path emerges, go left for just 10m on the track, and then right at Box Hill School playing fields. You come out at the clapperboard and brick *Running Horses* pub; cross over to the squat flint and stone **church**, drastically restored in the nineteenth century, though there's been a church here since Saxon times. Facing the main door is the grave of Richard Bedford Bennett, an Anglophile Canadian Prime Minister who died in Mickelham in 1947. You'll see two very worn fourteenth-century Longobardic tombstones in the porch.

  Resuming the walk, go up the path through the **cemetery**, to the left of the church as you face it. The path bears left between hedges thick with ivy, then leads along a paddock and onto a narrow paved lane. Cross the lane and go straight ahead up the path towards a clapperboard cottage with lattice windows. Facing the cottage, take a right onto the path up the hill – there's a National Trust Long Walk sign on the telegraph post here. After 100m you come out onto a wider track – go straight ahead, with the substantial shuttered villa to your right. Immediately beyond you come to a gravel track; bear left here, past the Church of England school. You emerge at a road, with the dual carriageway down to the left – turn right to reach the tile-hung *King William IV* **pub**.

The *King William IV* (☎01372/372 590) is an appealing country-
cottage style pub, with an open fire, a bright cosy interior and a
sheltered terrace. The hearty grub on offer includes steaks, pies,
ploughman's and veggie specials (£7–12) and there's Adnams and
Badger Best on handpump. Mon–Sat 11am–3pm & 6–11pm, Sun
noon–10.30pm (food served till 5pm).

Mickleham Downs

2km

Take the steep steps that lead alongside the pub and beyond,
taking you up onto **Mickleham Downs**. The path soon emerges
at a crossroads by an old flint wall; go up the bridleway ahead
of you, the narrow path climbing up through the trees. (As you
ascend the hill, look back for the sweeping views of the North
Downs to the west.) Follow the National Trust **Long Walk** sign
along the secluded, gently winding path through beech woodland.
Eventually, 600m from the crossroads, you come out at a wooden
post signed Downs Road. There's a blue arrow pointing you
straight ahead, but turn right here, up the track through the woodland. The track soon begins to lead gently downhill. You're now
on the **Thamesdown Link**, signed with a yellow arrow on a post.

You come out at a crossroads by a **National Trust** sign. Turn
left, up the hill. After 300m the path, enclosed by dark yew trees,
curves round to the right, following yellow arrows. The path
begins an initially gentle descent of the hill, before veering left
for a precipitously steep descent via wooden steps to the car park.
The path comes out on the road, opposite Whitehill car park. Go
straight ahead, up Whitehill.

Box Hill

2.5km

Go up the track for 300m, then take the right-hand turning onto
the **public footpath** signaled by a yellow arrow on a black background. The path climbs steeply uphill, through woodland. After
350m on your right you'll see a fencepost marked with a purple
arrow and a double-headed yellow one. Ignore these arrows and
turn left, on the path that leads up the hill. After another 250m
you come to a T-junction – turn right and carry on up the hill.
Eventually you come to a round flint folly, **Broadwoods Tower**.

Go straight ahead past the tower, on the narrow path through the
undergrowth. The path soon begins to lead downhill and curves
left, to join a hairpin bend on the tarred **zigzag road**. Take the
right-hand route, downhill for 500m – to your left is a steep bank

dotted with box trees, to the right is the sharp incline of **Box Hill**. At the next hairpin bend, you need to climb up the escarpment via the long run of wooden steps. You come out at a flint track where you should turn left to reach the summit and visitor centre. After 600m you come out at the long low walls of Box Hill **fort**, built in 1899 for protection from French invasion. Storage chambers under the fort are now home to a protected colony of bats.

The cream-coloured low brick building to the left of the fort contains the National Trust shop and **servery**, where you can get tea, home-made cakes, hot dogs and ice cream. After suitable refreshments, you need to **descend Box Hill** – instead of returning on the flint track, go back to the fort, keeping it to your right. At the far end of the fort buildings, take a left on a slightly tangled path that leads through undergrowth for a short stretch. You then

Box Hill in literature

Emma had never been to Box Hill... she wished to see what everybody found so much worth seeing.

Emma, Jane Austen

In the event, the eponymous heroine of **Jane Austen's** novel has a dispiriting time on Box Hill – the trip is marred by ennui and bad temper. Emma is rude to Miss Bates and the outing ends, quite literally, in tears. Austen may have been inspired to set the scene here by her admiration for the novelist **Fanny Burney**, who lived nearby and was married in Mickleham church.

The novelist and poet **George Meredith** lived near the zigzag road and reflected the sublime element of the landscape, writing, "anything grander than the days and nights in my porch you will not find away from the Alps: for the dark line of my hill runs up to the stars, the valley below is a soundless gulf". The great poet of the sublime, **John Keats**, stayed at the *Burford Bridge Hotel* (then the *Fox & Hounds*), and climbed Box Hill in the moonlight; he completed his epic poem *Endymion* here: "I like this place very much. There is Hill and Dale and a little River. I went up Box Hill this Evening after the moon... came down and wrote some lines."

While both these poets stress the solitary pleasures of Box Hill, **Daniel Defoe** in *A Tour through the Whole Island of Great Britain* (1724–6) writes of crowds and chaos – the clamorous scene he describes might strike a chord with today's summer visitors:

"...every Sunday, during the summer season, there used to be a rendezvous of coaches and horsemen, with abundance of gentlemen and ladies from Epsome to take the air, and walk in the boxwoods; and in a word, divert, or debauch, or perhaps both, as they thought fit, and the game increased so much, that it began almost on a sudden, to make a great noise in the county."

join a wide clay path that runs along the high ridge for 500m, with wonderfully sweeping views to either side.

Back to the station
1km

The path begins its slow descent of the hill. Ahead you'll see a couple of routes that lead straight ahead on the highest part of the hill, running down to solitary box trees. Take the path that veers left, heading down towards a **roundabout**. The path runs down the escarpment, dips into woodland and then takes you onto the road. Turn left, past what is now the sadly bland *Burford Bridge Hotel* – it is said to be the place where Nelson met with Lady Hamilton, and where he spent his last night in England before the Battle of Trafalgar. Wordsworth, Robert Louis Stevenson and Keats (see box opposite) also stayed here.

Beyond the roundabout, head along the path next to the busy A24, then after 250m follow the **cycle route** signs to the station via the subway. This takes you onto Westhumble Street, which leads, after 450m, to the **station**.

GUILDFORD AND THE NORTH DOWNS

Guildford to Compton and back

Distance and difficulty 9.75km; moderate.
Duration 2hr 20min.
Trains London Waterloo to Guildford (every 15 min; 35min); return from Guildford to London Waterloo (every 15 min; 35min.
Map OS Landranger 186: *Aldershot & Guildford*; OS Explorer 145: *Guildford & Farnham*.

This circular route takes you from the leafy fringes of the handsome county town of **Guildford**, through gentle North Downs countryside to the village of **Compton**. Here you can see the Arts and Crafts Watts Gallery, dedicated to the work of G.F. Watts; it's a wonderful showcase for his paintings and sculpture, and has the advantage of a very appealing **tearoom**, housed in what was the building's pottery. (Note that while the gallery is closed until summer 2010, the tearoom is staying open.) This tiny village is also home to the **Watts Chapel**, its interior designed by Watts's wife Mary in a unique fusion of the homespun and the visionary. From Compton, the route loops through Loseley Park and the hamlet of **Littleton**, back to the sylvan fringes of Guildford.

Getting started

1.75km

Coming out of the station at **Guildford**, follow the "way out" sign that points you towards Guildford Park Road. Turn left on the road and walk for 100m to reach the roundabout – cross straight over and follow the path that leads up the hill, passing terraces of red-brick Victorian houses. When you come out onto Mareschal Road, cross over and carry on up the path straight ahead of you – it leads to a flight of steps; descend these and turn right and carry on up the hill.

After 500m you pass a church on the left; turn left immediately after it, following the public footpath that cuts through the **cemetery**. Some 350m further on you reach a rocket-like octagonal tower at the edge of the cemetery. Follow the gentle curves of the road that takes you downhill, past comfortable suburban villas and their well-established gardens.

Another 600m down this road, cross over the wide road ahead and continue down Chestnut Avenue. Initially gravelled, it becomes paved and curves left, past St Catherine's Village Hall,

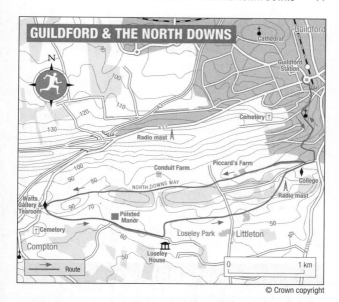

© Crown copyright

bringing you to a wide busy road. Turn right here before taking the first right onto Sandy Lane, opposite *Ye Olde Ship Inn*. Keep your eyes peeled for the narrow path to the right, 350m further on, signed "North Downs Way".

The North Downs Way

3km

Turn onto the **North Downs Way**, which leads straight ahead for an easy 3km to Compton, along tracks and farm lanes and through woodland and pastures. The only markers along the way are a couple of large farms – Pickard's Farm which you come to after 600m, and a kilometre beyond this, Conduit Farm (unsigned). The route is clearly waymarked with yellow arrows.

Some 400m beyond **Pickard's Farm**, the route veers left for just 20m, and then right, through a metal gate and up a sandy track. You'll see Conduit Farm along a track on your right, but take the left-hand fork. From here onwards, although the path is beautifully secluded, leading through beech woodland, your ears will begin to pick up the thunderous roar of the A3, which passes by Compton.

Another 750m after Conduit Farm the path slopes down to a crossroads, cutting over a public bridleway. Carry on straight ahead. From this point the little sandy track slopes downwards between two banks to emerge at some farm buildings. Carry on straight ahead along the track – this section of the walk leads between dense hedgerows towards **Compton**. Through a picket fence on the right, you'll soon see the long low outlines of the Watts Gallery.

Compton

A driveway sweeps up from the end of the path to the low grey Arts and Crafts building that houses the **Watts Gallery**, purpose-built in 1904 to house the work of G.F. Watts (1817–1904), the prolific sculptor, painter and symbolist who lived in Compton with his wife Mary from 1890 until his death. The building is currently undergoing major restoration to repair the roof, conserve the artwork and strengthen the gallery's education programme (to find out when the gallery will reopen, see Ⓦ www.wattsgallery.org.uk).

The **teashop**, housed in what was Mary Watts's pottery, shouldn't be missed. It's a rickety gem with a barn-like roof, dishing up

England's Michelangelo

The reputation of **George Frederic Watts** is beginning to recover after a long decline; in his time he enjoyed dazzling success, feted by critics as **"England's Michelangelo"**. While this may seem rather hyperbolic, Watts's portraits, particularly of celebrated women such as Ellen Terry (to whom he was briefly and disastrously married), his patron Lady Mary Augusta Holland and society beauty Lillie Langtry, are both glamorous and sympathetic. His enormous output in oils and later sculpture immortalized his Victorian contemporaries and friends – among whom were Ruskin, Tennyson and Julia Margaret Cameron – but he was also known for more allegorical works and for mystical landscapes.

Born in London in fairly humble circumstances, and a self-taught painter, Watts was politically a radical, though his connections with upper-class patrons gave him crucial access to an intellectual and aristocratic milieu. He married Mary (who was 36 years younger) in 1886, and in 1890 they moved out of London because of his poor health, settling on Compton in order to be close to friends. They built a mock-Tudor home, Limnerslease, and a few years later work began on the building that was to become the Watts Gallery. It was purpose-built as a gallery, but also housed Mary's pottery students.

Watts's Hall of Fame portraits, begun in the 1850s, include Carlyle, Browning and Rossetti; he left the collection to the National Portrait Gallery in 1895. The gallery in Compton is still run on his deeply held socialist principles, and with the village chapel that he and Mary built (see opposite), form an eloquent and intriguing testimony to his ideals.

▼ Watts Gallery

crumbly scones with home-made jam, large slices of traditional cakes made with free-range eggs, and pots of tea for a pound. The decor is eccentric but appealing, with plastic tablecloths, mis-matching china and old photos on the walls.

The Watts Gallery tearoom is open daily from 10.30am–5.30pm.
Watts Chapel is open daily from dawn till dusk.

At the entrance to the Watts Gallery, the North Downs Way joins the road into the village. To **continue the walk**, turn left onto the road; after just 10m, turn left onto a narrow path, which is the return route to Guildford. However, it's well worth continuing for another 500m up the road, to see the exceptional Watts Chapel.

Watts Chapel

Watts Chapel sits in the hillside cemetery to the left of the road. Follow the brick path through the cemetery, between tall yew trees, to reach the elongated terracotta-coloured building.

The chapel was built between 1895 and 1898, under the instruction of Watts and his wife, who designed it. Constructed with the aid of local craftsmen and seventy villagers, it is a rapturous expression of the ideals of the **Home Arts and Industries Association**, which sought to improve social conditions through creative endeavour. Round the door is a cluster of angel heads, modelled from clay in moulds, each one created by a villager.

The **interior**, created under the direction of Mary Watts between 1901 and 1904, achieves a majestic effect that is remarkable for a small structure. Her decorative scheme was sculpted in gesso, its sea-greens, reds and golds glowing in the soft light provided by four pairs of tall stained-glass windows. The tendrils of the Tree of Life lead the eye upwards, via cherubim and seraphim and pairs of gravely beautiful winged messengers, to a pattern symbolizing eternity. Coming out of the chapel and descending the hill, look out for Mary's terracotta **well**, near the lychgate.

To connect to the return path to Guildford, turn right onto the road after you've descended the hill, back the way you came. Then take the public footpath just before red-roofed **Coneycraft Farm**, 200m beyond the chapel – it's a grassy path between sturdy wooden fences. Follow the path round the farm; follow the wooden public footpath signs up the broad concrete path away from the farm.

To Littleton

2.75km

Go out of the wooden gate away from the paddocks and fields of Coneycraft Farm, and follow the public footpath sign that leads straight ahead, rather than the one that points down to the right. Head past gently rolling fields towards the buildings that comprise **Polsted Manor**. At the far edge of the manor grounds, wide wooden steps lead down to a path. Turn right here for 10m, and then left, following the public footpath sign.

The track, flanked by horse chestnuts, leads for 800m beyond Polsted Manor to **Loseley Park** (where a herd of Jersey cows produce milk used for yoghurt and ice cream). At the gate to Loseley Park the path leads down to the left, and then right, to skirt the grounds of the house. Cross the stile over a farm track, and carry straight across the field – to the right there are views of Elizabethan Loseley House, whose outlines will probably be familiar from ice cream tubs.

From the pond that borders the park, go through the metal gate and across two fields to the attractive jumble of houses that comprises **Littleton**, passing a timber-framed building to the left. Go straight ahead at the crossroads, down the lane.

Back to Guildford

2.25km

You pass a turning to a mansion called Orange Grove, to your right. Beyond this, instead of crossing the cattle grid, go left up a grassy public footpath. You soon come to a post with yellow arrows – take the path to the left, which is overhung and narrow at this point, leading uphill along the edge of a **wood**. It emerges onto a road – go straight ahead through the gap in the wall, following the public footpath sign.

This stretch of the path takes you through more woodland, then runs down on to the road – go straight ahead downhill, passing, after 400m, the turn-off to the North Downs Way you took earlier in the day. From this point you need to retrace your steps to get back to the station.

Turn left at the bottom of the lane, opposite *Ye Olde Ship Inn*, a snug, traditional pub where you might fancy stopping for a pint. Otherwise, take a left onto **Chestnut Avenue**. At the top of the avenue cross the road and go left, up **Beech Lane**. Climb the long steady curve of Beech Lane to the octagonal tower, where you turn right, back through the cemetery.

Turn right down the road once you've gone through the cemetery, and head down the hill. At the end of the descending terrace of Victorian houses, go left up the flight of steps. Cross Mareschal Road and then cross over Wodeland Avenue to head down the path, from where you'll have spectacular views of the brick bulk of **Guildford Cathedral**, designed by Sir Edward Maufe and built between 1936 and 1961. When the path reaches the roundabout, go straight back up Guildford Park Road and turn right into the railway station.

GOMSHALL AND THE NORTH DOWNS

Gomshall to Shere and back

Distance and difficulty 9km; easy–moderate.
Duration 2hr 15min.
Trains London Bridge or London Waterloo to Gomshall (hourly; 1hr 10min); return from Gomshall to London Bridge or London Waterloo (hourly; 1hr 10min).
Map OS Landranger 187: *Dorking & Reigate*; OS Explorer 145: *Guildford & Farnham.*

This circular walk begins and ends at the village of **Gomshall**, which sits on the Tilling Bourne stream between the green ridge of the North Downs and the Low Weald – given the proximity of Guildford and Dorking, the gentle, rolling countryside is surprisingly unspoilt and pretty. The route runs to medieval **Shere** and then climbs up onto the **North Downs**, continuing along the forested ridge of the downs before descending back into Gomshall to emerge opposite the *Compasses Inn*. This is a good place for **lunch**; there's also an attractive old pub in Shere, but the *Compasses'* food is better.

Getting started

1.5km

From platform 2 of tiny **Gomshall station**, head down the path to join the road, and then turn right (if you want to go straight to the *Compasses Inn*, go under the railway bridge and down the road for 500m). To get to Shere take the track to the left, just before you get to the railway bridge – it's marked with a wooden public footpath sign. Cross a stream and pass **Southbrook Farm Cottage**. Where the track turns sharply to the left, take the signed footpath to the right.

After 300m you emerge at a lane; turn right underneath the railway bridge, with a Tudor house ahead. Turn left up the minor road on the other side of the railway bridge and, at the junction 200m ahead, go straight on up Gravel Pits Lane. You are now following the signed **Shere Parish Millennium Trail**. Continue along the road, curving round to the left, after which you'll come out at a junction by Gravel Pits Farmhouse. Turn right here, following the sign for the Millennium Trail. The path beyond here is narrow and leafy, running through rolling countryside with good views of the downs to the right.

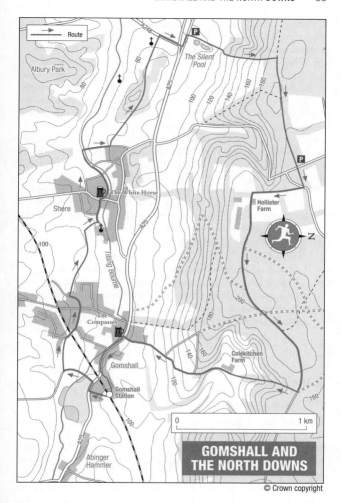

Route

Albury Park

The Silent
Pool

The White Horse

Shere

Tilling Bourne

Hollister
Farm

N

The
Compasses

Gomshall

Colekitchen
Farm

Gomshall
Station

Abinger
Hammer

0   1 km

**GOMSHALL AND
THE NORTH DOWNS**

© Crown copyright

Shere

Follow the path along a line of trees until you come to **Shere**. Take
the Millennium Trail sign to the right, through a gate that takes
you to **St James' Church**, entered via a handsome lychgate built by
Lutyens. The church is mainly Norman, with a fine, plain interior
and a beautiful font (dating from around 1200), its bowl patterned
with scallop shapes. Inside the church on the north wall is a qua-
trefoil with a squint, which allowed the local anchoress, **Christine
Carpenter**, to see the altar – her only view of the outside world.

Christine was walled up in a cell attached to the church in 1329; she was released after three years, but later succeeded in having herself imprisoned again. Contemporary documents describe her desire to evade the "rapacious wolf" outside her cell – it's unclear whether she was guilty of some transgression that caused her to be imprisoned in the first place, or whether it was a self-imposed act of devotion. Christine's cell no longer exists, but its low outline can still be seen on the exterior wall, giving some sense of its hideously claustrophobic proportions. Also worth looking out for inside the church is the thirteenth-century **Crusader chest**, one of a number placed in churches by order of Pope Innocent III to raise money for the Crusades; a small devotional medieval statue of a Madonna and Child is displayed nearby, while fragments of medieval glass adorn the windows.

From the church, head towards the village; the *White Horse* **pub** is straight ahead of you. To the right down the hill is the main body of the village, mostly comprising pretty fifteenth- and sixteenth-century timber-framed cottages. The Tilling Bourne stream, which is usually full of bobbing ducks, runs through the village.

The characterful and popular *White Horse* pub (Mon–Sat 11am–11pm, Sun 11.30am–10.30pm; ☏01483/202518) is a handsome half-timbered building, labyrinthine inside, with fine Tudor stonework and sturdy oak seating. The cooked food, particularly the Sunday lunches, isn't great, so it's best to go for ploughman's-type options.

To the Silent Pool

2km

Go down **Lower Street** along the stream, passing some allotments on your right. At the ford go straight ahead through the gate, keeping the stream to your right. Go through **Vicky's Gate** and follow the minor road leading away from the stream, turning left onto the path after 200m.

After 200m you come out into a big field which opens up to reveal downland. Cross the field and go through a stretch of beech and birch wood, before crossing a stile into a field. Off to the left, you can see glimpses of **Albury Park**, a much altered Tudor manor house. After 200m you pass a very old church to the left, then go through the gate, and descend towards the A248. At the road, turn right. A narrow path runs along the side of the road, saving you from having to walk on the road itself.

At the end of the road is the busy **A25** dual-carriageway. Cross the road to get to the car park. Keeping the car park on your left, follow the path leading to the Sherbourne Pool, which is on the right after about 75m. The path then winds round to the **Silent**

Pool – both pools are pretty devoid of atmosphere, thanks to the roar from the A25. According to popular legend though, a woodman's daughter was bathing in the Silent Pool when a caddish nobleman appeared. He rode his horse into the water to reach her and she drowned in her attempt to escape him. Her father found the body and the nobleman's hat floating on the water, which, in a sinister twist, bore the emblem of Prince John, suggesting that the future king of England was himself the culprit.

The North Downs

4km

To the left of the Silent Pool, wooden steps bring you up to a wire fence along a field; turn right on the narrow path up the hill. It's a stiff and steep climb through the woods – only 500m, but it feels further. Keep going till you reach a stone public bridleway sign, then turn right to walk through a beautiful beech wood on a wide sandy path. After 750m you reach a car park; cross the road and go straight ahead, following the signs for the **North Downs Way**. After 150m you reach another road. Turn right and then almost immediately left onto the wide path.

After 250m, take a left onto a curving track, marked with a North Downs Way sign. At **Hollister Farm**, 100m beyond, turn left through the farm buildings on a wide track. Pass the stables, then go through an access gate, following the blue arrow straight ahead. Follow the track for 400m to the crossroads, and continue straight on. Just over a kilometre further on you come to a **crossroads** where you'll see a big circular concrete structure on your left. Turn right here, down the hill.

Back to Gomshall

1.5km

The path dips down through the trees for 500m. Eventually the trees thin and there's a lovely verdant clearing to the left. Go through a wooden gate, carrying on straight ahead, and you'll see picturesque **Colekitchen Farm** to the right, in the lee of a steep hill. Beyond the farm, a tarred road runs uphill through woodland before emerging onto a wider road; go straight ahead to reach, after 500m, the **Compasses Inn** in Gomshall. To get back to the **train station**, turn left and head through the village.

The *Compasses Inn* (Mon–Sat 11am–11pm, Sun noon–10.30pm; ☏ 01483/202506) sits on the mill stream, with a beer garden on the banks, and serves good bar food, along with guest beers such as Hop Back Crop Circle and Wychwood Shires.

THE PILGRIMS' WAY

Charing to Chilham and Canterbury

Distance and difficulty day one: 17.5km; day two: 11.5km;
moderate.
Duration day one: 4hr 25min; day two: 2hr 50min.
Trains London Victoria to Charing (hourly; 1hr 15min); return from
Canterbury East to London Victoria (every 30min; 1hr 25min).
Map OS Landranger 189 and 179: *Ashford & Romney Marsh* and
Canterbury & East Kent; OS Explorer 137, 149 and 150: *Ashford,
Sittingbourne & Faversham* and *Canterbury*.

The route that became known as the **Pilgrims' Way** was an
amalgam of country roads and paths leading from Winchester
and serving pilgrims from the south and west of England and
continental Europe (via Southampton). At Harbledown, just outside Canterbury, this route merged with the much more ancient
Watling Street, the route for the main body of pilgrims from
London and the north. All were bent on seeing the gold- and
jewel-encrusted tomb of **Thomas Becket**, and perhaps, as the
Canterbury Tales testifies, having a bit of fun along the way.
    This two-day walk covers a particularly attractive stretch
of the Pilgrims' Way, and takes you to the goal of the
pilgrims – the magnificent **Cathedral** itself. The walk begins at
Charing in Kent, leading through lovely woods and farmland
to **Chilham**, an idyllic village where you can stay overnight,
before continuing on to **Canterbury** the next day. You can do
either day of this walk on its own, taking the train from or to
Chilham, but the most rewarding day in terms of landscape is
the first. This is fine, abundant countryside, especially appealing
in April – when Chaucer set his tales and when the fruit trees
are covered in blossom – or in late summer and early autumn,
when you can scrump for apples and pears. Although this is an
established walk, the signing (for the North Downs/Pilgrims'
Way) is minimal.

Day one

17.5km

Day one links two very pretty and historic Kentish villages:
Charing and **Chilham**. In between, Boughton Lees is home
to a pub that has been serving pilgrims for hundreds of years,
though a better **lunch** option on a sunny day is the nearby Perry
Court Farm Shop, where you can put together a picnic. The
country you walk through is for the most part domesticated but

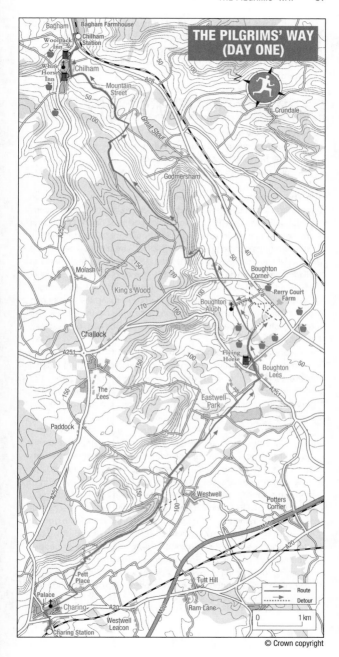

THE PILGRIMS' WAY
(DAY ONE)

Route
Detour

0   1 km

© Crown copyright

beautiful, with rolling vistas, orchards and the odd scattering of appealing tile-hung or half-timbered cottages. Towards the end of the walk you climb up into dense woodland, before descending into Chilham, where you can either take the train home or stay the night.

The Canterbury Tales

And specially from every shires end
Of England, down to Canterbury they wend
To seek the holy blissful martyr, quick
To give his help to them when they were sick.

In **The Canterbury Tales**, begun in 1386, Geoffrey Chaucer rolled together a rich bundle of stories – romances, animal fables, saucy yarns and sermons – by the simple expedient of having a group of characters, himself included, engage in a story-telling competition on a two-day pilgrimage to Becket's tomb. The pilgrims' host at the *Tabard Inn* in Southwark instigates the competition on the eve of the pilgrimage, launching Chaucer into his sparkling and pacy prologue, where he introduces his cast of characters, from the valiant knight, "his bearing modest as a maid", to the coy nun and the greasy pardoner. These vignettes are elaborated when the characters tell their tales, each one infused with the flaws, pretensions and, occasionally, nobility of the teller.

The framing device Chaucer employed for his tales represented a narrative revolution in English literature, as did the use of English in the telling, rather than courtly French or churchy Latin. For all their canonical significance though, the *Tales*, which seesaw between bawdiness and moral instruction, remain remarkably engaging.

The action of the book turns entirely on the stories themselves and the often tetchy interaction between the characters – one of the most disarming episodes is when the Host interrupts Chaucer's own *Tale of Sir Topaz* and begs him to quit his tedious "doggerel-rhyme" and tell a tale in prose. There's little mention of the topography of the route, except of the most incidental "Oh look, we're at Greenwich!" kind. So it hardly serves as a travelogue, but nonetheless it's quite fun to take the book with you on this walk. There are many versions available, from pared down and often pallid retellings for children to the full and (for most people) incomprehensible Middle English monty. The best choice, which will save you stumbling over too many *wympuls* and *lordynges*, is Nevill Coghill's rhythmic and vigorous modern verse rendering, published by Penguin Classics.

Getting started

1km

The walk starts at the village of **Charing**, tucked between the North Downs and the Low Weald. From Charing station, turn left onto Station Road and go straight ahead, crossing the busy A20 and continuing up the High Street into the village. Just past the post office, turn right down the lane to the **church** of St Peter and St Paul, which has a beautiful painted tie-beam roof, dated 1592. On the left are the remains of the **Archbishop's Palace**. These substantial and handsome ruins now incorporate picturesque houses, but once comprised a large manor house, built between the twelfth and the sixteenth centuries, which was given to Henry VIII by Archbishop Cranmer. A day's ride from Canterbury, the palace provided accommodation for more prestigious pilgrims.

Exit the church, turn left and follow the paved path behind the church that leads between houses and emerges at a playing field; go straight ahead across the field on the paved path, then go up the grassy path. Go straight ahead again, following the yellow arrow, across a field. Cross the stile and the field towards **Pett Place**, an early eighteenth-century mansion. Bear left when you reach the road, then follow the path to the right, marked with a green footpath sign, which leads via wooden steps into a field.

Pett Place to Boughton Lees

6.5km

The path climbs across the field, crosses a minor road, then cuts diagonally across another field to bring you to a huge beech tree. Turn right along the road here – you are now technically on the **Pilgrims' Way** itself. Follow the track ahead and then round to the right; it soon passes a quarry.

The route, marked with **North Downs Way** signs (also with acorns), runs for 1.5km through beautiful woodland; where it eventually forks, go to the left. It then joins a paved road; go left and carry on for nearly 1km until you come to a T-junction; cross the stile and turn left, then almost immediately right to cross the field. The path widens to become a track and dips through the fields, then climbs gently uphill. Turn right just before the white no entry sign then turn left to continue on the Pilgrims' Way.

Cross the stile and go through the field, with a large house up to the left. Coming out of the field, go straight ahead on the paved road, with the lake down to the right. At the T-junction, follow the footpath straight ahead across the field for 100m to reach a **National Trail** sign; After 600m you join the drive that leads down to a boundary wall of the nearby hotel and the A251.

Boughton Lees to Boughton Aluph

1.5km

Turn left onto the busy road and then take the right fork into **Boughton Lees**, along the village green. You'll see the *Flying Horse* pub across the green.

The *Flying Horse* (Thurs–Sat 10am–1am, Sun–Wed 10am–midnight; ☎01233/620914) at Boughton Lees was one of a chain of pubs designed to feed and water passing pilgrims. It's located in a fine old building right on the village green, where in summer you can sit outside and watch local cricket matches.

To continue, turn left out of the pub and then take a left, marked with a Pilgrims' Way sign, continuing down the road for 750m to reach a footpath sign that points in three directions: to continue on the Pilgrims' Way to Boughton Aluph, take the path to the left; to detour to the farm shop (see below), carry on up the road for 100m, then turn right and go through the gate with a yellow arrow.

The Pilgrims' Way leads across the fields for 750m, emerging in the tiny village of **Boughton Aluph**.

Detour to Perry Court Farm Shop

1.5km

If you don't fancy a pub lunch, the **Perry Court Farm Shop** is well worth a detour. You can put together a great picnic from the home-baked and locally grown goodies – cheeses, fresh bread, pear and apple juice, beers and all kinds of cakes, plus coffee and tea – and eat it in their adjoining orchard.

To reach the shop, having left the Pilgrims' Way and crossed the metal gate on the right-hand side, marked with a yellow arrow, follow the line of trees to your left; turn left and then right to cut through the field towards the busy A28 road. Cross the road to reach the shop, which is clearly signposted.

Perry Court Farm Shop is open daily 8.30am–6pm; ☎01233/812302.

To **continue to Boughton Aluph**, without retracing your steps, go back to the footpath but go straight ahead, not left. Cross the field, heading towards the church, then turn left onto the minor

road. After 50m turn right up the fenced path by the cattery, crossing the field towards the church.

Boughton Aluph and King's Wood

6.5km

The fourteenth-century church of **All Saints** in **Boughton Aluph**
is not in regular use, and as a result has an attractively ramshackle
and solitary air. The church is sturdily built of flint, with brick
buttresses and a stocky tower, though it's surprisingly lofty inside.
Look out for the fourteenth-century glass in the east window, and
for the memorial to the men of the Wye Fire Brigade, who saved
the church from destruction by incendiary bombs in September
1940 at the height of the Battle of Britain.

To continue the walk, exit the main gate, cross the road
and go over the stile. After 500m you come to a narrow path
through an arch of greenery. Ignore the stile on the left and
carry on straight ahead, passing through a metal kissing gate
onto a road; cross the road and head down a track towards a
picturesque **farmyard**. After you pass the farm, turn left and head
up the steep field.

Go through a metal gate, with hedgerows to either side, and into
King's Wood, particularly spectacular at bluebell time in April/
May. At the crossroads, follow the marked path to the right (a signed
detour from what the Ordnance Survey map designates as the
Pilgrims' Way). The track descends the hill for 100m and then forks;
take the route to the left and, after 500m, follow the signs back up
to the left, then, after 1.5km, bear right to rejoin the Pilgrims' Way,
following the red arrow. You'll see a stone waymarker here. The
path continues through the woods for 2.5km, then drops down off
the ridge, and curves round to the left. After 250m you come to a
wooden gate that leads you onto a small road: **Mountain Street**.

Chilham

2km

Head left along Mountain Street, passing the first of **Chilham**'s
timbered houses. After 1.5km or so you reach the village proper,
a high wall to the left marking the boundary of Chilham Castle.
At the end of Mountain Street, School Hill leads up the hill to
the left to the village square; to reach the *Woolpack Inn* or *Bagham
Farmhouse* (see box, p.92), turn right.

Chilham is a perfect English village, the main street climbing
from the *Woolpack Inn* past picturesque timbered houses to the flint
church and a handsome central square. Tall and forbidding gates at
the far end of the square all but conceal **Chilham Castle** – actually
a Jacobean manor house.

Places to stay and eat in Chilham

Chilham has plenty of B&Bs, but make sure you book well in advance, especially in summer. **Castle Cottage** is a comfortable B&B option in a 300-year-old building within the walls of Chilham Castle (☏ 01227/730330, ⊛ www.castlecottagechilham .co.uk; £75/85 for an en-suite twin/double). **Bagham Farmhouse** (☏ 01227/730306; £60 for an en-suite double), lies 750m east of the village, in neighbouring Bagham. It's a large and handsome fifteenth-century farmhouse, done out in period style, with huge breakfasts served on an antique table in the beamed dining room. There are pricier rooms in a converted stable block at the friendly **Woolpack Inn** (☏ 01227/730351, ⊛ www.woolpackchilham.co.uk; doubles from £85). This is the place to come for **dinner** – the food is decent and the atmosphere lively. For a quieter drink, go up the hill to the welcoming **White Horse Inn** in the village square.

If you're only doing this as a one-day walk, at the eastern end of the village take the main road toward Bagham to reach Chilham **train station**, with regular services to Waterloo, Charing Cross and London Bridge (hourly; 1hr 35min); it's a right-turn past the cluster of B&Bs.

Day two

11.5km

Day two is less bucolic than day one, and the orchards you pass through are on a rather commercial scale. There are some lovely sights along the way, though, and as the walk is relatively short there's time to meander around Chilham in the morning and still get to **Canterbury Cathedral** in time to have a look round. There's a decent pub at Chartham Hatch for **lunch**.

Chilham to Old Wives Lees

2km

The second day's walk starts from the **church** in Chilham. Go round to the left-hand side of the church and follow the path that leads behind it, cutting down through the graveyard. Where the path forks, go left down the slope and onto a narrow track. Turn right, and follow the track until you come to a busy road. Cross the road and carry on up the lane directly opposite.

When you reach **Old Wives Lees** (which isn't nearly as pretty as Chilham), you come to a junction; cross the road and go up Lower Lees road. This leads through straggling houses for 750m until you come to a couple of oast houses on the left. Just beyond, a sign

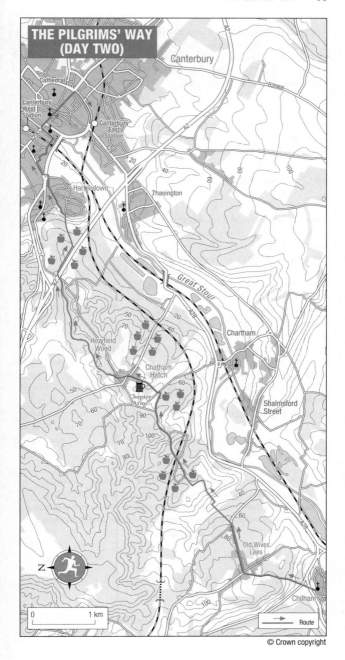

THE PILGRIMS' WAY
(DAY TWO)

Canterbury

Cathedral

Canterbury
West
Station

Canterbury East
Station

Harbledown

Thanington

Great Stour

Howfield
Wood

Chartham

Chatham
Hatch

Chapter
Arms

Shalmsford
Street

Old Wives
Lees

Chilham

Z

0   1 km

→→→   Route

© Crown copyright

If you are doing this as a **one-day route**, start the walk by turning left out of Chilham station. Follow the curve of the busy road and, after 300m, take the (unsigned) left-hand fork towards the village. Climbing the "The Street" beyond the *Woolpack Inn* brings you to the church, where the route starts.

points you off to the left. Go to the end of the road and turn right for a few metres – there's a kissing gate on the opposite side that leads you back onto the Pilgrims' Way.

To Chartham Hatch

3km

From here, a wonderful **avenue** of lime trees leads downhill, forming a dense, leafy tunnel. At the end of the avenue, cross the stile leading into a field, where you'll see tall poles used for growing hops. At the bottom of the hill turn right, then almost immediately left, climbing up the hill ahead, with the line of huge beech trees to your right.

At the top of the ridge continue straight on, then follow the yellow arrow on the wooden post which leads you left along the field. Then go right, down the field in the direction of the wooded hill. The path ascends a slope, then dips to a sprawling fruit farm. At the farm, turn left under the **railway bridge**.

Go up the track towards the tiled oast houses. Before you reach them, take a right up the gravel track. As you continue, the path becomes paved. Follow it until the path forks; take the right-hand fork, signed with a wooden post. Carry on past some houses, towards the electricity pylon. Walk up the gravel path following the "no cycling" signs through the houses to a minor road – turn left and then, almost immediately, right. This is the road into Chartham Hatch.

The eighteenth-century *Chapter Arms* free house (Mon–Sat noon–2.30pm & 7–9pm, Sun noon–3pm; ☏ 01227/738340) is before Chartham Hatch on the left-hand side. It serves generous-sized meals made using local produce (around £8–12) and has a pretty garden.

Chartham Hatch and Howfield Wood

2.5km

Continue down the road into **Chartham Hatch**, turning left onto Howfield Lane when you reach a T-junction. Soon after, follow the public footpath sign that leads away to the right. The narrow path emerges onto a road – cross this and continue on the path ahead, signed "The North Downs Way".

Go along the edge of the playing field, continuing along the path and into **Howfield Wood**. You eventually emerge in a clearing, with an orchard on your right and an avenue of trees ahead; ignore the stile to the left and continue straight ahead. At the end of the avenue of trees, in **No Man's Orchard**, you'll see a large, weatherbeaten wooden sculpture of a snake curving through the grass. Coming out of the orchard, follow the sign that points down to the left: just keep following the yellow arrows. Go straight ahead; the path comes out at a junction onto a short paved section of path; turn right, and walk a few steps until you reach the North Downs Way signpost and a road. Turn left and cross the bridge over the **A2**.

Harbledown

1.5km

Turn right at the end of the bridge, following the bridleway sign. The path leads up the hill, running alongside the A2. After 500m the path curves left into woodland, and through an orchard. Cross a little bridge over a stream, and then follow the steep path up into **Harbledown**, mentioned in the *Canterbury Tales* as "Bob up and down", presumably for its hilly geography. The route joins a tarmac path; bear left and go straight ahead.

Into Canterbury

1.5km

The path comes out at a large roundabout; cross the road via the subway and go straight ahead, following the blue cycle-path sign to the city centre (you are now diverging from the official Pilgrims' Way to follow a more scenic route into the city). After 800m, go through the gate into **West Gate Gardens**, just right of the sign for Whitehall Road. Cross the footbridge over the Stour, turn left and walk through the gardens to emerge at the medieval **West Gate**. Many pilgrims ended their journey at a canter – the word derives from the phrase "at a Canterbury pace" – to reach the West Gate before dusk, when the portcullis descended. Turn right here and go straight up **Canterbury**'s main street, where there's an all-pervasive smell of fast food from the grotty selection of kebab and burger joints that has colonized the otherwise appealing mixture of old buildings. About 200m up the street, the road crosses the river – look up to the left and you'll see a **ducking stool**. Turn left at Boots, down narrow Mercery Lane, for the cathedral.

Canterbury Cathedral

The Cathedral

Mercery Lane leads into the Buttermarket, where pilgrims once bought religious relics. Before you is the wonderfully elaborate sixteenth-century **Christ Church Gate**, and beyond that lies **Canterbury Cathedral** itself. Canterbury Cathedral has been central to the history of the English Church since St Augustine's sixth-century mission from Rome to establish Christianity in the country. The original Saxon church was rebuilt by **Archbishop Lanfranc** in the eleventh century, but was severely damaged by fire a hundred years later. The choir was then rebuilt by William of Sens, a French master-mason, and extended by his successor, William the Englishman, in the 1180s. The rebuilding and remodelling of the nave and aisles continued into the early fifteenth century.

Canterbury Cathedral is open Easter to Sept Mon–Fri 9am–5.30pm, Sun 12.30–2.30pm; Oct to Easter Mon–Fri 9am–5pm, Sun 12.30–2.30pm; £7. Evensong (during which admission is free) is at 5.30pm Mon–Fri & 3.15pm Sat & Sun.

From a distance the cathedral appears rather ethereal, but close up what impresses is its colossal physical presence. The bulk and length of the Gothic **nave** is lightened by the soaring Bell Harry tower, added in the late fifteenth century. Inside, the stately nave is full of light, the ribs of its roof fanning out to join the long, central rib, punctuated by gold ceiling bosses. A flight of steps leads to the elaborate fifteenth-century choir screen, and beyond that another flight of steps ascends to the altar.

The **choir**, one of the longest in England, was built by the two Williams in transitional Norman style, with both round and pointed arches. It is separated from the aisles by ornate screens and canopied **tombs**. Among them are the splendid tomb of Henry IV (d.1413) and his second wife Joan of Navarre (d.1437), and a portrait effigy of Edward, the Black Prince (d.1376), hung with his flamboyant armour.

To the left as you face the choir screen is the area of the cathedral called "**Martyrdom**", where Thomas Becket was hacked to death as vespers were sung on December 29, 1170. A jagged modern sculpture symbolizes the bloody instruments of his murder. Becket, the Archbishop of Canterbury, had been chancellor and friend to Henry II, but they argued about the king's jurisdiction over the Church – few contemporary or modern commentators can explain Thomas's belligerence in reviving tensions between Church and state. Henry launched a furious outburst against Thomas, supposedly exclaiming, "Will no one rid me of this turbulent priest?" This, perhaps the most famous rhetorical question in English, prompted four knights to cross the Channel to kill the archbishop.

Stricken with guilt, Henry II did penance for the murder in the cathedral and soon after the English defeated the Scots at the battle of Alnwick, the first of a series of "miracles" which were associated with the shrine. Thomas was **canonized** three years after his death, and his lavish tomb became the most significant pilgrimage site in England. The tomb was destroyed by Henry VIII during the dissolution of the monasteries, but the cult of Becket survived. To the east of the cathedral lies the spacious fourteenth-century chapterhouse where T.S. Eliot's austere verse play *Murder in the Cathedral* was first performed in 1935.

The lofty arched **crypt** features lively Norman carving on its capitals – the stonemasons, perhaps as a form of spiritual insurance, incorporated some distinctly pagan figures into the mix. The **Great Cloister** features beautiful Early English arcading; beyond it is a series of rambling buildings belonging to the King's School, a monastic foundation established in the seventh century – the Elizabethan playwright Christopher Marlowe was a pupil.

Leaving Canterbury

1km

There are two train stations in Canterbury – **Canterbury West**, just outside the West Gate, from where trains leave for London

Bridge, and **Canterbury East**, where faster trains leave for Victoria (change at Ashford for a quicker journey). To reach Canterbury East, go up the High Street till you reach the roundabout and the city walls. Turn right and walk round the walls, with the handsome **Dane John Gardens** down to the right. After 700m, a footbridge leads to the left, over the busy road that circles the walls, taking you right into the station.

3

The Weald

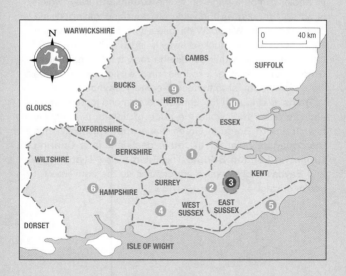

The Eden Valley
Penshurst to Chiddingstone
and back...................................... 101

The Greensand Way
Borough Green to Knole via
Ightham Mote............................... 107

The High Weald Walk
Tunbridge Wells to Groombridge
and back...................................... 112

Bayham Abbey
Wadhurst to Bayham Abbey and
Hook Green................................... 119

The quintessential image of the **Weald** – the low but undulating stretch of wood and farmland between the North and South Downs – is of orchards, country cottages, oast houses and hop gardens. The system of medieval land tenure used in the area meant that estates were divided rather than inherited wholesale, with the result that this fertile land was split into smaller and smaller plots, creating a patchwork quilt of little fields and orchards enclosed by impenetrable hedgerows. A correspondingly modest architectural style predominates, with tile-hung and timber-framed cottages the norm, giving the landscape a domestic appeal that is hard to resist.

The name "weald" derives from the Anglo Saxon word for forest, and remains of the woodland that originally covered the region can be seen on the walk through the aptly named **Eden Valley**, where great oak trees dot the now thoroughly cultivated landscape. A longer route, from Borough Green to Knole, climbs a ridge on to the **Greensand Way**, which is as spectacular as the generally low and rolling Weald gets. The **High Weald Walk** takes you from picturesque Tunbridge Wells via tucked-away villages, hills and woodland to the spectacular sandstone rock formations around Groombridge. Another excursion in the High Weald is the walk from Wadhurst to thirteenth-century **Bayham Abbey**.

Trains are frequent throughout the area and journey times short (around 1hr), while the price of tickets is relatively low. Trains to Borough Green leave from **Victoria**, while the departure point for the other destinations is **Charing Cross** via **London Bridge**. The Eden Valley, High Weald and Bayham Abbey walks are circular, so are convenient if you're driving.

THE EDEN VALLEY

Penshurst to Chiddingstone and back

Distance and difficulty 11km; moderate.
Duration 2hr 45min.
Trains London Bridge or London Charing Cross to Penshurst (every 30min; 1hr); return from Penshurst to London Bridge or London Charing Cross (every 30min; 1hr).
Map OS Landranger 188: *Maidstone & Royal Tunbridge Wells*; OS Explorer 147: *Sevenoaks & Tonbridge*.

This walk leads in a satisfying circle through rolling Kent countryside, across fields and meadows and past orchards, vineyards and great solitary oaks, remnants of what was once thick forest. The route takes you from **Penshurst station** to the remarkably intact Tudor village of **Chiddingstone**. From here, paths and farm tracks lead across the **Eden Valley** to Penshurst, home to the mighty manor house **Penshurst Place**, which boasts a well-preserved medieval hall. It merits a separate, longer visit so isn't described in any detail here. From the house, the route runs through parkland and finally by road back to Penshurst station.

Getting started

3km

Exit the station opposite the *Little Brown Jug* pub and turn left. Walk down the road for 250m, then take the path to the left marked by a green **public footpath** sign; it's just before the post office and red phone box. The path leads along the edge of a field and crosses the railway. Walk along the edge of the next field, with the line of trees on your right, until you get to a gate after about 100m; go through the gate on your right and straight across the next field and over the stile.

Walk diagonally across the following field, towards the right side of the **oast houses**; go over the stile and cross the driveway that leads to the farm, passing in front of the decrepit but picturesque buildings, their orange-tiled roofs draped with foliage. Continue straight ahead, over the stile and down the edge of the field (ignoring the stile on your left). Go into the next field – diagonally across it you'll see a house with chimneys sticking up through the trees. Head across the field towards the house, then, with the little brook on your left, veer right to the metal gate and stile.

Cross the stile and turn left up the **tarred road**, heading uphill. After 100m, take a right onto a track: on the left of the track is a red-brick house and, on the right, a crumbling, tiled garage.

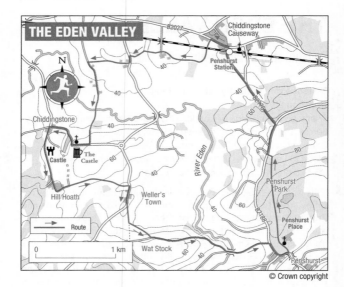

© Crown copyright

You soon come to a stile with a yellow arrow; cross over and turn right, walking along the edge of the field. At the end of the field is another wooden stile; carry on straight ahead and cross another stile, continuing straight ahead, with a long avenue of ash trees to your left. At the end of this field cross yet another stile to emerge onto an oak-lined **track**. Turn left onto the track, with North Cottage on your left-hand side.

Following the track for 500m, you'll come to a wonderful tile-hung house on the left, with lattice windows and the date 1601 over the door. Shortly beyond the cottage, the track narrows, leading to a bridge over the **River Eden**. Carry on up the path, keeping the little wood to your left, until you emerge onto the road – turn right for Chiddingstone.

Chiddingstone

1km

Just before you get to **Chiddingstone**, a marked path to the left makes the short detour to the **Chiding Stone**, the much-graffitied and weathered rounded outcrop for which the village is named. The stone itself, brought from Tunbridge Wells, was, according to legend, a seat of judgement for **druids** (see box, p.203). It then became the place where villagers brought their grievances against each other and were "chided" for their transgressions.

The village itself was extremely prosperous, first thanks to pig farming – the pigs grew fat on acorns in the nearby oak forest

– and then through a basic form of iron smelting. The timber-framed and tile-hung **houses** dating from the village's heyday in the sixteenth and seventeenth centuries are perfectly preserved and, although the place swarms with tourists in summer, it retains great beauty and character. Look out too for the tower of the fourteenth-century **Church of St Mary**, adorned with comically grotesque stone gargoyles who stick their tongues out at the village below. There are many memorials inside the church to the Streatfields, who owned Chiddingstone Castle (see below) and whose eighteenth-century sandstone mausoleum sits in the churchyard.

Across the road from the church sits the half-timbered *Castle* pub, which has occupied the Tudor building since 1730 and now makes a good **lunch** stop. To continue on the walk, come out of the pub and go straight ahead, following the signs for Chiddingstone Castle. After 200m, follow the road as it curves round to the left. At the crossroads, take the signed left-hand fork which leads to **Chiddingstone Castle** – it's really just a house, originally medieval but rebuilt in the seventeenth century and renovated and castellated in 1805.

The Castle (Mon–Fri 11am–11pm, Sun noon–11pm; ☎01892/870247) has an upmarket and fairly pricey restaurant (mains £9–14); alternatively, on a sunny day head round to the left of the building to the Garden Bar, which serves drinks and cheaper pub lunches. The proprietors take advantage of Chiddingstone's olde-world pulling power – the food is mediocre and over-priced – but the garden setting is gorgeous.

Across the Eden Valley

4km

To reach the **Eden Valley**, continue on the road past the turn-off to the castle. After 500m, the road meanders into the appealing hamlet of **Hill Hoath**. Instead of turning right into the tiny heart of Hill Hoath – marked by a rickety sign that says "private road" – take the left-hand track up the hill. At the top of the hill, turn left on the farm track, passing a black wooden converted barn on your right; you should be able to see Chiddingstone Castle down to the left.

Where the track peters out into a field, go straight ahead, following the yellow arrow (rather than the Eden Valley Walk, which is signed to the right). Cross the stile into a field and take the path straight ahead. There's another stile under a large oak tree. Go straight ahead; you'll see the conical towers of four oast houses over to the left. Follow the curve of the field round to the right.

Oast houses

You can't go far in the Weald without seeing **oast houses**, the distinctive brick towers with conical tiled roofs that are so characteristic of the area's landscape and agricultural heritage. Oast houses were originally used for the drying and packing of **hops**, whose flowers imbue beer with its bitter tang. Most have been converted into homes, and not one is now used for its original purpose.

The eccentric design of the oast house was imported from Flanders in the sixteenth century, when hops first began to be widely used in brewing in England. A **kiln** (in old English, oast) was located at the base of the tower, with a drying-room floor set a few metres above it, spread with a horsehair cloth onto which the hop flowers were laid. Smoke from the kiln was released from the building via a cowl surmounting the cone of the roof. Almost all oast houses were connected to a two-storey building: hops were cooled on the upper floor then stamped down into long sacks that dangled through holes in the floor. As well as accommodating the dangling sacks of hops, the ground floor also provided access to the kiln, which was stoked and serviced from here.

Nearly all the surviving oast houses date from the nineteenth century, when the growth of a drinking culture in the expanding cities created a huge demand for **beer**. In a neat exchange, the consumers of most Kentish beer – Londoners – augmented the huge work force needed for harvesting; indeed until the 1950s harvesting was the closest thing that most working-class Londoners had to a holiday. Hops are still integral to the beer-making process (though they are now processed into pellets rather than being laboriously dried), and the starkly regimented lines of tall chestnut poles on which they're grown are as much a feature of the Kent countryside as the cosily converted oast houses themselves.

At the bottom of the field, turn right onto the road. Ignore the green public footpath sign that points to the left and carry on up the hill through the hamlet of **Weller's Town**. Go past a long row of terraced cottages to the right then, 50m further on, follow the green footpath sign to the left through the field.

Take the path down the middle of the field. At the bottom of the field, instead of heading up to the pinkish corrugated-iron barns at the top of the hill, turn left, with the trees on your left. You emerge into another field; turn right and go up the hill. At the top right-hand corner of the field you come out onto a narrow farm track. Turn left here – the track, which runs along a ridge and has lovely views, leads all the way to Penshurst. After just over a kilometre the track joins a little paved road; turn left and cross the bridge over the River Eden.

Penshurst

3km

Five hundred metres beyond the river crossing, the road joins the much busier B2176; turn right for **Penshurst**. Just beyond the *Fir Tree House Tearooms*, at the T-junction opposite the *Quaintways Tearooms*, turn left to visit the **Church of St John the Baptist**, which has a distinctively squat Perpendicular tower, surmounted by cone-shaped pinnacles. The church is tucked away beyond a courtyard of ramshackle but appealing half-timbered buildings, and houses the vault of the Sidney family, owners of Penshurst Place. Also worth looking out for is the fine but damaged late thirteenth-century marble effigy of **Sir Stephen de Penchester**, Warden of the Cinque Ports and one-time resident of Penshurst Place, who is depicted drawing his sword.

The *Fir Tree House Tearooms* (March–Easter Sat & Sun 2–5.30pm; Easter–Jan Wed–Sun 2.30–5.30pm) serves up loose-leaf teas and tasty home-made cakes and scones; tables in the back garden are set among flower beds and under a weeping willow.

You now have the option of continuing the walk straight back to Penshurst **station**, or detouring to **Penshurst Place** (see box below). To continue directly to the station, take the skinny path that curves round the church to the left (as you face it). Go straight ahead through the squeeze-gate and into the rolling parkland of Penshurst Place – you walk along its boundary wall.

Detour to Penshurst Place

1km

To visit **Penshurst Place** (March Sat & Sun; April–Oct daily: house noon–4pm; formal gardens 10.30am–6pm; £8.50), go back onto the road leading to the church, turning left to reach the long drive into the park. The house was built by the London draper and merchant Sir John de Pulteney in the 1330s, and in 1552 became the home of the Sidney family, whose most famous son is the Renaissance poet and statesman **Sir Philip Sidney**. Sir Philip – who died aged 32 from a wound received at the Battle of Zutphen, where he famously refused a drink of water in favour of another wounded man – praised the "firm stateliness" of the house in his pastoral romance *Arcadia*. The original house was much extended in Tudor times and again in the nineteenth century, but the overall impression of the romantic, crenellated exterior is coherent and majestic.

To **rejoin the walk**, go back up the drive away from the house and pick up the route from the church.

Cross the narrow road that leads to the house from the B2176. Keeping the cricket pitch and pavilion to your right, go straight ahead, heading uphill through the park and passing a large **pond** to the right. Go through the squeeze-gate (ignoring the yellow arrow that points right) and carry on uphill, aiming for the red-brick building straight ahead. This high ground provides great views of Penshurst Place itself.

At the top of the park, go over the stile to the left, which clips a little corner of woodland before joining the busy B2176. Head right here for 350m, then turn left at the junction for **Penshurst station**. After another 650m the road forks – take the left fork for the final 500m to the station itself.

THE GREENSAND WAY

Borough Green to Knole via Ightham Mote

Distance and difficulty 15.5km; moderate.
Duration 3hr 50min.
Trains London Victoria to Borough Green (every 30min; 45min);
return from Sevenoaks to London Bridge (every 20–30min; 25min).
Map OS Landranger 188: *Maidstone & Royal Tunbridge Wells*;
OS Explorer 147: *Sevenoaks & Tonbridge.*

This rewarding walk takes you down narrow country lanes,
through lush orchards and across fields, from the village of
Borough Green to secluded **Ightham Common**, where the
Harrow Inn serves up classy locally sourced pub food. From this
point, the walk becomes not just pretty but spectacular. First you
pass the wonderfully atmospheric medieval and Tudor manor
house of **Ightham Mote**, which looks like a quaint half-timbered
cottage writ large, ringed by a moat. You might want to make
an early start in order to visit the house, which is crammed with
treasures. From Ightham Mote, the walk ascends a high ridge,
following part of the established **Greensand Way**, with terrific
views south to the High Weald. From the ridge you enter the
magnificent deer park at **Knole**, walking past the high ragstone
walls of Knole House itself. As the house has 365 rooms – one
for every day of the year – it's best saved for a separate visit, so
isn't described in any detail here.

. . . .

Although this walk starts and ends on different lines, it's possible
to get a return ticket to Sevenoaks rather than two separate
single tickets.

. . . .

Getting started

1.5km

Turn right out of the station, past the co-op, and take a right
across the railway bridge. Carry on straight ahead, down **Borough
Green**'s main street. After 250m you come to a busy intersection;
cross over and carry on straight ahead, up Quarry Hill Road.
Continue for another 250m to a roundabout, then go straight
ahead on Thong Lane. The road leads downhill, under a disused
railway bridge, before curving left to Basted, running alongside a
stream.

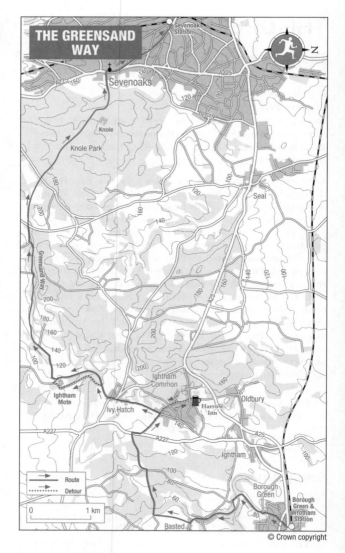

THE GREENSAND WAY

Route
Detour

0   1 km

© Crown copyright

Basted to Ightham Common

3km

After 800m the stream widens into a picturesque weir at the village of **Basted**, which has some pretty eighteenth-century houses alongside modern pastiches.

Go straight through the village and follow **Plough Hill**, which leads up to the left. Immediately beyond the *Plough* pub, follow the public footpath sign to the right. Head straight across the field ahead of you. At the end of this you'll see a decrepit corrugated-iron building; turn left and continue along the bottom of the field to the hedge, where a path leads down to the right and joins a narrow lane.

Turn right onto the lane, which leads through apple orchards for 750m to a junction. Turn left and follow the road, which curves to the right onto Bewley Lane. Turn right onto the busy A227, then turn left almost immediately onto Back Lane, which leads to **Ightham Common**. You pass a turning to Ivy Hatch on the left; this is the quickest way to Ightham Mote, but if you want to detour to the **pub** for lunch, carry on up the lane and past the Sandy Lane junction to the edge of Ightham Common. The *Harrow Inn* lies 500m beyond Sandy Lane, on the right-hand side of the road.

. . . .

The cosy *Harrow Inn* (Tues–Sat noon–3pm & 6–11pm, Sun noon–3pm; ☎01732/885912) serves up hearty quantities of well-presented food, from simple but succulent bangers and mash to full roast dinners; it's slightly more expensive than your average pub grub, but worth the extra.

. . . .

To Ightham Mote

3km

From the pub, turn left to retrace your steps to the turn-off to the picture-book village **Ivy Hatch**, 750m further on; at the junction at the end of the lane turn left onto the bigger road, then after 100m take a right opposite the oast house to Ightham Mote. After 200m, take the turning to the house if you're planning to visit – otherwise you skirt the outside. The lane leads downhill between high banks scattered with wild flowers in summer, and provides a stunning view of the finely proportioned house.

Ightham Mote

Ightham Mote is a gem of an English manor house, its bluff stone tower and half-timbered Tudor walls set prettily in a square moat. The interior is an intriguing warren of relatively small-scale and intimate rooms. Sensitive preservation reflects the house's eight hundred years of occupation from medieval to Victorian times (which only ended when its American owner bequeathed the house to the National Trust in 1985): the Victorian billiard room with its mighty table and overblown flounced lamps has been restored, as has the 1880s housekeeper's room and the parts of the house that date back to the fourteenth century.

....

Ightham Mote is open early March to Oct daily except Tues & Sat;
10.30am–5.30pm; £9.50 (NT).

....

The entrance, from the internal courtyard, takes you into the oldest part of the house: the outer hall and panelled **Great Hall**, built in the 1330s. Look up to the beams in the Great Hall, where the face of a green man is carved. A passageway built in the 1340s takes you past the **housekeeper's room**, an engaging exercise in Victorian nostalgia, into the **butler's pantry**, with its mighty fire-proof safe and system of bells. The adjoining **crypt** was also built in the 1340s, and is the only part of the house to retain its original appearance.

A handsome wooden staircase takes you from the Crypt to the **Oriel Room**, named for its projecting window. Beyond is the barn-like **Old Chapel**, with lustrous wooden floors and furniture and latticed windows – looking up, you can see it was originally split into two floors (the line of what was a ceiling is above you). Next you come to a series of attractive bedrooms with Victorian furniture, and then to the well-preserved **New Chapel**, which features pews carved with poppyheads and a ceiling painted with naïve but appealing images of Tudor roses, stylized castles and quivers full of arrows. The long **drawing room** boasts exquisite eighteenth-century Chinese wallpaper, dancing with exotic birds and dragonflies, and a cheerfully gaudy seventeenth-century overmantel. From here you descend, via the billiard room, back into the courtyard.

The Greensand Way

4km

Pass Ightham Mote and continue up the road, turning right after 100m at Mote Farm and heading towards some oast houses; follow the waymarker with a blue arrow. The track curves to the right at the oast houses and continues up the hill. At the second fork, after 750m, continue to the left, following the signs for the **Greensand Way** – this leads all the way to Knole. You pass an idyllically sited cottage; the path leads past it to the right, via a flight of wooden steps, before continuing into beech woods and then emerging on a road after 750m. Turn right up the road, following the signs for the Greensand Way, and soon afterwards picking up the path opposite Rooks Hill Cottage.

The path forks after the stile at One Tree Hill, leading to a little clearing with wonderful views across the **Kent Weald**. Pick up the path across the clearing and, at the next road, turn left, then take a right opposite Carter's Hill House. The path is much narrower at this point, skirting a field to the left and woods to the right. It emerges onto a track; turn right, following the yellow signs, and cross the stile on the left into a field, which is sometimes used for

▼ Knole House

horse trials. Walk to the far edge of the field and skirt round it; about three-quarters of the way down the field you'll see signs for the Greensand Way on the left. Follow the path until it comes to a road; cross the road and go through the metal gate into Knole Park.

Knole Park
1.5km

The path leads for 200m through **Knole Park** to a crossroads – go straight ahead to reach Knole House. You'll soon see the long wall enclosing the house to your right.

The hundred-acre park was created for the archbishops of Canterbury to hunt in (the house itself was built as an archbishop's palace in 1456–80, but was pounced upon by the acquisitive Henry VIII). The fallow and sika **deer**, which have been residents of the park for centuries, look adorable, but they shouldn't be approached as they can be dangerous.

Knole House is open mid-March to Oct Wed–Sun noon–4pm; £9 (NT).

To Sevenoaks station
2.5km

To leave the park, take the paved path that leads from the front of the house and curves to the left, keeping the domed brick ice-house to your left. The path leads for 500m to twin gatehouses; turn right and keep going straight ahead till you come to ornate signposts in the middle of a traffic island. Take the left-hand fork for the rather dull 1.5km trek through **Sevenoaks** to the station, which lies on the left-hand side of the road.

THE HIGH WEALD WALK

Tunbridge Wells to Groombridge and back

Distance and difficulty 17.5km; moderate.
Duration 4hr 15min.
Trains London Waterloo or London Bridge to Tunbridge Wells (every
30min–1hr; 50min–1hr 15min); return from Tunbridge Wells to London
Waterloo or London Bridge (every 30min–1hr; 1hr–1hr 15min).
Map OS Landranger 188: *Maidstone & Royal Tunbridge Wells*; OS
Explorer 135: *Ashdown Forest*.

This circular Kent/Sussex route for the most part follows the well-
signed **High Weald Walk**, which links a chain of pretty, secluded
villages via dense woodland and more open, gently hilly countryside. An unexpected feature of the walk are imposing sandstone
cliffs, including Harrison's Rocks and High Rocks, more *Picnic
at Hanging Rock* than what you'd expect in southeast England. The
walk takes a while to leave the spa town of Tunbridge Wells
itself, but this is no hardship as its handsome pastel-coloured villas,
quirky boutiques and cafés reward exploration. There are plenty of
food shops for **picnic** supplies (though these aren't open on Sun),
or you can have lunch at the *Abergavenny Arms* **pub** in Frant; there's
also an excellent old boozer at the lovely village of Groombridge.

Getting started

2km

Coming out of the rear of **Tunbridge Wells** station, turn left and
then almost immediately right, down the attractive sloping **High
Street**, following signs for the tourist information office. After
350m, at the bottom of the High Street, you'll see a sign for The
Pantiles to the right, and Mount Sion to your left. Go straight ahead,
down narrow Chapel Place, with its Georgian houses and quaint
shops. Descend the steps to emerge opposite a red-brick building
with a sign for **Cumberland Walk**. Turn left here, up the brick path.
The leafy path leads you past some magnificent tall villas; you
come out onto a suburban street – turn right for 20m, then left onto
Upper Cumberland Walk. This soon emerges onto a quiet suburban lane – go straight ahead, between the houses. After 200m this
narrows to a path – keep on straight ahead. The path leads up beyond
a wooden house to your right, through some woodland, with a fence
to the left. Cross the bridge over the railway line and follow the
narrow path, which emerges onto a street of low brick villas. Turn
right and carry on down Delves Avenue for 400m. Where Delves
Avenue begins a gentle curve to the left you'll see a green **public**

footpath sign to your right, between the houses. Follow this and at the end of the path go through the wooden gate and straight ahead along the line of trees, up the grassy hill to the road.

Go through the wooden gate at the top of the hill, up the steps and cross the busy road, then follow the pavement to your right for 100m. Tucked away to the left is a little lane with a green public footpath sign. You go through some trees, the path running gently downhill, and then curving right and uphill to join a paved lane, where you need to turn left. After 350m there's a golf club on your right, with stone cow's heads on brick pillars to either side of the drive. Immediately before it, and easy to miss, is a narrow path signed **The Tunbridge Wells Circular High Weald Walk**: this is where the walk proper begins.

Towards Frant
2km

The path initially runs along the back of the golf club. Head down the edge of the golf course; the route crosses the B2169 and resumes immediately across the road, on the track to **Brickhouse Farm**. Go straight through the farm buildings – just beyond these, the track narrows to become a path and leads left for 10m, after which you turn right, through the trees.

The path runs along the treeline, towards a wooded dip and a little stream, crossed by a footbridge. You are now in **Chase Wood** – the path splits 100m beyond the footbridge at a woodland clearing. Take the narrower left-hand fork, initially unsigned, down the hill. After just 30m the path crosses a submerged stream and you'll see a High Weald sign, indicating that you're on the right track. The path leads steadily uphill, through the tall fir trees and holly bushes. At the edge of the wood, a stile with the High Weald sign takes you into a field. Turn left up the edge of the field, then up some stone steps into a second field – keep going straight ahead. At the end of this field, a stile brings you out into the churchyard at Frant.

Frant
0.5km

Skirt early-nineteenth-century **Frant** church, with its unusual cas-tellated exterior, and exit the churchyard via the pavilion-like gate and go up the main street, with *The George* **pub** on your left. The village features an attractive jumble of Victorian cottages, clapper-board houses and mock-Tudor homes. You emerge after 150m at the sweeping village green – take the right-hand fork round the green, passing a tiled pavilion on your left. Just 30m beyond here, at the curving brick wall with the High Street, take a sharp right towards a lofty clapperboard house with tall chimneys. Turn right onto the major road for the **Abergavenny Arms**, or left to continue

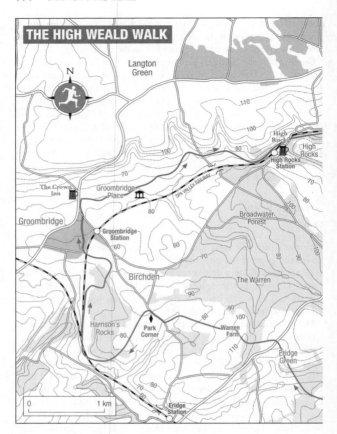

the walk. After 200m, 50m beyond the edge of the green, on the right-hand side of the road you'll see a narrow path leading downhill, marked with the High Weald Walk sign.

The friendly *Abergavenny Arms* (Mon–Fri noon–3pm & 6–11pm, Sat noon–11pm, Sun noon–10.30pm; ☎01892/750233) is located in an old coaching inn, and serves real ales and good food.

Whitehill Wood

3km

Head downhill, into **Whitehill Wood** and the fenced deer park, which you enter via the gate; this is the oldest enclosed deer

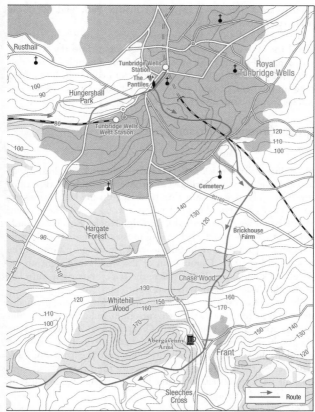

© Crown copyright

park in the country and was mentioned in the Domesday Book. Descend the hill, with the trees of Whitehall Wood to the right and gently rolling hills to your left. Signs advise you that there is a beef sucker herd grazing in the wood, but there's no corresponding advice on what to do if you encounter them. As you're alongside a fence for this stretch of the walk, a nimble jump over it should do the trick if you feel threatened.

After 2km you come to a large pond to the left; just beyond the pond the path bears left to cross the stream via a wooden **foot-bridge**. Some 200m beyond, you emerge into a field at a wooden kissing gate – turn right here for 50m and then go through the metal kissing gate and turn left along the trees. You come out at a metal cattle grid: turn right following the path straight ahead up the field – at the summit of the field there's a wooden post to keep you right. From the top of the field, you can look out to your right to see a lake, the grasslands of **Eridge Park**, and the house itself, rebuilt in Georgian style in the 1930s.

At the edge of the field you come out at a track – go straight ahead for 20m and then follow the sign right, into the wood. A raised path leads through woodland, across a couple of wooden footbridges. Crossing the second bridge you come out into a field – go up the field, towards the village of Eridge Green, which you can see from the summit of the field.

Eridge Green to Harrison's Rocks

3km

Head diagonally across the field, towards the track that leads up to a major road through **Edridge Green**. At the main road, turn right for 100m. Just past the bus stop turn left, up the lane, following the High Weald sign. Ahead of you is a wood called The Warren, where you'll see the smooth, high **Eridge Rocks**, distinctive sandstone formations which shelter rare mosses, liverworts and ferns. The signed path leads right off the track, running up through the woodland for 100m. Coming out of the wood, turn right up the paved track and, after 200m, where the track bears right, turn left at the sign. Warren Farm is to your right.

The route leads straight across two wide fields, sloping gradually downhill. At the edge of the field turn right and go down for 20m to the corner, where you bear left. Cross the wooden stile and then the footbridge over the stream. At the end of the field, cross the stile, join the lane and turn right for 300m into the hamlet of **Park Corner**. At the top of the lane, opposite the Eridge Road sign, take the track to the left. It's marked as the private road to Pinstraw Farm, but it is a public footpath.

You pass Pinstraw Farm to your right and carry on up the track, which curves to the right, enclosed by thick hedges. You then go through another stretch of woodland for 100m, emerging at Forge Farmhouse and a converted oast house – these and the neighbouring tile-hung houses make a very appealing cluster, with the rail line and the river running close by. Go straight ahead at the wooden gate, at the sign reading Birchden Forge. The path starts climbing above the railway – up to the right are the smooth outcrops of **Harrison's Rocks**, which are popular with climbers. The path follows the course of the railway for a kilometre – across the meadow to your right are long and dramatic sandstone steps, threaded with the roots of tall trees.

The path leads away from the rail line and back into woodland, by a metal gate and with a huge oak tree to the left. Ascend the hill for 100m, with a car park to your left; beyond the car park, turn left up the track to join a tarred road. You emerge at the edge of **Birchden** village; take a left at the stile, following the High Weald sign.

Groombridge

1km

A narrow path leads for 400m to **Groombridge**, crossing a wooden bridge over the railway cutting. At the end of the path, turn right into the village. Head down Corseley Road for 250m, past Victorian terraces. At the end of Corseley Road, opposite the village hall, turn left. At the roundabout, bear right up the B2110. After 350m you come to the village green, and its wonderfully picturesque mixture of clapperboard, tiled and chequered-brick cottages. At the corner of the green, the tile-hung sixteenth-century *Crown Inn* makes for a snug and attractive stop.

....

The atmospheric *Crown Inn* (Mon–Fri 11am–3pm & 5–11pm, Sat 11am–11pm, Sun noon–10.30pm; ☎01892/864742) has flagstoned, low-beamed rooms, and a terrace out front on the green. There's IPA and Greene King Abbot on handpump, and they do decent and reasonably priced bar food (£5–9).

....

Back to Tunbridge Wells

6km

Opposite the pub and just beyond the chapel, a narrow path with a wooden fingerpost sign leads right off the B2110. Follow it down a field and towards mid-seventeenth-century **Groombridge Place**; continue on the grassy path between the lake and the house. With its latticed attic windows, weathered brick and narrow portico, the moated house is a graceful combination of vernacular Kentish architecture and a grander aesthetic; it was built on the site of a thirteenth-century castle, and it's thought that Wren had a hand in the architecture. Conan Doyle stayed in the house to take part in séances, and made it the setting for the Sherlock Holmes mystery *The Valley of Fear*. In 2005, Groombridge Place was used as a location for the film *Pride and Prejudice* starring Keira Knightley.

Go along the side of the house, between the moat and a small stream, along a rusty metal fence. Beyond the house, go between the wooden picket fences, crossing a stream, and out of the gate. Carry on straight ahead, up a long meadow. The route runs north of and parallel to the **Spa Valley Railway** line – during the summer, you'll see little steam trains puffing along the track.

At the edge of the meadow cross the stile, go along a stream and over a little wooden footbridge. Go over the next field to emerge onto a lane; cross the lane and go straight ahead, following the **Tunbridge Wells Circular Link Route** signs. There's a non-too-scenic sewage works down to your right, but you're mostly shielded from it by woodland. Beyond the works, cross the road and go straight ahead up the track. After 200m this turns into a path. Go through the metal gate and follow the path as it curves right, into a patch of dense woodland. You come out of the woodland at a wooden stile – go straight ahead here, with the barbed-wire fence to your left. The path leads downhill; turn left over the stile under a huge oak. After meandering through woodland for 250m, the path crosses a wooden footbridge and runs under the stone railway bridge at **High Rocks Station**. The route joins a road for 150m at the *High Rocks pub*, an exuberant ivy-clad building with Alpine-style additions and an oak-framed barn. Beyond the pub, turn right up the path into Friezland Wood, under the impressive sandstone **High Rocks**, which were settled in the Stone Age.

From here, the secluded path runs through woodland, hugging the right-hand side of the rail line. Some 2km beyond High Rocks, the path opens out and then goes through some suburban houses. At the busy A26 bear left, under the railway bridge. Just past the entrance to the **Wyevale Country Gardens**, take the narrow path left off the road into Hungershall Park on the edge of Tunbridge Wells. The path climbs steeply – at the top, opposite a tile-hung cottage, take the first right along the paved path that runs above and parallel to the A26. You emerge onto a busy road – cross over to have a wander up the delightful colonnaded **Pantiles**, built in the town's eighteenth-century heyday, before making your way back up the High Street to the train station.

BAYHAM ABBEY

Wadhurst to Bayham Abbey and Hook Green

Distance and difficulty 11.5km; moderate–strenuous.
Duration 2hr 50min.
Trains London Bridge or Charing Cross to Wadhurst (every 30min;
1hr); return from Wadhurst to London Bridge or Charing Cross
(hourly; 1hr).
Map OS Landranger 188: *Maidstone and Royal Tunbridge Wells*; OS
Explorer 136: *The Weald*.

This route takes you through archetypally attractive Weald country,
divided into a patchwork of fields, meadows and woodland and
dotted with tile-hung and clapperboard cottages. From secluded
Wadhurst station you come to the **Sussex Border Path**, which
winds across streams and through woodland towards idyllic **Bartley
Mill**, with its fine oast houses. There's a stretch beyond here on a
possibly muddy and definitely hard-to-follow woodland path where
any Girl Guide/Boy Scout skills will come in handy – if you're after
a sedate walk this probably isn't for you. You emerge at the drive of
thirteenth-century **Bayham Abbey**, a peaceful and romantic ruin
(note that it's only open April to September). From here you can
continue to a fine traditional **pub** at the village of **Hook's Green**,
from where quiet winding country lanes lead back to the station. To
lengthen the route there's the alternative option of returning to the
station on the Sussex Border Path.

The Sussex Border Path

1.75km

Exiting the station from platform 2 of **Wadhurst Station**, turn
right onto the road, following the curve that leads up the hill.
After 150m you come to a cluster of white buildings on the left;
turn left here and go up the paved path that runs up the hill. You
soon come to some pretty white clapperboard cottages on the left
– just before you reach the cottages the path splits and you need to
take the left-hand route.

Cross a lawn, following the **bridleway sign** on the telegraph
pole. You pass an octagonal brick and wood house on the right
and cut across its drive. Go straight ahead, again following a
sign on another telegraph pole. The narrow path leads downhill
through some woodland and, 100m beyond the octagonal house,
joins a road. Take a right onto the road, heading right up the hill
away from **Rockrobin Cottages**. From here a dirt path leads you
through a patch of tangled woodland. After 100m, stone steps take

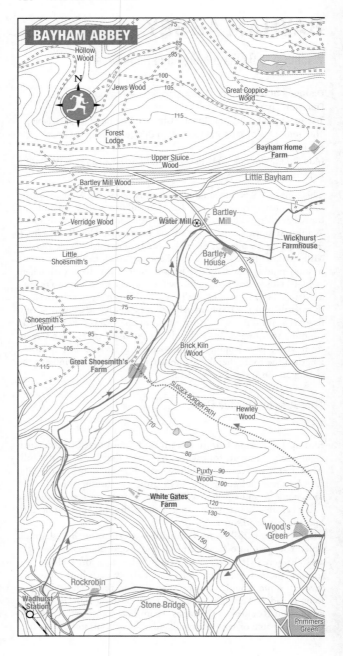

BAYHAM ABBEY

Hollow Wood
Jews Wood
Great Coppice Wood
Forest Lodge
Bayham Home Farm
Upper Sluice Wood
Little Bayham
Bartley Mill Wood
Verridge Wood
Water Mill
Bartley Mill
Wickhurst Farmhouse
Little Shoesmith's
Bartley House
Shoesmith's Wood
Brick Kiln Wood
Great Shoesmith's Farm
SUSSEX BORDER PATH
Hewley Wood
Puxty Wood
White Gates Farm
Wood's Green
Rockrobin
Wadhurst Station
Stone Bridge
Primmers Green

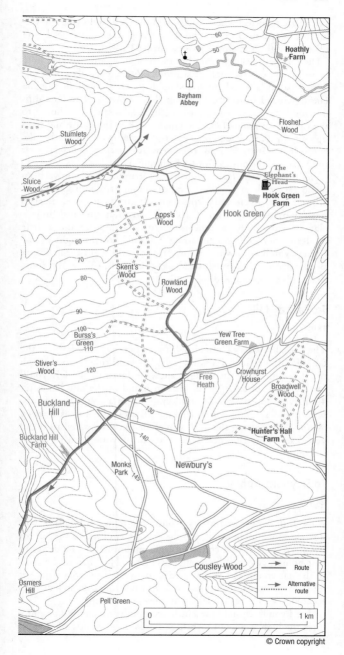

Hoathly
Farm

Bayham
Abbey

Floshet
Wood

Stumlets
Wood

The
Elephant's
Head

Sluice
Wood

Hook Green
Farm

Apps's
Wood

Hook Green

Skent's
Wood

Rowland
Wood

Burss's
Green

Yew Tree
Green Farm

Stiver's
Wood

Crowhurst
House

Broadwell
Wood

Buckland
Hill

Free
Heath

Buckland Hill
Farm

Hunter's Hall
Farm

Monks
Park

Newbury's

Cousley Wood

Osmers
Hill

Pell Green

	Route
	Alternative route

0   1 km

© Crown copyright

you down to a road where you should turn left, following the yellow arrow. About 75m beyond the turning, a fingerpost leads you off to the right, signed the **Sussex Border Path**.

The dirt path leads you for 500m through lightly wooded hilly countryside, cut through by a brook. You eventually come out onto a paved lane, where you should turn left downhill past the **clapperboard house** that's covered in wisteria. The lane dips downhill, with a treehouse to the left and a tile-hung house to the right with pointed Gothic windows. Pass the house and head uphill for 150m till you come to a right turning off the track – the entrance to **Great Shoesmiths Farm** (it's marked as private, but this is part of the Sussex Border Path route).

The track to the farm is on higher ground than you've been on so far, with expansive views of the prettily cultivated hills around you. Eventually you come to the farm gate, marked with a **bridleway sign**. Carry on through the buildings – clapperboard barns, a handsome stone farmhouse and a little modern brick cottage. Go straight ahead – to the right of the cottage you'll see a wooden post. Over to the right is the Sussex Border Path route, but instead of taking this, follow the route that leads straight ahead.

To Bartley Mill

1km

The walk leads along a field, with woodland to your left – at the far side of the field, cross the wooden footbridge. Go through the gate and carry on straight ahead – down to the left you'll see a curious circular pond with an island in the middle. After 400m you approach some buildings set in a watery landscape with ducks splashing and quacking all around – this is **Bartley Water Mill**. Passing the mill, you come onto the paved road and you'll see some fine oast houses ahead of you. Turn right, up the hill.

To Bayham Abbey

2km

After 150m you pass **Bartley House**, tile-hung with lattice windows. Some 20m beyond, take the paved **farm road** to the left for 200m. You come to a couple of signs indicating private drives to oast houses, cottages, barns and farmhouses. Just before the signs to the left you'll see a yellow arrow on a wooden fence on the left – follow the **narrow path** that leads down through an arch of trees for 200m. Cross the stile and continue down the hill.

Ahead you'll see and hear a little **weir** in the stream to the right – cross the high wooden **footbridge** across it. One option here is to go up the path to the hamlet of **Little Bayham** and turn right on the major road for a kilometre to reach Bayham Abbey. However it's not recommended as it's a busy road with a narrow verge and cars hurtle along it at high speed.

Instead, take the **narrow path** to the right immediately over the bridge and go along the water's edge, past the weir. Just beyond the weir, the path curves right and crosses the small tributary stream – it then carries on straight ahead before curving left, following the line of the **woodland**. Carry on for 800m, along a faint path that is sometimes very hard to follow. If in doubt, just

▼ Bayham Abbey

make sure that you stick as closely as possible to the deep stream that runs along the right-hand side of the woodland. You'll eventually be aware of the increasing road noise up to your left and you'll see a field ahead through the trees. Still sticking near the stream, you are brought to a bank that you need to climb to reach the road. To the right when you reach the road is the Kent county sign and a brown sign that points you left off the road to **Bayham Abbey**.

The abbey ruins

1km

A wide driveway leads you for 500m towards **Bayham Abbey** ruins (up to your left on a hill you'll see the grey stone 1860s Garden House, looking like something out of a Victorian Gothic novel).

You buy tickets for the ruins from the Georgian Gothick **dower house** on the edge of the site, and then are free to wander the rolling landscape, which was shaped by Humphrey Repton. Built in golden sandstone between the thirteenth and fifteenth centuries, Bayham Abbey **church** was destroyed during the dissolution of the monasteries in the sixteenth century; the most substantial survival is the tall south wall of the nave. The basic layout is still discernible, and here and there are little domestic and architectural details: a stone loo, carved heads and a rose window. Despite the destruction, the elegant precision of the masonry still bears witness to what must have been a wonderful building. The abbey was built by the "white canons" (named for their robes) of the Premonstratensian order, who were rather more laid back than the Benedictines; they were allowed to talk, didn't shave their heads, and interacted with the community, educating local people. The order's name derives from Prémontré in France, where the order's founder, Norbert, lived in a forest, eventually gathering a band of followers. On the fringes of the ruins is a scenic fourteenth-century gatehouse.

....

Bayham Abbey is open April–Sept 11am–5pm; £3.70 (NT).

....

To Hook Green

0.75km

Coming out of the abbey drive, turn left up the busy road. Some 200m beyond, where the road curves left, look out for the stone public footpath sign to the right and follow the path along the edge of the woodland. After 80m, cross the cute wooden **footbridge** over a stream, then go straight ahead, up the edge of the field.

After 150m, follow the yellow arrow at the rickety gate to the left and then cross the little stile straight ahead of you. Bear left at the bend of the track: to the left is a neat clapperboard cottage with a wacky topiary hedge shaped like a teapot. You come out onto a road – turn left here to get to **Hook Green**. At the junction down to the right is the timber-framed *Elephant's Head* **pub**.

The *Elephant Head* (Mon–Fri noon–3pm & 4.30–11.30pm, Sat noon–11.30pm, Sun noon–10.30pm; ☎01892/890279) serves Sussex ales, and hearty food such as steak and ale pies, fish'n'chips and so on for under £10.

Back to Wadhurst
5km

Go back on the road you approached the village on, signed for Free Heath. The road is more of a country lane – very quiet and edged with lush farmland and the odd tile-hung cottage. After 1.5km you come to the **Free Heath crossroads** – take the right-hand turning. At the next crossroads, follow the Wood's Green sign. Next you come to a "give way" sign – carry on following signs for Wood's Green and Wadhurst, the same applies at the T-junction ahead. Just beyond here you pass Buckland Hill Farm on the right-hand side – keep heading downhill.

The road dips up and down for another 700m beyond the farm, before running up steeply into **Wood's Green** – you'll see some tiled roofs up ahead. Take the first right on the road called Wood's Green, towards a white cottage. After 100m you'll see a red phone box and a fingerpost on your right. This **alternative longer route** takes you on to the Sussex Border Path and, after nearly 2km, back to Great Shoesmiths Farm, from where you retrace your steps to Wadhurst. For a much shorter return to the station, albeit mostly on tarmac, carry on straight ahead. After 500m you reach a crossroads – bear left for 10m, and then turn right over the stile, following the yellow arrow up the footpath.

The narrow dirt path takes you gently downhill through **woodland** – you cross a brook and go past a white house on your right before coming out onto the road. Turn right, into the hamlet of **Stone Bridge**. Here you'll see a sign for Wadhurst Station. Stay on the narrow paved lane for 700m till you see, to your right, Quarry Cottages. A few metres beyond on the left there's a gate marked **"The Briars"**. Follow the stone public footpath sign here and go up the narrow path, past the houses. You come out onto a paved lane – turn left and you come out at a riding stable. To your left there's a gap in the fence with a yellow arrow. Follow this to a little T-junction. Turn right, and you'll soon encounter the white **clapperboard cottages** you saw at the beginning of the walk. Head downhill past the modern buildings you passed earlier, and turn right on the road towards the **station**.

4

The South Downs

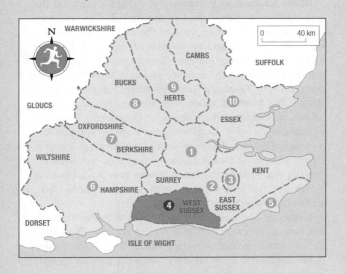

Along the Arun

South Stoke via Burpham to
Arundel 129

Cissbury Ring

Goring-by-Sea to Worthing........... 135

**Mount Caburn and the South
Downs**

Lewes to Southease via Firle 141

The South Downs Way

Lewes to Eastbourne via Alfriston ...147

The "blunt, bow-headed, whale-backed" **South Downs**, as Kipling described them, run from Winchester in the west, terminating in the east at the spectacular high white cliffs near Eastbourne. Walking along the ridge of the downs, with the crescents of smooth, green-gold hills ahead, the sea to one side and the winding rivers to the other – and maybe a trilling skylark above – you can feel an exhilarating sense of space and isolation. The vegetation is low and from a distance appears sparse, lending the landscape a rather austere quality – the beauty, as far as plant-life goes, is in the detail, from butter-coloured cowslips to tiny, delicate orchids. The downs are cut through by a series of river valleys – the Arun, the Ouse, the Adur and the Cuckmere – dotted with wonderful medieval villages which, partly owing to the economic depression that characterized the area until intensive farming was begun after World War II, remain remarkably unchanged and unspoilt. They offer plenty of diversions, from Saxon churches to excellent old country pubs.

All the walks in this chapter are in Sussex, around the less-developed eastern part of the downs. The first walk leads between the steep walls of the downs, following the lush banks of the **Arun** river towards Arundel's extraordinary castle and cathedral. Goring-by-Sea is the starting point for a downland hike which takes in a couple of pretty villages as well as mighty **Cissbury Ring**, the second-largest hillfort in Britain. The **Mount Caburn** walk ascends the downs from Lewes, dipping into the villages of Gynde and Firle, and including a detour to Charleston, the home of Vanessa Bell and Duncan Grant. The final walk in this chapter is a two-day stomp (though you can easily treat it as two separate one-day walks) along the **South Downs Way**, from Lewes to Alfriston on day one, and then on to dramatic Beachy Head, via the Cuckmere Valley, on day two.

Trains for all these walks leave from **Victoria**, stopping at Clapham Junction, and take around an hour. The Mount Caburn walk is probably the best option if you want to **drive** – you can park at Lewes and then take the train for the very short journey back there from Southease.

ALONG THE ARUN

South Stoke via Burpham to Arundel

Distance and difficulty 11.5km; moderate.
Duration 2hr 50min.
Trains London Victoria to Amberley (hourly; 1hr 10min); return from
Arundel to London Victoria (hourly; 1hr 25min).
Map OS Landranger 197: *Chichester & the South Downs*;
OS Explorer 121: *Arundel & Pulborough*.

Winding through the lush Arun Valley, this route links three
ancient Sussex settlements: picturesque **South Stoke**, tucked in a
bend of the Arun, with its lovely Saxon church; **Burpham**, which
sits above the river and was fortified during the Danish invasions
of the area during the tenth century; and **Arundel** itself, whose
fantastic Gothic castle dominates the valley. It's best to time your
walk to have **lunch** at the *George & Dragon* in Burpham. Bear in
mind that the path can become waterlogged after heavy rain.

Getting started

2.5km

Emerging from **Amberley station**, turn left down the road,
past the telephone box, and take another left on to the main road
towards the long stone bridge; to the right are some little shops
and cafés – the *Riverside Café and Bistro* has outside seating by the
river and is a good place to fuel up before you start the walk.

Cross the bridge over the Arun. You'll see signposts to the
left – take the one marked with a yellow arrow, and then cross
the stile into a **meadow** which borders the river (it can get very
splashy underfoot). A path to the right leads up to a small flint
church, but keep going straight ahead across the meadow, to
an overgrown area on the far side, where a bridge leads over
a brook. From here the boardwalk path runs along the gently
flowing **Arun**, bordered on either side by nettles, elderflower
trees and – in June – banks of dog roses, irises and buttercups
mixed in with the wild foliage. Dense reeds run along the river
side of the path. Eventually you emerge from the undergrowth
on to a wider stone path. Turn left and continue along next to
the chalk escarpment. Just over 750m from the start of the path,
a large beech tree stands on the slope to the right, with intricate
exposed roots and a rope swing.

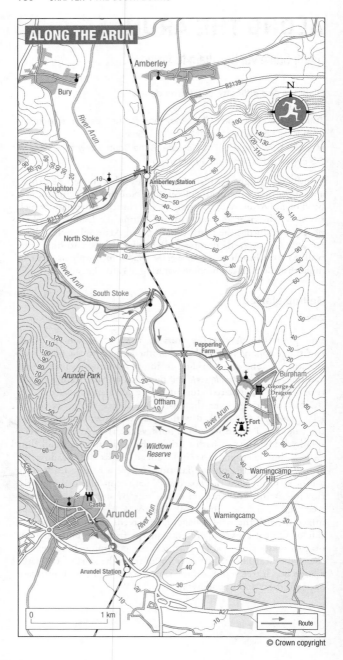

ALONG THE ARUN

N

Amberley

Bury

River Arun

B2139

Houghton

Amberley Station

North Stoke

South Stoke

Peppering Farm

Burpham

George & Dragon

Arundel Park

Offham

Fort

River Arun

Wildfowl Reserve

Warningcamp Hill

Castle

Arundel

Warningcamp

Arundel Station

0   1 km

→ Route

© Crown copyright

To South Stoke

1.5km

Just past the swing the path opens out, with chalky cliffs to the right and the houses of North Stoke visible on the other side of the river. At the point where the river widens you'll reach the flint boundary wall of **Arundel Park**, created in 1806 by Charles, Duke of Norfolk, out of common land. Farmers lost the right to graze their sheep here, with the result that prosperity – and eventually the local population – declined sharply. Don't go through the gate into the park, but carry on along the path, keeping the flint wall to your right. The path begins to climb away from the river, zigzagging upwards to a stile where you cross over into a field.

The view now opens out, with a sloping field to the right and the South Downs beyond. Carry on down the field and follow the farm track to the left, through a gate where you'll see a wooden public bridleway sign.

The path climbs up through woodland then continues through another field to reach a farmyard. You're now in the village of **South Stoke**, which was owned by the earls of Arundel from the Norman Conquest till the reign of Elizabeth I. When Earl Philip Howard (later St Philip) refused to renounce Catholicism, his possessions – including South Stoke – were seized by the Crown. After years of imprisonment, he eventually died in the Tower of London.

Go past the mid-Victorian Chapel Barn, just beyond the farm-yard, and turn left on the tarred road and then left again. The road bends to the left; follow it and take the narrow pebble foot-path on the right just beyond the postbox (set into the side of a wall) to reach the beautiful flint church of **St Leonard's**. Although restored in the nineteenth century, St Leonard's is essentially Norman, with an aisle-less nave. The interior is appealingly rudimentary – the church has no electricity – and features a wonderful wooden-beamed ceiling. The churchyard is exceptionally pretty; the Georgian facade of the **rectory** conceals a house dating back to the fourteenth century.

To Burpham

2.5km

Rejoin the tar road, ignore the "Private no entry" signs – these relate to the field on the left – and continue along the macadam path which takes you over the Arun on a little metal bridge. Turn right at the end of the narrow path leading to the church, then right again at the wooden public footpath sign (the fallen trees by the river here provide good seating for a **picnic**). Cross the metal bridge over the Arun then take a right over the wooden stile immediately beyond. You're now walking along a raised bank of the river, which is wide and fast-moving. Cross a wooden stile and pass through dense foliage; if it's too overgrown, just climb down the bank and carry on through the metal gate – either way you'll emerge onto a stretch of **pasture**.

Continue along the bank of the river. Where the river splits, head up to another wooden stile where the route crosses the railway line towards Burpham. On the other side there's a pretty meadow; the river is much narrower and slower-moving at this point. When you meet the track, take the left-hand fork up the **hill**, passing flint houses on the left-hand side. Carry on up the track, which merges with a tarred road; follow the road and, where it divides, turn right opposite the sign for Peppering Farm.

From here you'll see the fairy-tale shape of **Arundel Castle** to the right across the valley with, bizarrely, a field of bison in the foreground.

Burpham

Carry on along the road to enter **Burpham** (pronounced "Burfam"); turn left at the bottom of the road for the **pub**. Like South Stoke, Burpham is an extremely old settlement and the site of one of the five **forts** built by King Alfred (see box, p.188) to repel Danish invaders who used to sail up the Arun Valley, which was then a tidal estuary.

Burpham Church was substantially rebuilt between 1160 and 1220, the vaulted chancel being emphatically French in style, though the north wall of the nave and parts of the walls between the arches predate the Norman Conquest. A fine old copper beech stands in the churchyard, where you'll find the grave of the writer **Mervyn Peake**, who lived in the village; Gormenghast Castle in Peake's outlandish Gothic fantasy *Titus Groan* was inspired by Arundel Castle.

....

Just up the road from the church, the *George & Dragon*
(Mon–Sat 11am–11pm, closed 3–6pm winter, Sun noon–4pm;
℡01903/883131) makes a perfect lunch stop, serving fine bar
snacks as well as expensive three-course Sunday lunches. Wash
it all down with a pint of Burpham Best Bitter.

....

Across the Arun Valley

5km

From the *George & Dragon*, head back past the church, but instead of turning right and retracing your steps, go straight ahead down the road with the dead-end sign. Turn left where the wooden public

▲ Arundel Castle

footpath sign points in two directions and follow the path through the woods; the river now lies to your right and the raised ground up to the left conceals the remains of Alfred's **fort**. Excavations here have revealed the foundations of Saxon buildings, as well as the remains of a mint, which operated up until the Norman Conquest, but there's little to see now – just a wooded mound.

Beyond here, the path emerges at a stile. Cross this, ignoring the track that climbs up the hill to the left, and follow the path as it heads down a meadow and across the **Arun Valley**, with Arundel Castle straight ahead. Over to the left you'll see the terraces of **Warningcamp Hill**, possibly built and named by ancient Britons who feared Roman invasion.

The path continues, passing over dykes via a series of stiles and bridges, and crossing the railway line once more. Ahead, across the river, is the *Black Rabbit* pub at Offham, idyllically situated with a white cliff rising up behind and boats moored in front; Turner painted a mist-shrouded Arundel Castle from this point. Beyond here the path continues to run alongside the river – which is very wide at this point – as it curves away from Arundel, back towards Warningcamp. The surrounding area belongs to the Wildfowl and Wetlands Trust and is home to several unusual species, including the blue duck and the world's rarest goose, the nene, a black-and-grey short-winged Hawaiian bird.

You approach the railway line again but, instead of crossing it, climb over the stile marked by a post with yellow arrows, and continue round to the right. Cross over the V-shaped wooden stile; you're now heading back towards the castle. Up ahead, the busy **A27** breaks the peace – the path skirts it, curving round towards the town. Approaching Arundel, the river lies to your right, with little boats in various states of decay moored to fragile wooden jetties.

Arundel

The castle and nineteenth-century cathedral lose much of their Gothic glamour on closer inspection, being clearly faux-medieval, but nevertheless **Arundel** is a pretty little town, sitting on a hill in the middle of the Arun valley. Once an inland port linked to the sea by the Arun, Arundel's current staid atmosphere belies the fact that it was a vibrant shipbuilding centre until the Edwardian period, and was also the scene of fights between smugglers and excisemen.

If you want to skip the town and head straight for the **train station**, cut through the car park to the left of the riverside path, just before it emerges into Arundel. Head down to the busy road and cross over, with the police station straight ahead; then take a left, continue down the road to the roundabout and follow the A27 to the left. The station lies 200m up the A27 on the right-hand side.

Arundel Castle

Arundel Castle (April–Oct Tues–Sun noon–5pm; £13; Ⓦ www .arundelcastle.org) was originally a Norman structure but was blown up during the Civil War and lavishly reconstructed in the 1860s by Henry, fifteenth Duke of Norfolk, an immensely wealthy eccentric who dined on swans but dressed like a tramp. Inside the castle, make a beeline for the lofty **Baron's Hall** and the **library**, which is hung with works by Gainsborough, Holbein and Van Dyck. The fourteenth-century **Fitzalan Chapel** contains the tombs of past dukes of Norfolk, including two effigies of the seventh duke – one depicting him as he was when he died, the other his emaciated corpse. The chapel adjoins the fourteenth-century parish church of **St Nicholas**, entered from London Road; the chapel is, very unusually, separated from the altar of the Anglican church by a glass screen and an older iron grille.

Arundel Cathedral

West from here along London Road is **Arundel Cathedral**, gloriously French-looking and romantic from a distance, but rather dull close up. Built in the 1870s by Duke Henry, the cathedral's spire was designed by John Hansom, inventor of the hansom cab. Inside is the tomb of St Philip Howard, exhumed from the Fitzalan Chapel after his canonization in 1970.

CISSBURY RING

Goring-by-Sea to Worthing

Distance and difficulty 14km; moderate–strenuous.
Duration 3hr 30min.
Trains London Victoria to Goring-by-Sea (every 30min; 1hr 25min);
return from Worthing to London Victoria (every 20min; 1hr 20min).
Map OS Landranger 198: *Brighton & Lewes*; OS Explorer 121:
Worthing & Bognor Regis.

This route starts from **Goring-by-Sea**, at the far edge of the sprawling seaside town of Worthing, west of Brighton. It runs via a small hillfort and the village of **Clapham**, through woodland to attractive **Findon**, where the *Gun Inn* is a reliable pub lunch stop. From here you climb up to **Cissbury Ring**, a vast hillfort with sweeping sea views. The path then descends to **Worthing**, with some urban sprawl to get through before you reach the station.

The route doesn't give you the feeling of unspoilt isolation common to the other South Downs walks in this chapter – aside from Cissbury Ring the downland here has been cultivated and its long contours divided into strips of field. But there are plenty of attractions: the thirteenth-century church at Clapham; the venerable boozer with its World War II associations; and the majesty of Cissbury Ring itself. Plus, if it's a sunny day, you can round things off with a swim from **Worthing Beach**.

Getting started

1.5km

From **Goring-by-Sea** station, come out onto the road by the railway crossing and follow the green public footpath sign on the path parallel to the railway track, leading away from the station and along the edge of the field. After 700m follow the wooden **public footpath** sign that points up to the right, along a line of trees. Some 200m further on the path comes out onto the bend of a road – cross over onto the pavement and turn right, following the curve of the road towards the downs – you pass some flint cottages to the right. After 200m you come to the dual carriageway, which you need to cross. Turn right and, after only about 10m, follow the green bridleway sign that points to the left.

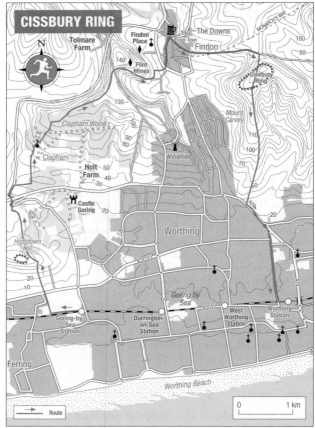

© Crown copyright

Highdown Hill

2km

The flint track now begins the ascent of **Highdown Hill** – at the top of the track by the metal gate, enter the National Trust boundary and turn left. (Down to the left you should now be able to see the sea – and you may also be able to see and hear larks above you.) After 200m bear right, ascending the gentle curve of the hill and heading for the wooden fingerpost.

At the fingerpost, follow the public bridleway sign, which points to the right and leads to Highdown Hill's **Bronze Age fort** – it was once thought to be an outpost of Cissbury Ring, but in fact long predates it. After 200m go straight ahead to continue the walk, or make the short detour to the left to explore the fort. Steps cut into the bank take you to the centre of the small ring-shaped structure from where you can see what a good strategic position this was, with lofty 360° views of the surrounding countryside. A Saxon cemetery was found inside the fort, with cremations and burials, spearheads, knives and glass drinking horns – these finds can be seen in Worthing Museum.

Back on the route of the walk, the path veers left into woodland. It then curves right and begins a gentle descent of Highdown Hill. After 500m, the track emerges from the woodland; the roar of the A27 is ahead. Just beyond the substantial house to your right, the path joins a wider track – carry on straight ahead, continuing on the **bridleway** down the hill to the busy tarred road.

This section is little short of hideous due to busy roads – turn left towards the roundabout and then right, crossing one roundabout and the bridge over the **A27**, towards a second roundabout. Go straight ahead here, on the road signed towards Clapham and Findon. Stay on the left-hand side of the road where there's a pavement but, after a mercifully brief 150m, turn right on the narrow road signed for the Clapham depot – there's also a green public footpath sign.

Walk past brick and flint cottages, straight ahead towards the unpromising looking depot. Just before the entrance gates of the depot you'll see a scrubby area to the right, with a faded yellow arrow on a post. Follow this, down the side of the depot. At the end of the buildings turn immediately left through the **woodland**, with the green metal fence to your left. Head down the hill – you soon come out of the woodland and you'll see Clapham village ahead of you.

Clapham village and wood

2km

At the bottom of the hill you come to a wooden kissing gate and then a metal gate – the path leads from here up the field to the village of **Clapham**. At the end of the field a wooden gate at a long flint wall takes you up the track into the village. You emerge onto a paved road, with a picturesque tiled barn down to the right. Go straight ahead here, following the public footpath sign for the church, **St Mary the Virgin**.

A tiled lynchgate leads to the church – if the gate is locked just go through the portcullis-style gate to the right. The substantial flint church with its bulky tower is mainly thirteenth-century and was sympathetically restored by Sir Gilbert Scott, the brilliant Gothic Revivalist architect of St Pancras Station and the Albert Memorial. Inside, look out for the lovely William Morris tiles over the altar, and the sixteenth-century brasses and tombs that commemorate the Shelley family, ancestors of Percy Bysshe.

To continue the walk, circle round to the back of the church and you'll see a wooden stile with a yellow arrow – go over the stile and cross the field. Go over a second stile into **Clapham Wood**, which mainly consists of oak and hazel trees. After just 200m you come to a clearing in the wood – go over the stile and cross the clearing. Carry on up the path, which in spring is carpeted to either side with bluebells, celandine and primroses. The path curves right – follow the yellow arrow, which leads along a clearing, with the woodland to your left. A few metres beyond, follow the yellow arrow across a stile and another clearing. On the far side there's another wooden stile – continue on the path, which leads gently downhill through the woodland.

You cross another clearing – through the light woodland to your left you'll be able to see rolling downs and hear traffic noise from the A280 at the bottom of the hill.

Towards Findon

2km

The dirt track leads straight ahead, exiting the woodland – the views suddenly open out and you can see the soft but dramatic contours of the surrounding **downs**. Some 200m beyond the woodland you'll see a blue arrow where the path converges with another route – carry on straight ahead. You come out at a track – there's a wooden fence post with burgundy arrows. Turn right and, after 20m, take a left, following the blue arrow.

The track leads through light woodland, heading downhill along the side of a ridge; to the left is the site of an ancient **flint mine**. The track runs on for a slow steady kilometre downhill, with a low flint wall to the left. It comes out at South Lodge, a little white cottage. Go straight ahead down the hill, with South Lodge to your left. Turn left after 100m onto the wide track, and keep heading downhill towards the road and the cluster of buildings that comprise Findon.

Findon

2km

You come out at a dual carriageway – cross here and bear left and then head on up Findon's **High Street**, passing the *Black Horse pub* to your left. The village is a handsome and affluent little place, with a mixture of Thirties bungalows, Victorian Gothic houses, Georgian mansions and terraced cottages. You pass the *Findon Manor Hotel* on the right and eventually, on the left, you come to the fifteenth-century **Gun Inn**. A plaque outside the pub commemorates the Glengarry Fencibles, a Canadian D-Day division who, whilst drinking in the pub, originated the popular battle cry "up the Glens".

The *Gun Inn* is a low-beamed traditional village inn (Mon–Fri 11am–11pm, Sun 11am–10.30pm; ☎01903/873206) with a good lunchtime menu featuring lamb chops, rump steaks, salmon, guinea fowl and so on for £9–12, plus puds like sticky toffee pudding for under a fiver.

Coming out of the pub, go straight ahead, following the sign to *John Henry's Inn*. Head up the road for 500m; at the edge of the village, at a bend in the road, follow the blue pedestrian sign for Cissbury Ring. Go up the paved road for a kilometre, ignoring the Monarch's Way signs to either side.

Cissbury Ring
0.5km

You soon get views of **Cissbury Ring**, the unmissable vast oval mound to the right. Turn right off the road at the National Trust sign. Go straight ahead through the wooden gate to ascend to the top of the **fort**. (Signs warn you that rather scarily long-horned **cattle** sometimes graze within the boundary of the gate, so if you have cow issues you might want to circle the structure using one of the lower paths – see map, p.136.) Head up the stepped path till you reach the top – ahead is a stone that marks the **summit**. From the summit, head south along the length of the inner part of the fort, along the broad grassy path that runs gently downhill.

You come to two mounds at the far side of the fort, with steps built into their inner edges. Exit the fort through the gap in between the mounds.

Cissbury Ring

Epic in scale, **Cissbury Ring** has an enclosed area of 65 acres, with an inner bank 1.5km in circumference. It was constructed some time before 300 BC and would have been surmounted by a timber palisade. The sea views, from Beachy Head to the Isle of Wight, made it a wonderful vantage point, but the fort may have been used to protect livestock rather than for military purposes. The site is dotted with deep flint mines of even greater antiquity: they were mined by Stone Age people using antler-horn tools around 3000 BC. Cissbury Ring was abandoned and then farmed by the Romans, later becoming an Armada beacon site and an anti-aircraft emplacement during World War II.

To Worthing

4km

Some 250m beyond the ring, you come out at a National Trust
sign and a fingerpost pointing variously to Steyning Bowl, Findon
and the Findon Valley. Ignore these routes and go straight ahead,
through the wooden kissing gate. The wide path heads gently up
the rounded hill called **Mount Carvey** and then slopes downhill.
Ahead you'll see a gas tower in Worthing, and beyond this the sea.
Eventually, the path leads through a golf course. Keep heading
downhill till you reach a wide road, where you need to turn left.
After 500m you come to the Grove Lodge roundabout – take the
right-hand turning on the A24 towards Worthing.

Go down the right-hand side of the expansive triangular
green, and head down South Farm Road for a kilometre to reach
Worthing station – once you cross the rail line bear left on Cross
Street for the station. To get to the beach, go straight ahead on
Clifton Road for another kilometre.

MOUNT CABURN AND THE SOUTH DOWNS

Lewes to Southease via Firle

Distance and difficulty 14.5km plus 5km detour; strenuous.
Duration 3hr 40min plus 1hr 15min detour.
Trains London Victoria to Lewes (every 30min; 1hr); Southease to Lewes (hourly; 8min); return from Lewes to London Victoria (hourly; 1hr 5min).
Map OS Landranger 198 and 199: *Brighton & Lewes* and *Eastbourne & Hastings* (the latter is only needed if you do the detour to Charleston Farmhouse); OS Explorer 122 and 123: *Steyning to Newhaven* and *Newhaven to Eastbourne*.

This walk takes in the most pleasing features of the Sussex country-side: unspoilt villages, undulating chalky downland and a couple of decent pubs. From the handsome and prosperous town of **Lewes**, it climbs **Mount Caburn**, with its Iron Age earthworks, then descends to the idyllic villages of **Glynde** and **Firle**, both complete with cricket greens and delightful seventeenth- and eighteenth-century buildings. The *Ram* at Firle can provide a hearty **lunch** or you could pick up a **picnic** in foodie-heaven Lewes. From Firle there's a great **detour** through the grounds of Firle Place and across the fields to **Charleston Farmhouse**, the country retreat of the Bloomsbury Group. Beyond Firle, a steep path leads up onto the downs, with the **South Downs Way** running east for 5km along a high ridge to the village of Southease, from where there are trains to Lewes. Alternatively, to **shorten the walk**, return to Glynde from Firle and take the train back to Lewes from there.

Getting started
1.5km

From the main entrance of **Lewes station** turn right to cross the railway bridge. At the *Landsdown Arms*, go uphill on Station Street then turn right on to the High Street and go straight ahead for 750m. (On the right-hand-side, just over the bridge, Bill's is a great place to pick up picnic goodies.) Carry on to the junction with South Street and then go straight ahead up steep and narrow Chapel Hill. At the top of the hill, with the golf club on your left, is a wooden waymarker with yellow arrows. Follow this through the gate and turn left, following the fence for 50m, then go straight ahead across the field, to a sturdy wooden post where you head down into the valley.

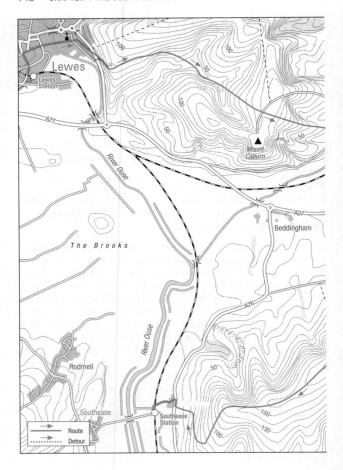

Over Mount Caburn

3km

This is where the walk proper begins, through the valley that bisects **Mount Caburn**. There are no views from here, but the enclosing valley walls create a wonderfully still atmosphere, which intensifies the sound of lark song. Look out for yellow cowslips in April and May. Head downhill, through two gates, then continue down across a field following the yellow arrow. Go straight ahead at a third gate by some feeding troughs, then follow the bottom of the slightly ridged hill round to your right. Cross a stile by the green sign that welcomes

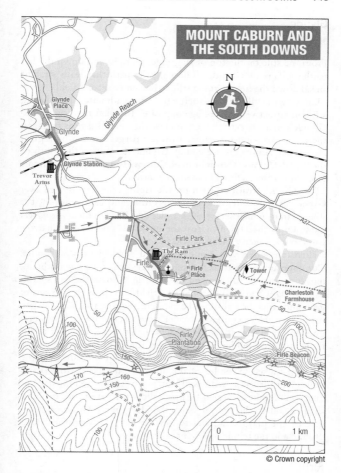

© Crown copyright

you to Mount Caburn, after which the path begins to climb steeply.

At the top of the hill you cross another stile, from where there's a panorama of the long ridge of the South Downs, the route of the second half of the walk. A short detour to the right leads to the fort itself, whose encircling **defensive ditches** are still clearly visible. Caburn (from the Celtic *caer bryn*, or "fortified hill") was the site of an Iron Age fort, erected around 500 AD. The fort is thought to have contained about seventy wattle-and-daub houses, gathered around a great hall.

Glynde

3km

From the stile on the top of the ridge, go right and down the hill to the village of **Glynde**, following the path that leads straight ahead down the field. Cross a stile to descend a second field.

Entering the village you emerge from the path onto a paved road, with an attractive pink cottage opposite. Turn left then right onto Glynde's main street where, amongst the beautiful flint cottages, there's an Arts-and-Crafts-era working **forge**, fronted by a giant horseshoe (visitors are welcome). Glynde lies just to the south of the world-famous **Glyndebourne Opera House**, and is also home to Glynde Place, a fine Elizabethan mansion.

Pass Glynde **train station** on the right, cross the bridge over Glynde Reach, a tributary of the Ouse, and carry on past the *Trevor Arms*, which serves Sussex ales and has a garden with great views up to the Downs. Cross the busy A27 and take the narrow paved track directly ahead of you.

Turn left when you come to a wall marked Preston Court. Continue along the track, passing a flint barn and some outbuildings on your left. Just beyond this is a stile (also on the left) – cross it, turn right and walk through the field. Go through two sets of gates and cross the field ahead of you, then swing round to the left, past a barn. Here you join a wider farm track; turn right towards Firle. After 300m, at the five-way junction, take the track to the right, marked "public footpath". This leads you into the grounds of **Firle Place**, a picturesque house built in the late fifteenth century, tucked in the lee of the downs to protect it from strong winds and furnish it with well water; it was later remodelled and given an elegant Georgian facade. Follow the paved path for 50m, then cut off to the right towards the playground. Go through the gate by the playground and follow the path between the cricket ground and the tennis courts into the village.

Firle

The route brings you out at the back of the seventeenth-century *Ram* at **Firle**, a good **lunch** or pint stop. The oldest part of the building is thought to be medieval, and there is, needless to say, a resident ghost, that of an old washerwoman with a wooden leg who lived in an attic in the eaves. She was found dead one day in her laundry basket; it's claimed she can sometimes be heard stomping across her tiny room.

The *Ram* (Mon–Sat 11.30am–11pm, Sun noon–10.30pm; ☏01273/858222) has a large garden at the back and serves good gastro pub lunches (from £10 for a main) plus Harveys Bitter, guest ales and cider on tap.

To rejoin the walk, carry on up Firle's main street following the sign for St Peter's Church, past rows of neat seventeenth- and eighteenth-century cottages. Just before you come to St Peter's at the top end of the village, there's a detour (2.5km each way) left off the main street to **Charleston Farmhouse**, the painter Vanessa Bell's immaculately restored home, which was a focus for the activities of the Bloomsbury Group.

Detour to Charleston Farmhouse
5km

Go through the gate into the grounds of **Firle Place** and head to the right, passing the house, which lies to your right. There are a couple of wooden posts with yellow arrows in the field showing the route through the estate, though they're easy to miss; you need to head for the high ground to the right, which is surmounted by a tower. At the edge of the estate go through the wooden gate, up the driveway between two **flint cottages**, and then through a metal gate. Carry on ahead along the thin chalk path that leads up the field, to the right of the flint wall. At the top go through the wooden gate (a chalk track heads left to the tower, which is a private house). From the wooden gate, carry on straight ahead on the second track that leads across the fields. From here you can see the barns and orange roof of Charleston ahead of you.

Charleston Farmhouse

In 1916, on the recommendation of her sister Virginia Woolf, Vanessa Bell moved to **Charleston Farmhouse**, along with the painter Duncan Grant, her two children and the writer David Garnett. The house initially provided a rural retreat from World War I, but soon became the country home of the **Bloomsbury Group** and a social and artistic stimulus for the Woolfs and other intellectuals including the artist and curator Roger Fry, the biographer Lytton Strachey and the economist John Maynard Keynes.

Charleston Farmhouse is open April–Oct Wed & Sat 11.30am–5pm, Thurs & Fri 2–5pm (11.30am July & Aug), Sun 2–5pm; £7.50; ⓦwww.charleston.org.uk. Obligatory one-hour tours run every 20min.

Grant and Bell decorated every surface of Charleston – both were admirers of the emphatic lines and bold colours of the Post-impressionists – so that the house became a work of art in its own right. However, by the time Duncan Grant died in 1978, Charleston had become dilapidated, and a reverential **restoration** of the house and garden was undertaken in the 1980s by the Charleston Trust.

The Mediterranean colours of the wall paintings were revived, the loveliest perhaps being the cock and hound above and below Bell's bedroom window, which Grant painted to wake her in the morning and guard her at night. Other experiments in the decorative arts were less successful, as the rather wobbly pottery of the off-shoot **Omega Workshop** testifies. But the house is still permeated with sensuous colour and light, and the lush gardens, with their quirky statuary, are enticing too; all can be seen on the impressively informative tours.

On to the downs

1.5km

From Firle, continue up the main street, passing the drive to St Peter's Church and the tradesmen's entrance to Firle Place, following the bridlepath signs. (If you've made the detour to Charleston Farmhouse, you could simply turn left up the track on the eastern edge of Firle Park and climb up onto the downs from there).

Plain **St Peter's** itself is worth a look; a stained glass window designed by John Piper depicting the Tree of Life features strong, sinuous lines and dazzling colour, and there's also an imposing Elizabethan tomb with a sombre double effigy.

Follow the track, which curves round to the left, for 500m, and then go along the gravel path up the hill to the right, skirting the aspen and silver birch woods of **Firle Plantation** on your right. The path makes the dizzying ascent up the escarpment of the South Downs, eventually joining the **South Downs Way** at the fence at the top. When you reach the top, the English Channel is revealed to the south; you might see a cross-channel ferry from Dieppe nipping into the port of Newhaven.

The South Downs Way

5.5km

At the top, take a right onto the **South Downs Way**, and continue for 300m till you come to a car park. From here the South Downs Way leads through a wooden gate marked with a sky-blue arrow and runs along the top of the ridge. There's no chance of losing your way here: just keep to the highest ground. After 700m you pass some radio masts on the left; from here the fort surmounting Mount Caburn is clearly visible.

After 1.5km, you start to descend, with Newhaven visible to the left. The track then plunges steeply, down Itford Hill towards **Southease**, to emerge near the A26. A footbridge takes you across the road to **Southease station**, from where trains make the short run back to Lewes. Alternatively, you can call a **taxi** on ☏ 01273/477015 to take you back to Lewes (around £8).

THE SOUTH DOWNS WAY

Lewes to Eastbourne via Alfriston

Distance and difficulty day 1: 18km; day 2: 19.5km; strenuous.
Duration day 1: 4.5hr; day 2: 5hr.
Trains London Victoria to Lewes (every 15min; 1hr 38min);
return from Eastbourne to London Victoria (every 30min; 1hr 30min).
Map OS Landranger 198 and 199: *Brighton & Lewes* and
Eastbourne & Hastings; OS Explorer 122 and 123: *Steyring to
Newhaven* and *Newhaven to Eastbourne*.

The **South Downs Way** runs for 160km from Winchester to
Eastbourne; the two-day section described here covers the spectacular
eastern extent of the route. It starts from **Lewes** and ends at
Eastbourne: each day's walk can be done separately, or you can stay
at **Alfriston** and make a two-day walk of it. On **day one** you walk
across the Ouse valley, crisscrossed with water channels, via a couple
of venerable Sussex villages – Iford and Rodmell. You then go onto
the Downs for a longish hike before descending to picturesque
Alfriston, where there are plenty of places you can stay overnight (see
p.153). **Day two** leads through the lush Cuckmere Valley to the
undulating cliffs at Beachy Head and on to Eastbourne. This second
day should only be undertaken if you're fit: there are some
fantastically wiggly contours to contend with.

Day one

18km

The walk starts gently, from **Lewes** and down onto the watery plain
of the Ouse river – this can be a very muddy stretch. Surrounded by
downland views, you walk alongside water channels before climbing briefly onto the Downs and dropping down into **Rodmell**,
where the *Abergavenny Arms* is a good stop for a pint. The food isn't
up to much though, so it's better to bring a picnic. It's well worth

To do day one as a one-day walk, when you get to the end of the
walk take the bus from Alfriston's market cross to Berwick and the
train from there to Lewes. To do day two as a one-day walk, take
the train from Lewes to Berwick, and then the bus to Alfriston to get
started. The **bus service** is reliable and efficient and timed to coincide with Berwick trains, though the timetable is limited – be sure
to check it in advance so you don't get stranded (☏01323/870920,
🖳www.cuckmerebus.freeuk.com).

exploring Rodmell, to see **Monk's House**, the home of Leonard and Virgina Woolf, and to look at the twelfth-century church. The route continues to Southease, from where you ascend the Downs, walking along a high ridge for 10km then descending to Alfriston, a wonderful place for an overnight stay.

Getting started

1km

From the main entrance of Lewes station, turn left down Station Road, then right onto **Priory Road**. Turn left beyond the church, down **Cockshut Road**. You go underneath a bridge over the minor road; 50m beyond here, turn left and follow the sign if you want to detour to see the remains of the Cluniac St Pancras Priory. It was founded in the eleventh century by William de Warenne, builder of Lewes Castle, and his wife Gunrada, and destroyed in 1538 during the Dissolution of the Monasteries.

  Back on the route, head down the path and, with the bank ahead of you, turn right following the cycle sign to Kingston, through the **concrete tunnel** under the major road. Turn right and then left, following the **public footpath** sign on the fingerpost. Go through a wooden kissing gate, and then climb up the bank immediately to your right.

To Itford and Rodmell

5km

Walk along the bank, with the stream to your right and playing fields beyond. After 800m, where the playing fields peter out, the path draws close to the road. Take the path that cuts across diagonally and up to the left. You're heading for the **wooden gate** at a gap in the hedge.

Go through the gate, and straight across another field. At the edge of the field you go through a gap in the hedge onto a **narrow dirt path**, with trees to the left and gardens with rabbit hutches to the right. You pass a small sewage works to the left and come out onto a track. Turn right for just a few metres, then left up the bank via some wooden steps. You go over a stile at the top of the bank and go to the summit of the field and straight ahead, following the **yellow arrow** on the post you will see in front of you. The road is to your right, with a spectacular downland ridge beyond.

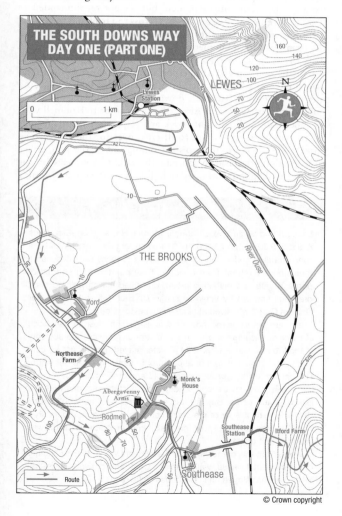

© Crown copyright

You emerge, 700m beyond the sewage works, at the hamlet of **Itford** – go up the track between a converted barn and a flint cottage. Cross the tarred road and the stile, marked with a public footpath sign. Go through the field, with the long flint wall to your left – behind the wall is a beautiful white villa. Go across a drive, through a couple of gates and then you emerge with a pink villa to your left under an arched pine tree. You join the road for just 20m, then go over the stile on the right, back into the fields.

Across another couple of fields you join a track where you turn right to join the road. It's possible to turn left along the road here for a quicker route into Rodmell, but it's not recommended as there's no verge to walk on. Instead, cross the road and turn right for a few metres, then turn left on a paved **farm track**. Follow the farm track for a kilometre – it curves round to the left with a bank rising up to the right and impressive open views to the left. Eventually you come to a fingerpost marking a crossroads with the **South Downs Way**. Turn left here; after another 600m you come out at a little road. Turn left down the hill, following the green public **right of way** sign. After 700m you come to Rodmell with its appealing jumble of flint, brick and clapperboard cottages and villas. You come to a wider road; cross over for the *Abergavenny Arms*, a good pit stop for a **pint**. Coming out of the pub, either turn left along the road to continue the walk to Southease or, for an enticing detour, take a sharp right following the sign to **Monk's**

Monk's House

Leonard and Virginia Woolf bought **Monk's House** (April–Oct Weds & Sat 2–5.30pm; £3.70 NT) in 1919 when Virginia was 37, and the "unpretending house, long & low, a house of many doors" became their country retreat from London. They painted it in shades of pomegranate and pistachio green, and filled it with painted tiles, drawings and oils by Virginia's sister Vanessa Bell and her partner Duncan Grant, who lived at nearby Charleston (see p.145).

It's hard not to be moved by the house which, despite the charm of its colour scheme and decoration, strongly conveys the austerity of the Woolfs' lives – when E.M. Forster stayed here he got so cold that he burnt his trousers on the bedroom stove trying to get warm. The colours of the **garden** are as bold and striking as those inside the house, and it's cleverly divided into intimate sections that feel like separate rooms. Beyond it is an orchard with, as Woolf wrote, "the grey extinguisher of the church steeple pointing my boundary". The little wooden lodge was Virginia's writing room, and its loft was used to store apples.

It was from this paradisal place that Virginia Woolf, fearing another onset of mental illness, walked to the Ouse and drowned herself in 1941. Leonard stayed on in the house till he died in 1969.

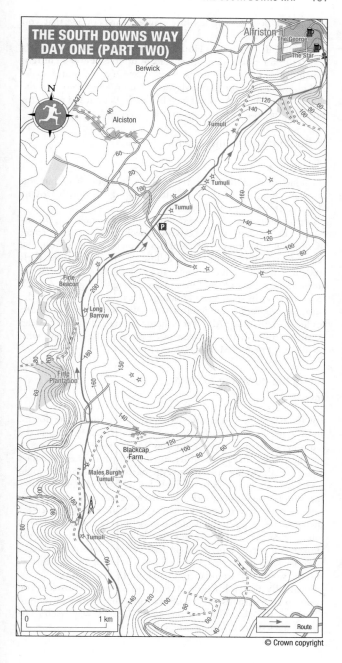

THE SOUTH DOWNS WAY
DAY ONE (PART TWO)

Alfriston
The George
The Star

Berwick

N

Alciston

Tumuli

Tumuli

Tumuli

P

Firle
Beacon

Long
Barrow

Firle
Plantation

Blackcap
Farm

Males Burgh
Tumuli

Tumuli

0   1 km

→ Route

© Crown copyright

House (see box, p.150), a white clapperboard cottage that you reach after 550m.

Coming out of Monk's House turn left and immediately left again onto the public footpath that leads up to **St Peter's church**, which dates back in part to the twelfth century; it features medieval glass and an eight-hundred-year-old font. Coming out of the church, turn left up the street into Rodmell. Back at the pub, turn left along the road to get to Southease.

To Southease and the downs

2km

Go along the road for 700m; the road is a little busy here, but you can walk along the verge. Turn left, following the **South Downs Way** and the Southease village sign.

Southease is a small and extremely pretty settlement, distinguished by a round-towered **Saxon church**. Inside are faint traces of thirteenth-century wall paintings depicting scenes from the life of Christ. From the church, follow the minor road that leads straight down through the hamlet and over the River Ouse. At the **station**, cross the railway line and go through the gates. A track leads up towards some farm buildings – just before you reach the barn, turn right onto the South Downs Way, crossing the wooden bridge over the busy A26. From here you start the steady, steep ascent of the downs, until you reach the top of the ridge, with good views north to **Mount Caburn** (see p.142).

Along the downs to Alfriston

10km

For the next 10km, the path sweeps along the top of the downs, and you get a real sense of quiet and isolation here. Apart from the radio mast ahead, the other features you'll notice on this stretch are the tumuli that lie to either side of the path. These rounded grassy burial mounds are **Bronze Age barrows** – the largest would originally have stood up to 6m high, but all have been eroded over the centuries and opened either by thieves or antiquarians. The barrows were built by a people known as the **Beaker Folk**, named for their custom of placing a drinking vessel beside entombed bodies – bronze daggers and spearheads were left, too, suggesting that the Beaker Folk were preparing their dead for the afterlife. The bodies were arranged in a curled, foetal position, as if the rounded barrow was the womb that would carry them into the next world.

Eventually the path begins to descend towards Alfriston. You come to a **crossroads**, with paths radiating out in five directions. Carry on straight ahead on the South Downs Way itself. The chalky track drops down into the village.

Alfriston

Once in **Alfriston**, you join a wide tarred road called King's Ride. Go straight ahead until you see the Tudor *George Inn* ahead of you; the *Star* is on the left — you are now in the heart of the village, on the High Street. This handsome village has more the feel of a small town, with plenty of accommodation and eating options (see below) and some great independent shops, including an award-winning bookshop, Much Ado Books, on the High Street. The main sights are the church and the **Clergy House** (see p.155).

To end the walk here, go to the market cross at the east end of the High Street from where **buses** leave for Berwick (£1.40; 15min) — there are two services, the Rambler Bus and the Cuckmere Community Bus. The timetable is posted up in the square.

Day two

19.5km

This is a hugely rewarding walk, taking in the verdant **Cuckmere Valley**, secluded forest, and the undulating chalky cliffs of the **Seven Sisters** and **Beachy Head**. There's the option of a three-kilometre detour for a pub lunch at the celebrated *Tiger Inn* at East Dean, though if you don't fancy lengthening what is already a stiff walk then buy a picnic in Alfriston.

To do this as a **one-day walk** from London, take the train to Berwick via Lewes, and then the bus (see p.147) from Berwick station to Alfriston.

Where to stay and eat in Alfriston

If you're on a budget, a good **accommodation** option is *YHA Alfriston* (☎01323/870432, ⊛www.yha.org.uk; £13.95), located in **Litlington** (see p.156) in a sixteenth-century house. There are several attractive **B&Bs** in the village – try *Chestnuts* (☎01323/870298, ⊛www.chestnuts-alfriston.co.uk; £55 twin, £65 double) on the High Street; Georgian *Rose Cottage* (☎01323/871534, ⊛www.rosecott.uk.com; £90) on North Street; or *Pleasant Rise Farm* (☎01323/870545, ⊛www.pleasant-rise-farm.co.uk; £70) at the western end of Alfriston.

For good **pub food**, try the *George* (☎01323/870319, ⊛www.thegeorge-alfriston.com) or the *Star* (☎01323/870495, ⊛www.star-inn-alfriston.com). Both are housed in fine timber-framed fourteenth-century buildings on the High Street – the *George* has the edge for atmosphere. Otherwise, there's upmarket *Moonraker's* **restaurant** (☎01323/871199, ⊛www.moonrakersrestaurant.co.uk), also on the High Street, which serves Sussex ales and locally sourced produce.

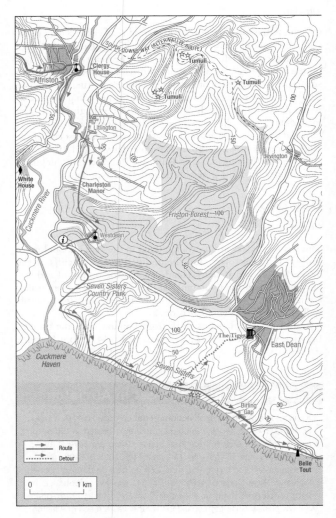

Back to the South Downs Way

0.5km

The walk starts from the square at the east end of the High Street in Alfriston, where you'll see the village's market cross. Opposite the little post office building there's a road off to the right, marked with a South Downs Way marker. This leads to the **Cuckmere River**. Turn right here, down towards the

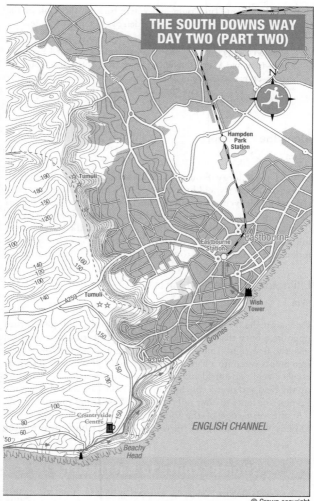

THE SOUTH DOWNS WAY
DAY TWO (PART TWO)

Hampden
Park
Station

Tumuli

Tumuli

A259

Eastbourne
Station

Eastbourne

Wish
Tower

Groynes

B2103

Countryside
Centre

ENGLISH CHANNEL

Beachy
Head

© Crown copyright

unexpectedly imposing **Church of St Andrews** – known as
the "Cathedral of the Downs", it dates from the mid-fourteenth
century and has a spacious cruciform interior.

From the church, head through the graveyard towards the
fourteenth-century **Alfriston Clergy House**. This is a Wealden "hall
house" – the central hall is flanked by two-storey bays that jut out to
the front – and the whole building is surmounted by a thatched roof.
Turn left before you reach the house, then go straight ahead, with the

church behind you. Turn right and you're back on the bank of the Cuckmere, which skirts the cottage garden of the Clergy House.

....

Alfriston Clergy House is open early to mid-March Sat & Sun 11am–4pm; mid-March to end Oct Mon, Wed, Thurs, Sat & Sun 10am–5pm; end Oct to mid-Dec Mon, Wed, Thurs, Sat & Sun 11am–4pm; £3.70 (NT).

....

Along the Cuckmere

1.5km

Beyond the Clergy House, the **Cuckmere** winds through an exceptionally pretty and lush valley – it's hard to believe that contraband goods were once run up this lazy little river from the sea (see box, p.158). Just before you reach the wooden bridge over the Cuckmere at Litlington, you can see a white **chalk horse** on the hill ahead, created in 1924 by three brothers who cut the horse by moonlight one night so as to surprise the locals the next morning.

Litlington to Westdean Forest

3km

Once over the bridge, turn right. After 150m the path joins a road opposite a huge thatched house; turn left into **Litlington** and then take the first right. Immediately to the right, a South Downs Way sign points you onto a narrow path, through a kissing gate. The path climbs steeply up a field and through another kissing gate. Carry on up the field and over a stile into another field – then head downhill, keeping the fence to your right, towards **Westdean Forest**.

At the very edge of the forest, turn left to follow the South Downs Way – handsome thirteenth-century **Charleston Manor**

Shorter route to Eastbourne

The **South Downs Way** splits into two at Alfriston, with one route (10km) taking you to Eastbourne over the downs and avoiding the spectacular but testing (and longer) cliff walk described below. To join this branch of the South Downs Way, cross the bridge over the Cuckmere shortly before you reach the Church of St Andrew and turn left after 100m, following the South Downs Way signs. After 2km you pass the **Long Man of Wilmington**, a seventy-metre-high ancient chalk giant cut onto the hill. Some 3km further on you go through the ancient village of **Jevington**, beyond which the route descends for 5km to the western edge of **Eastbourne**.

is visible ahead through the trees. A little further on, wooden steps lead up into the trees. South Downs Way signs direct you through the forest to the secluded medieval village of **Westdean**. Ignore the road that curves round left to the church and go straight ahead to continue on the South Downs Way. Go past the green phone box on the left, climb the steps ahead of you through the trees and follow the public footpath sign towards Cuckmere Haven.

Cuckmere Haven
2.5km

Coming out of the forest you'll see the Cuckmere river ahead of you, snaking through the silted estuary at **Cuckmere Haven**. Go straight ahead down the field towards the visitor centre. Across the busy road and over the cattle grid, the path splits, the South Downs Way climbing high up the valley wall and a second track leading beside the river. If you want to save yourself a strenuous climb, it's quite possible to follow the track along the river, picking up the South Downs Way just over a kilometre further on – you can make a little detour on to the beach from the lower path.

The track and the other paths join and then diverge once more; the South Downs Way follows the steeper route to the left, taking you onto the downs again.

The Seven Sisters, Birling Gap and Beachy Head
7km

From here on you need to brace yourself for the dramatic walk over the switchback sequence of cliffs known as the **Seven Sisters**. The path runs close to the edge of the chalky cliffs, with the only break in the clifftop walk provided by **Birling Gap**, a small settlement featuring a row of nineteenth-century coastguards' cottages. Beyond, the clifftop walk takes you on a further rollercoaster ride to **Beachy Head**, the highest point of the cliffs (160m). The wildness of the surroundings helps to explain why Debussy came here to complete *La Mer*, his masterly evocation of the sea; he stayed at the Grand Hotel on the front in nearby Eastbourne. Look out for the red and white candy stripes of the glorious **lighthouse**, built in 1902, just off the coast at Beachy Head.

....

Around 400m before you reach the Birling Gap turnoff, a bridleway leads uphill for just over a kilometre to East Dean, where you can have lunch at the *Tiger Inn* (Mon–Fri 11am–3pm & 6–11pm, Sat 11am–11pm, Sun noon–10.30pm; ☎ 01323/423209). The inn, which enjoys an idyllic location on the village green, serves Harveys Best and locally sourced food.

....

Jevington Jigg

Smuggling has a very long history in Sussex – wool-running, known as "owling", started in the thirteenth century following the imposition of a severe tax on wool under Edward I, and continued into the eighteenth century. By this time, smuggling had developed into a serious industry, with goods, from brandy to lace and tea, being smuggled in from the Continent.

Many gangs of smugglers were bankrolled by City of London financiers, and whole villages, from estate owners to innkeepers, were involved. One such innkeeper was James Pettit, known as **Jevington Jigg**, who operated out of the *Eight Bells* in Jevington, running contraband from Birling Gap. Jevington Jigg was a kind of Sussex Ned Kelly, and led a lawless and incident-packed life – when once trapped in an inn surrounded by armed constables, he managed to escape by slipping into a petticoat and feigning girlish hysterics. In 1789 he was arrested with his friend Cream Pot Tom for stealing a mare in Firle. Tom was hanged at Oxford, but Jevington Jigg was released, leading people to suspect he had betrayed his friend. He was later nearly lynched at Lewes for informing on other associates. Eventually Jevington Jigg's luck ran out: he was convicted of horse theft and transported to Botany Bay in Australia, and probably died there.

Today the exploits of the smugglers, including a small gang that operated out of Alfriston, are much romanticized, despite their violent and sometimes murderous treatment of excise men. Traces of tunnels beneath inns and manor houses – and even the church in Jevington – built to hide contraband goods from the excisemen, are the last reminder of the trade.

Into Eastbourne

5km

At the *Beachy Head* pub just to the left of the route, you begin to descend into Eastbourne. Take the tarred path that leads off to the right, via a viewpoint. Cross the metal gate and descend the narrow wooded path for 1.5km. Below you is **Eastbourne**, whose Edwardian villas can look unexpectedly glamorous in the evening light. The last gasp of downland walk takes you down a steep grassy slope, and lands you right on Eastbourne's seafront.

Follow the seafront for just over 1.5km, heading towards the pier; turn left onto Terminus Road for the **station**. If you're flagging at this point, a **taxi** (☎ 01323/725511) to the station from the seafront will cost around £5.

5

The Saxon Shore

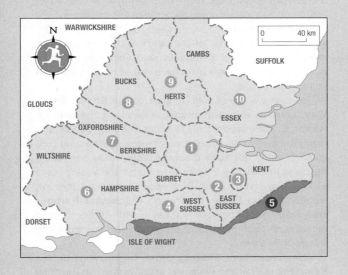

The Saxon Shore Way
Hastings to Winchelsea
via Cliff End.................................. 161

The 1066 Country Walk
Pevensey to Battle via
Brownbread Street........................ 168

Chichester Harbour
Fishbourne to Bosham.................. 178

Leading along the coast from Hastings in Sussex to Gravesend in Kent, the **Saxon Shore Way** is named for the string of late-Roman fortifications that protected the coast against Saxon invasion, and whose remains you can still see today, as at Anderida, which features on the second walk in this chapter. The stretch of Sussex shoreline covered in this chapter has always been particularly vulnerable to invasion; indeed, it was at Anderida that William the Conqueror landed – the 1066 Country Walk follows the route of his army inland to Battle.

The **levels** are the defining physical feature of the first two walks in this chapter: a landscape of fields and banks, reclaimed from the sea and crisscrossed by little man-made channels (known, rather off-puttingly, as "sewers"). Reclamation was an expensive and therefore very gradual process, begun by the Romans, revived in the eighth century by monastic houses that owned tracts of marshland, and continued into the eighteenth century. The result of this piecemeal development is an idiosyncratic landscape of small and irregularly shaped fields, scattered with shells, which offer a reminder of the land's watery origins. The marshy, reed-fringed **peninsula** near Fishbourne Palace illustrates how the levels must have looked before they were reclaimed.

The first walk leads along part of the **Saxon Shore Way**, starting with a strenuous hike along the cliffs at Hastings, then descending to cross the Pett Levels and reach the lovely little town of Winchelsea. The second (and longest) walk, the **1066 Country Walk**, takes you along the route followed by the Normans from their landing place at Pevensey, across the Pevensey Levels and through wooded hills to Battle. Finally, the **Chichester Harbour** walk leads from Fishbourne Palace, with its fine Roman mosaics, through marshland and pasture to the appealing village of Bosham.

Trains leave from **Charing Cross** for Hastings on the Saxon Shore Way and Pevensey and Westham on the 1066 route, with stops at London Bridge. For the Chichester Harbour walk, trains leave from **Waterloo**, stopping at Clapham Junction. The easiest walk for **drivers** is the circular Chichester Harbour one.

THE SAXON SHORE WAY

Hastings to Winchelsea via Cliff End

Distance and difficulty 17km; strenuous.
Duration 4hr 15min.
Trains London Charing Cross to Hastings (every 30min; 1hr 20min);
return from Winchelsea to Hastings (hourly; 15min), then Hastings to
London Charing Cross (every 30min; 1hr 20min).
Map OS Landranger 199 and 189: *Eastbourne & Hastings* and
Ashford & Romney Marsh; OS Explorer 124: *Hastings & Bexhill*.

This glorious walk is very much a day of two halves, starting as a
strenuous stomp along the clifftops near Hastings before descending to the pancake-flat "levels" beyond. The route follows part of
the **Saxon Shore Way**, a long-distance path that runs for 260km
in its entirety, from Hastings all the way round the coast to
Gravesend. Starting in tattily charismatic **Hastings**, a funicular
takes you up to the sandstone cliffs that soar above the town into
the pristine downland of the **Hastings Country Park**. From
here, the route follows the clifftops for 5km, taking in sweeping
sea views and dipping down into luxuriant wooded glens before
terminating at the prosaically named village of **Cliff End**; a short
detour leads from here to a long sandy **beach**, where it's
sometimes safe to swim. From Cliff End, the walk runs across
Pett Level, reclaimed from the sea and crisscrossed by water
channels. Though the scenery is less obviously dramatic than
along the clifftop walk, the levels have an enticingly still
atmosphere and are prettily framed by hills to the north and the
long bank of the sea wall to the south. The walk ends at
Winchelsea, an attractive little town with a fascinating history.

There are lots of wonderful **picnic** spots along the way, but
you'll need to wait till Winchelsea for a good **pub**. It's cheapest
and quickest to return from Winchelsea via Hastings, taking either
the bus or the train, meaning that you can buy a return ticket to
Hastings. Alternatively, infrequent trains run from Winchelsea to
London **via Ashford**, but if you go for this option you have to buy
two single tickets rather than a return.

Getting started

2km

From **Hastings station**, go down Havelock Road, then straight
ahead down Wellington Place, through a pedestrian underpass
and towards the old town. Turn left along the sea front and
continue for 700m, past Hastings' appealingly shabby jumble

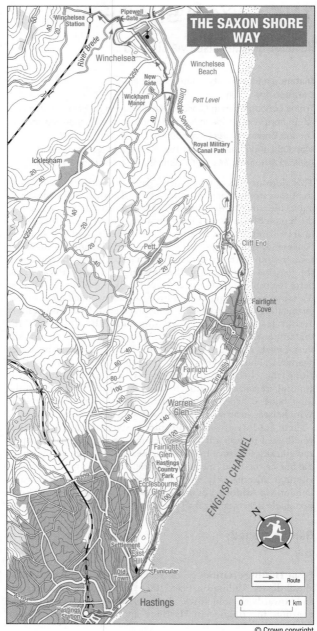

THE SAXON SHORE WAY

© Crown copyright

of Regency and Victorian buildings, amusement arcades and fish'n'chip shops. Follow the signs towards the East Hill Cliff Railway. This picturesque part of town is known as the **Stade**, from the old English for "landing place" – Hastings still has a working fleet and you'll see brightly coloured boats on the beach, among the unusually tall black wooden fishing huts that lend the area a quirky Gothic air. These were built in the nineteenth century to store nets and ropes – as the sea came in much further at that time, fishermen were forced to capitalize on the available space by building up rather than out.

Hastings Country Park

5km

Opposite the cluster of fishing huts, the East Hill **funicular railway** (April–Sept 10am–5.30pm; Oct & Nov 11am–4pm; £1), Britain's steepest at 39 degrees, runs up the cliffside at surprising speed. If you want to start walking before the funicular starts running, or if it's poorly, which happens from time to time, you'll have to climb the cliff via Tamarisk Steps to the left of the train tracks, by the *Dolphin* pub. The funicular provides tremendous views of the town and lands you neatly in **Hastings Country Park**, whose cliffs tower up to 90m above the sea and are bright with yellow gorse in the summer. You pick up the Saxon Shore Way here, though it's not signed; follow the brown signs towards Firehills. If in doubt at any point in the park, head for the path closest to the cliffs.

Go straight ahead and up the hill, which is surmounted by a low, circular-banked structure, the remains of an **Iron Age fort**. The views are tremendous, with the sea to the right, Hastings to the left and the cliffs you'll walk along ahead. Just beyond the fort, head right to the long wooden fence that runs along a field. From here, simply follow the path as it hugs the cliff edge and dips down first into **Ecclesbourne**, **Fairlight** and **Warren Glens**, wooded clefts in the cliffs, following the brown signs to Fairlight and/or Firehills. There's a nudist beach at Fairlight, although the council recommends that you avoid it because of recent cliff falls – even so, there always seem to be a few hopeful teenage boys keeping a lookout on the cliffs just in case. Coming out of Warren Glen, follow the wide grassy path that leads up the hill and veers left, away from the cliffs, following the signs to Fairlight Church and Firehills. Some 400m beyond here you'll pass a radio mast on top of the hill; carry on straight ahead to Firehills on the cliffside path to the right, not the one that leads inland.

Fairlight to Cliff End

3km

From the country park, you emerge into staid **Fairlight**. Go
straight ahead along Channel Way, a track that leads between the
rows of bungalows and the sea. Some 500m along Channel Way,
turn left onto Shepherd's Way, and after 100m turn right onto
Bramble Way. After 250m turn left onto Smuggler's Way then,
after 200m, take a right onto Lower Wait's Lane. This lane cuts
through the village for 750m; at the T-junction, turn right. About
100m further on you'll see a National Trust sign. Go through the
gap in the hedge here, onto the path that leads through a field, and
climbs away from Fairlight.

The cliff-top walk resumes from this point. Out of the National
Trust area, follow the yellow arrow on the fence post – you'll see
a gorgeous golden strand ahead. You're now in **Cliff End**. Head
down the hill for 400m, past two pretty thatched cottages – ignore
the turn-offs and go straight ahead downhill until you get to the
road. Turn right and keep going for 300m to get to the **beach**, but
don't swim if the red flag is flying.

Pett Levels

4km

To continue along the Saxon Shore Way, turn right at the
point where the path joins the road through Cliff End and head
towards the beach. After 100m, where the road curves, take the
footpath to the left along the **Royal Military Canal**, built by
William Pitt for defence against a Napoleonic invasion that never
materialized. After 200m you come to a little bridge – don't cross
over here, but go straight ahead up the left bank of the canal, on a
narrow and slightly scruffy path. After another 200m you'll see a
brick pillbox on the left – just before you reach it, turn right over
a second bridge to cross the canal. (The official route continues
on the left bank here and crosses at the third bridge, but the path
can be very overgrown so it's better to cross here.) Continue up
the right bank of the canal. At a third bridge, cross the road and
carry on up the canal.

From here you're on **Pett Level** and the views open up – the
canal heads gradually away from the sea and the noisy seafront
road, drawing closer to the hills to the north, where you'll see a
windmill. At a kink in the canal the Dimsdale Sewer (actually a
water channel, so not as unappealing as it sounds) appears on your
right, so you're walking between the two stretches of water.
Where the canal curves to the right there's a bridge – don't cross
over here, but continue for another 700m until you begin to draw
near to a white clapboard house on the left.

Winchelsea: storms, smuggling and sacking

The pretty and now rather sedate town of **Winchelsea** was shaped over the centuries both by natural disasters and by brutal attacks. The town originally sat on a long shingle spit that poked out into the sea from Fairlight cliffs. However, by the thirteenth century the spit was being eaten away by erosion. A huge **storm** in 1252 and a freak high tide swallowed up three hundred houses, while another storm in 1288 converted the spit into an island. It was decided to move Winchelsea to higher and safer ground – the remains of the old town are now completely submerged, and even their exact whereabouts are unknown.

Edward I employed a French architect, who designed the new town along the lines of a French *bastide* (fortified town) on a neat grid plan that still survives today. The town was built primarily for commerce and was a vital link in the wine trade with Bordeaux, as well as being a place from where fish, wool, cheese and salt were exported, plus iron and wool from the Weald. There was a good road to London, and each merchant was given wharf space on the River Brede, which was then wide and flourishing. The king imposed a perpetual rent on the town in return for the building costs, and a sum of just over £14 – a figure that has remained unchanged through the centuries – is still collected annually.

Prior to the rebuilding, the strategic significance of Winchelsea had already been recognized by its inclusion in the **Cinq Ports** confederation. This was a grouping of five towns – Hastings, New Romney, Hythe, Sandwich and Dover – to which Winchelsea and Rye were later added. At a time when Britain had no navy, the Cinq Ports were the only line of defence against a possible invasion of southern England. In exchange for providing ships and men for a certain number of days a year, the ports were granted freedom from taxation and the governance of their own affairs. This arrangement was open to abuse, however: Winchelsea carried on a lively trade in the **smuggling** of tax-free goods and also engaged in piracy – its sailors were notorious for preying on English and foreign ships.

The town's wealth and strategic location made it vulnerable to **attack**. In 1359, while the inhabitants were at Mass, the French stormed Winchelsea, killing forty people and burning and looting the town. They returned exactly a year later, and again in 1380 and 1449, on similarly violent missions. But it was natural forces that were to prove the undoing of Winchelsea. Early in the sixteenth century, great masses of shingle from the Channel caused the River Brede to silt up and narrow and the town's days as a port were finished.

Following the silting up of the river, Winchelsea went into economic decline for more than three centuries, the gaps in its grid

continued next page

of streets caused by the French attacks leading both Daniel Defoe and John Wesley to liken the place to a skeleton. This melancholy shade of a town began to draw writers and artists from the end of the nineteenth century: Turner and Millais painted here; Henry James, Thackeray, Conrad, Ford Madox Ford, Rumer Godden and Radclyffe Hall were visitors; and the actress Ellen Terry lived in Tower Cottage at the north end of town. Although they were attracted by Winchelsea's air of romantic decay, their presence in the town undoubtedly contributed to its transformation into the prosperous little place you see today.

Cross at the **concrete bridge,** marked with yellow public footpath arrows. Go straight ahead across the field towards the road, then follow the curve of the track up the hill to the left. Go through the gate and turn right onto a minor road. After 100m you come to **New Gate**, one of the medieval entrances to Winchelsea. Go through it, then look back – you'll see that the arch of the gate perfectly frames **Wickham Manor**, a fine early sixteenth-century farmhouse. Follow the road for 700m and bear right at the T-junction for Winchelsea.

Winchelsea

3km

On your right as you enter the main part of town is the great **Church of St Thomas**. The transepts and nave were entirely destroyed by the French; as a result, the remaining part, the chancel, feels bizarrely abbreviated. Its scale, however, is still grand and the detail splendidly ornate. To either side are sombre fourteenth-century effigies – two depict admirals of the Cinque Ports and the others are generic, representing a knight, a lady and a civilian. The 1920s stained glass adds splashes of colour. You can take a **bus** (hourly; 25min; £4.10) from in front of the church to return to Hastings.

Opposite the church is the *New Inn*, a scenic spot for a pint, and nearby is a scion of **Wesley's Tree**; John Wesley frequently preached at Winchelsea and delivered his last sermon, against smuggling, under the original tree in 1790. The town mainly consists of well-proportioned sixteenth- to eighteenth-century town houses, with some harmonious early twentieth-century imitations. The only surviving medieval building-work, apart from the much-damaged church, is in the wine cellars concealed beneath many of the houses.

From the church, go straight ahead for 150m until you come to a post with a **1066 sign** pointing to the left. If you follow the sign for 900m you can avoid walking on the main road and there are fine views across the marshes – this was a lookout point during the medieval wars with the French. Cross the main road and go straight ahead, following the 1066 Country Walk signs which lead you in a loop down to the minor road that runs to the station. Otherwise, turn right down the main road, through Pipewell Gate. At the hairpin bend, follow the minor road signed towards the station, which zigzags for a kilometre to **Winchelsea station**, from where trains depart to Hastings (hourly; 15min) or on to London Charing Cross, changing at Ashford (every 30min; 2hr).

THE 1066 COUNTRY WALK

Pevensey to Battle via Brownbread Street

Distance and difficulty 26km; strenuous.
Duration 6hr 30min.
Trains London Bridge/Charing Cross to Pevensey and Westham (every 30min; 1hr 50min, change at St Leonard's Warrior Square); return from Battle to London Bridge/Charing Cross (every 30min; 1hr 10min).
Map OS Landranger 199: *Eastbourne & Hastings*; OS Explorer 124: *Hasting & Bexhill*.

This long and wonderfully varied walk is part of the **1066 Country Walk**, which follows the route taken by the Norman army from Pevensey, where they landed and established a castle within the walls of a Roman fort, to Battle, where they defeated King Harold's army (the official route then continues for another 28km through Winchelsea to Rye). The walk starts at **Pevensey and Westham station** – a little further down the line there's a station simply called Pevensey which is slightly closer to the castle and the start of the walk proper, but trains don't run there at weekends. **Pevensey** was the landing place of Duke William of Normandy (although the sea receded over time, leaving the town high and dry), who established himself in the great circular Roman fort of **Anderida** – the ruins of the Roman fort and the Norman castle constructed within it are well worth a wander. From the castle, 1066 Country Walk leads across the Pevensey Levels, where you're likely to see a mass of water birds.

Leaving the levels you climb uphill to the edge of **Herstmonceux**, whose castle grounds are a good place for a picnic. Beyond Herstmonceux, the route runs across fertile hilly country to the village of **Boreham Street** where there's an excellent pub, *The Ash*; from here paths and minor roads lead through verdant, undulating countryside, punctuated by small settlements such as **Ashburnham Forge** and **Steven's Crouch**. Eventually the walk heads uphill, skirting the site of the most momentous battle in English history, and lands you at the fine fortified gatehouse of **Battle Abbey**.

The route is easy to follow – just look for the circular red **1066 signs**, whose stylized Norman arrows point you in the right direction.

Getting started

1km

From **Pevensey and Westham station**, follow the signs towards the castle then turn right onto the High Street, passing two

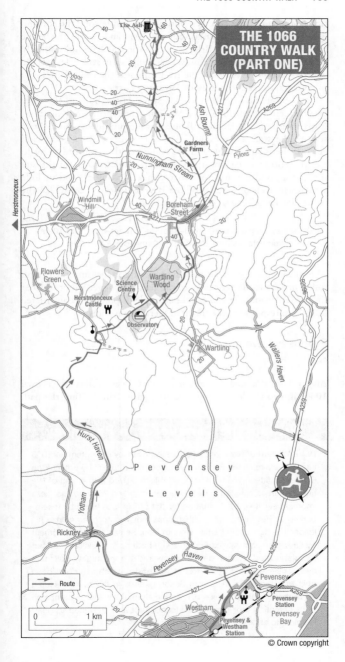

THE 1066 COUNTRY WALK (PART ONE)

The Ash

40

60

40

20

Pylons

20

40

40

20

Ash Bourne

A269

Pylons

Gardners Farm

Nunningham Stream

20

Windmill Hill

Boreham Street

A271

40

20

Flowers Green

Wartling Wood

Science Centre

Herstmonceux Castle ♜

Observatory

20

Wartling

20

B2095

Wallers Haven

A259

◀ Herstmonceux

Hurst Haven

Yotham

P e v e n s e y

L e v e l s

N

Rickney

Pevensey Haven

Pevensey

A27

Westham

Pevensey & Westham Station

Pevensey Station

Pevensey Bay

A259

20

→ Route

0   1 km

© Crown copyright

timber-framed Tudor cottages on the right. Just beyond the cottages is the **Church of St Nicholas**, built in 1080 and claimed to be the first Norman church in Britain, though it was later substantially altered, and what you see now is Early English in style. Beyond the church, follow the curve of the road round to the right, past a row of cottages, to reach the ruins of **Pevensey Castle.**

The combination of the Norman stone castle (built in the early twelfth century, probably by William's half-brother, Robert of Mortmain) and the ancient Roman walls provide as evocative a start to the walk as you could wish for; you can get a good look at both the Roman walls and the ruined castle without having to pay the entrance fee. Information boards erected around the site provide a good context for what you're looking at, and include a representation of a panel of the Bayeux tapestry, on which the name "Pevensae" can be clearly seen.

Pevensey Castle is open April–Sept daily 10am–6pm; Oct 10am–4pm; Nov–March Sat & Sun 10am–4pm; £4.20 (EH).

From the castle, go back past the row of cottages and turn right, following the road as it curves round past the rugged outer walls of the castle – from here you can see a couple of pillboxes, constructed in 1940 in response to the threat of German invasion.

Pevensey Levels

6km

After 600m, at a tiled house called "The Gables", follow the brown **1066 sign** to the left, down a narrow path. After 250m, the path

William the Conqueror in Pevensey

Duke William of Normandy landed in Pevensey in September 1066 intent on claiming the English throne, promised to him by Edward the Confessor fifteen years previously. William arrived with a fleet of five hundred ships carrying seven thousand men and 2500 horses. Less impressively, it was said that he fell flat on his face when he disembarked at Pevensey; with a sharpness that was to characterize his leadership during the battle a month later, he salvaged the moment by saying he had "seized England with both hands". William erected a prefabricated wooden defensive tower within the mighty walls that once encircled the Roman fort of **Anderida**, which itself had been built to withstand attack from Saxon pirates. In the month leading up to the fateful battle (see p.176), the Normans waged a campaign of systematic terror against the locals, probably designed to goad Harold into attack.

comes to the thunderous A259 – cross the road and follow the path as it resumes on the other side, running along the left bank of **Pevensey Haven**, one of the many channels cut to drain the levels. You should begin to spot some birds: herons, ducks, redshanks, warblers, swans, grebes and sandpipers. Plants line the havens, including great reed mace and yellow water iris.

The path follows the gentle curve of the haven for 3km to the quiet hamlet of **Rickney**. You come out onto a lane through the village; take the 1066 fingerpost straight ahead (not the Jevington route). The lane curves to the right, crossing a bridge over a little stream. Follow the 1066 sign soon after, and you're back in open country. From this point the character of the **Pevensey Levels**, framed by the South Downs to the south and wooded hills to the north, is much more apparent: a network of streams and ditches reflect the light, and herons and swans can be seen in profusion. The path runs for 3km through a series of gates, along the right bank of the wide and fast-flowing haven. Alongside the pedestrian gates that dot the route you'll see wider farm gates and, between them, horse jumps – this is very horsey country, and you're likely to see a few riders out and about.

Towards Herstmonceux

1km

A couple of kilometres ahead is the green dome of Herstmonceux observatory, which you pass later in the day, and the spire of the church at **Herstmonceux** – the name is a combination of the Saxon *herst*, meaning forest, and de Monceux, the name of the Conqueror's grandson, though it's now pronounced in a resolutely English fashion as "Herst-mont-zoo".

Keep your eyes peeled for the 1066 sign and follow it away from the haven to the right (there's another post with a 1066 sign just beyond to confirm that you're on the correct path). The path curves round to the left, over a stile, and then turns into a broad, grassy track, running between two ditches. The path joins another wide grassy track – turn left onto it and follow it round to the church.

Looking out over the Pevensey Levels from the southeast fringes of Herstmonceux village, **All Saints Church** was built around a century after the Conquest, although the dormer windows – which give the long nave roof a rather gingerbread-cottage look – were a Victorian addition, designed to bring more light to the interior. Inside, look out for the sturdy medieval trussed roof and the long brass on the chancel floor (it may be concealed by a carpet) depicting Sir William Fiennes and dating from 1402 – he wears a mail shirt and sword and his pointy feet rest on a lion. The Gothic **Dacre Chapel** to the left of the altar was built with funds provided in 1534 by the Dacre family, who were then living at Herstmonceux Castle (see below). The chapel shelters an unusual double effigy, restored in brilliant colour, which commemorates Thomas, the eighth Lord Dacre (1470–1533) with his feet resting on a bull representing the Dacres, and his son, Sir Thomas Fiennes, whose feet are supported by a wolfhound, the symbol of the Fiennes family (now of actor and explorer fame). It's thought that the carving originally represented a pair of half-brothers, but was brought from Battle Abbey following the dissolution of the monasteries and adapted to represent Lord Dacre and Sir Thomas.

Herstmonceux to Boreham Street

3km

Go straight ahead across the road from the stile by the churchyard and follow the 1066 sign towards Herstmonceux Castle. The path goes downhill through some pine woods before emerging into an open field. From here, you can see the green dome of the observatory looming ahead of you and **Herstmonceux Castle** to the left – a bizarre juxtaposition, resembling the backdrop to one of Tintin's adventures. The beautifully symmetrical castle, really more of a manor house, was one of the earliest brick structures in England. It was built by Sir Roger Fiennes, who obtained the necessary "licence to crenellate" in 1440, but it fell into disuse and disrepair and was dismantled in 1777, before being reconstructed in 1932 by Sir Paul Latham. In 1946, the estate was purchased by the Admiralty as a home for the Royal Observatory; and, in 1993 both the observatory and castle were purchased by a Canadian university.

Head towards the **observatory**, up the steepish enclosed path through some woodland. On the left at the top of the hill you'll see smaller steel and copper domes belonging to the Herstmonceux Science Centre; the place is now run as an education facility rather than a serious observatory (the main telescope was shifted in the 1980s to the Canary Islands, where the weather is obviously more reliable). The path goes straight ahead through beech and pine wood, then joins a minor road. Turn right onto the road for 200m, then left just before the orange-tiled cottage.

The path runs down the edge of a field, with Wartling Wood on the left, then climbs up a field and curves to join another minor road. Turn right on the road and then almost immediately left over a stile into a field, then cross a series of stiles over paddock fences as you head diagonally across the field towards a black barn. The path then curves left towards a line of trees – cross the stile on the far side of the field, and you'll soon see a farm and some houses. Cross the stile leading onto the road on the right, just before you get to the barn. Head down to the road and turn right into **Boreham Street**, an attractive village with some fine Georgian houses and cottages.

Towards Brownbread Street

4.5km

Just outside Boreham Street, a 1066 sign points left to Brownbread Street – the path heads very steeply down a field, with superb views ahead made more dramatic by the line of giant pylons that marches across it. At the bottom of the hill you come to a stream; cross this and carry straight on up the hill, following the 1066 sign, past **Gardners Farm**, where the path becomes a farm track. A kilometre beyond the farm the track joins a minor road. Go right and continue for another kilometre to come out at a grassy triangle with a red-brick house on the right-hand side. Turn left and follow the sign to **Brownbread Street** for 200m, where you come to the *Ash Tree Inn*.

....

The *Ash Tree Inn* (Tues–Sun 11am–2.15pm & 7–9pm; ☎ 01424/892104) is a free house and makes an excellent stop for a pint, with outside tables in a pretty garden.

....

To Ashburnham Forge

2km

Some 500m beyond *The Ash Tree Inn* you come to **Ashburnham Village Hall**; just beyond this, on the right, follow the 1066 sign that points away from the road towards Ashburnham Forge. The path leads through a wooden kissing gate, then down the field and on to the road – turn left for a few metres, then right onto another minor road. Continue for a couple of kilometres along this very quiet minor road as it rolls up and down through fields. Descend the hill and you'll see a red post box; on the right is Forge Cottage. You're now in the hamlet of **Ashburnham Forge**. Cross the brick bridge over the weir and climb the road up the hill. Follow the path that leads off the road to the right, passing a red-brick house and pond before heading across a wide field.

To Catsfield via Steven's Crouch

5km

Go down the field, then cross two little plank **bridges** over streams and pass through some woodland. Climb the steep hill ahead of you, heading for the signed wooden posts. The path levels out and emerges into a large open field. Cross the faint track ahead through

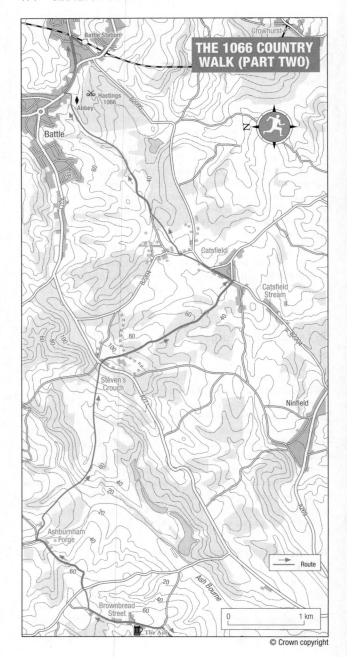

THE 1066 COUNTRY
WALK (PART TWO)

Battle Station

Crowhurst

Hastings
1066

Abbey

Battle

Catsfield

Catsfield
Stream

Steven's
Crouch

Ninfield

Ashburnham
Forge

Ash Bourne

Brownbread
Street

The Ash

→   Route

0   1 km

© Crown copyright

the field: it leads diagonally left towards an island of woodland, to the right of which there's a fingerpost (further to the left is a Victorian Gothic stone cottage). Head towards the post at the long line of woodland ahead. You go through the tip of the woodland and then up through the field – there's an enormous horse chestnut ahead, with heavy branches that touch the ground and look as if they're rerooting themselves. Follow the 1066 sign on a post to the left of the tree, which points you up the hill, towards the road. Just to the left is a stone gatehouse and a set of gateposts topped by statues of greyhounds.

A hundred metres beyond you join a road at the village of **Steven's Crouch** – you'll see some picturesque thatched, timber-framed cottages to the right. Cross a stile and turn left onto the road, then cross the road almost immediately and follow the sign that leads away from the road towards Catsfield. This leads down an avenue lined by tall Wellingtonia trees. After 350m you reach a junction. Go through the gate on the left, then turn right down the track towards Catsfield, rather than curving up to the left. The track leads downhill into pine woodland, passing a couple of lakes on the right after 800m. Some 800m further on, go through a gate, with a pond on the left, and join the lane towards **Catsfield**.

On to Battle

3.5km

At the junction turn left and walk along the road for 400m through the undistinguished village. On the far side of the village you'll see a **1066 sign** on a fingerpost. Turn left off the road at this sign and cross the field to the road. Cross the road and turn left for 50m, then follow another 1066 sign that points off to the right along a track. Follow the track for 100m, continuing straight ahead over a stile and into a field. Go through a pine plantation – beyond the pines in the corner of the field is a stile; follow the sign here that points through some woodland and, after 100m, leads sharp left.

The path leads steeply downhill for 200m. Cross a stile onto a little gravel track and turn right, then eventually go through a metal gate and up the path. Go through another metal gate and the path opens out into a field. Follow the sign that points ahead up the steep grassy hill. At the far side the path joins a gravel track – the houses at the top of the hill are in Battle, while the line of trees to your right conceals the site of the battle beyond. At the top of the track, immediately ahead of you, lies Battle Abbey.

Battle

Battle is a small and inoffensively touristy town, dominated by the gatehouse of the abbey around which it was built. Facing the

▲ Battle Abbey

abbey is the good if slightly pricey *Pilgrim's* restaurant (£15 for a two-course dinner), located in a magnificent thirteenth-century timbered building – there's a high, barn-like timber roof and a vast fireplace inside. You can sit outside in summer and admire the abbey gatehouse. The food is all prepared using fresh local ingredients.

The entrance fee to **Battle Abbey** allows you to explore the ruined monastery buildings and also to tour the battle site. The papal authorities insisted that William build the abbey as penance for the deaths resulting from the battle; building started in 1070 and the abbey was consecrated in 1094. You enter via the gatehouse, built in 1338 in an elegant synthesis of form and function – the high polygonal turrets are both formidable and beautiful. Of the complex of buildings beyond the gatehouse, the most intriguing and best preserved (with the exception of the Abbot's Hall, which is now a school and not open to the public) is the airy dormitory, its three chambers descending to accommodate the sloping ground and its long lines punctuated by slender lancet windows. You can also see the foundations of the abbey church, whose high altar is supposed to mark the spot where Harold fell.

. . . .

Battle Abbey is open daily: April–Sept 10am–6pm; Oct–March 10am–4pm; £6.50 (EH).

. . . .

The most intangible feature of the site – the **battle** itself – is nicely evoked by an audio tour. You look out over the battle site from the high ground occupied by the shield wall of the Saxons, or can take an extended version of the tour and walk round the battle site. The Saxon army was famously exhausted by their victory over the Norwegians at the Battle of Stamford Bridge, and by the hasty march south to take on the Normans. The tactics of the Normans – as recalled by the outraged audio thane – included faked retreats by the mounted knights and the consequent slaughter of the pursuing Saxon foot soldiers. The Saxon line was broken and Harold was killed, though he's more likely to have been bludgeoned to death than killed by an arrow in his eye as shown in the Bayeux Tapestry.

Turning right out of the abbey gatehouse you soon come to the **Church of St Mary the Virgin**, which features a Romanesque nave, Norman font, rare fourteenth-century wall paintings and the gaudy gilded alabaster tomb of Sir Anthony Browns (to whom Henry VIII granted the abbey).

To reach the **train station**, follow the road beyond the church for 500m, then take the signed road down the hill to the left.

CHICHESTER HARBOUR

Fishbourne to Bosham

Distance and difficulty 9km; easy.
Duration 2hr 15min.
Trains London Victoria/Waterloo to Fishbourne (every 30min;
1hr 40min; change at Havant); return from Fishbourne to London
Waterloo (every 30min; 1hr 55min; change at Havant).
Map OS Landranger 197: *Chichester and the South Downs*;
OS Explorer 120: *Chichester*.

The short stretch of land covered by this walk is rich and distinctive, both in appearance and history. The walk leads from
Fishbourne, site of **Fishbourne Palace**, one of the grandest
Roman villas in Britain, across a sheltered peninsula to the Saxon
settlement of **Bosham**. There are no open seascapes, but water
is a constant presence, from the marshland south of Fishbourne,
where dense clumps of reeds tower above you, to salty Bosham
itself. Here the houses cling together as if to resist the tide that
races up Bosham Channel – one of a series of inlets that comprise
Chichester Harbour – and then recedes to leave a tangle of sea-
weed, shells, tiny crabs and other marine detritus.

To get to Bosham in time for lunch, you'll probably need to leave
a visit to Fishbourne Palace to the end of the walk. Bear in mind
also that the route can get extremely muddy and come prepared.

Getting started

0.5km

From **Fishbourne station**, turn right, crossing the railway
line, and go straight ahead down the road in the direction of
Fishbourne Palace (see box opposite); you'll see the palace signed
off to the left, up Roman Way. To carry on to Bosham, go straight
ahead, turning left at the end of the road onto the A259 towards
Chichester. After 200m, cross to the *Bull's Head* pub. Immediately
beyond the pub, take a right onto Mill Lane.

South along Chichester Channel

0.75km

Mill Lane leads to **Mill Pond**, opposite a beautiful thatched cottage.
Take the right-hand path that goes past the pond and then winds
through the high, rustling reeds, crossing a series of wooden bridges
and trackways. This section is very watery at high tide – you may
have to wait a little for it to recede. Eventually you come out onto

Fishbourne Palace

Fishbourne Palace (Jan Sat & Sun 10am–4pm; Feb, Nov & Dec daily 10am–4pm; March–July, Sept & Oct daily 10am–5pm; Aug daily 10am–6pm; £7) was one of the very few Roman villas in Britain whose size and grandeur bore comparison to its Continental counterparts. Originally a supply depot for the Roman army, the site was developed in the second half of the first century as the splendid palace of the Romanized Celtic aristocrat **Cogidubnus** (the villa may have been granted to him in reward for his loyalty to Rome during the onslaught of Boudicca). The villa was similar to those in Pompeii, featuring gardens and a courtyard surrounded by a colonnaded walk, and a vaulted audience chamber where the owner would receive guests. It also boasted baths and pools, and was adorned with mosaics, stuccowork, marble panels and elaborately painted frescoes, all thought to have been the work of highly skilled foreign craftsmen, though only the mosaic floors survive in anything but fragmentary form. The villa was destroyed by fire in the third century; charred door-sills are still visible between the mosaic floors. Bodies were buried in the ruins some time after the fire, and the skeleton of one still lies in situ in a shallow grave.

The palace's highlight is its series of fine **mosaic floors**, by far the most flamboyant and beautiful being the one that depicts Cupid riding a dolphin, surrounded by fantastic sea creatures. A jumble of artefacts is displayed in the palace **museum**, including roof tiles which acquired imprints of human and animal feet as they dried two thousand years ago, and a dainty intaglio onyx ring, engraved with a tiny image of a horse, a palm-frond waving above it. Otherwise, the palace is a bit of a disappointment. The surrounding houses and unattractive museum and shop have eradicated any atmosphere that may have clung to the site, and the style of interpretation throughout is a little past its sell-by date.

a high bank on the edge of the mud flats that border the Chichester Channel. The landscape opens out and you can see boats either reposing on mud or bobbing in the water, depending on the state of the tide. You eventually descend from the bank and the path winds through a glade of low oak trees with a pond on the right – a good sheltered spot for a **picnic**.

Across the peninsula to Bosham

3km

Just beyond the glade, the path veers off to the right to cross the **peninsula** that separates the Chichester and Bosham channels. The path is wide and grassy at this point; where it reaches a T-junction after 300m, turn right and, 200m further on, turn left at the line of

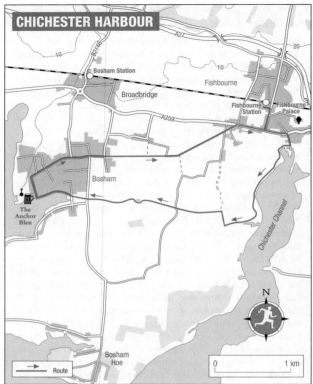

© Crown copyright

lime trees. After 500m, you cross a minor road; continue straight ahead, through wide, flat fields, broken up by patches of dense woodland. After passing a white cottage, the path joins a rough road. Where it curves round to the left, continue straight ahead, over a couple of little wooden bridges. Cross the field ahead, towards a flint cottage.

Steps lead down to a minor road – cross this and carry on straight ahead between a house and a garage. The path leads through the back gardens of Bosham and emerges at the harbour, where you get a sudden blast of salty air. Go straight along the edge of the harbour to the heart of Bosham.

Bosham

0.75km

The seventeenth- and eighteenth-century cottages of **Bosham** (pronounced "Bozzum") have a wonderfully organic quality, more redolent of a Cornish village than anything you'd expect to find in southeast England. The road round the harbour, **Mariner's Terrace**, takes you past terraced cottages and comes out at Beach Cottage (1708) – head straight up the road to reach the *Anchor Bleu* pub, and look out for the protective panels at the doorways of the houses you pass, which slot into stone grooves and protect against flooding at high tide.

The *Anchor Bleu* (Mon–Sat 11.30am–11pm, Sun noon–10pm; ℡01243/573956), licensed since the 1700s, is a characterful place with low beams, flagstones and a wheel-operated bulkhead door (for protection from high tides) leading to a little terrace with sea views. For lunch, it's best to go for the ploughman's rather than the cooked food, which can be pretty stodgy.

▼ Holy Trinity Church, Bosham

Turn left out of the pub to reach **Holy Trinity Church**, which sits on the lush Quay Meadow facing the water. The church is thought to be the oldest Christian site in Sussex, its unbuttressed, rocket-like tower unmistakably Saxon. Inside the church, the wide chancel arch gives the structure unexpected scale. The remains of an 8-year-old girl discovered in a tomb in the church in 1865 are thought to be those of **King Canute**'s daughter, who drowned in a mill stream behind the church. (It was also at Bosham that Canute famously ordered the sea to retreat. Contrary to popular belief, Canute knew he would fail, his purpose being to demonstrate both the limited powers he exercised as king and his humility as a convert to Christianity.) The church's great antiquity is also reflected by its appearance in a panel of the **Bayeux Tapestry**, a replica of which hangs in the church, depicting King Harold leaving Bosham for Normandy in 1064, with the church in the background, so stylized as to be unrecognizable. It was an ill-starred trip, which ended in shipwreck and Harold being forced to swear an oath of allegiance to William, the future conqueror of England.

Back to Fishbourne

4km

If you're in a rush to get back to Fishbourne to see the palace before it closes, you could take the short but rather uninspiring circular return route from Bosham described below. However, if you're not in a hurry, the recommended **return route** is the way you came – the views of Chichester Cathedral, the intricate track through the marsh and the immense skies that seem magnified by the nearby water are well worth savouring twice.

To **return directly to Fishbourne** from the church, turn left past the *Anchor Bleu* back down to Beach Cottage. Turn left again and carry on straight ahead through the village. At the *Millstream Hotel*, follow the road round to the right. If you want to get to **Bosham station** (which, confusingly, is actually in the neighbouring village of **Broadbridge**), take a left up Delling Lane, 600m beyond the point where the road curves; the station is just over a kilometre up the road. Otherwise, keep going up the road for another 500m.

Where the road curves round to the left, head along the path straight ahead, between the flint cottage and Rectory Farm – it's marked with a green public footpath sign. Ignore the public footpath sign to your left after 500m and just keep going.

Where the path ends, continue ahead up the track. There's a row of high lime trees to the right and the houses of Fishbourne are visible to the left. After another 600m, at the end of the track, go straight ahead up the road for 200m. Turn right at the busy road and then left to reach the **station** and **Fishbourne Palace**, either on the cycle path or on the road you came down earlier.

6

The North Wessex Downs to the New Forest

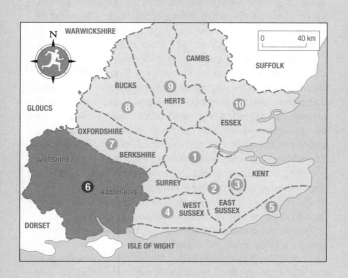

The Ridgeway

Foxhill to Wantage and Goring...... 185

The North Wessex Downs

Kintbury to Inkpen and back.......... 195

Stonehenge

Salisbury to Stonehenge
via Old Sarum 199

The New Forest

Lymington to Brockenhurst........... 206

Much of the area covered by this chapter has a conspicuous sense of antiquity, dotted with stone monuments, burial mounds and hillforts which comprise the earliest evidence of the impact of Britons on their natural environment. Nowhere is this more apparent than at **Stonehenge**, the most famous prehistoric structure in Europe, which sits in the middle of the downs of Salisbury Plain while, just to the north, the **North Wessex Downs** – a vast tract of chalky downland and ancient woodland, stretching from the edge of the Chilterns in the east to the Vale of the White Horse in the west – are home to a rich assortment of ancient monuments. To the southeast of Salisbury is the **New Forest**, a swathe of forest, heath and bog that has a striking wilderness feel, belying the fact that it has been systematically managed since the Norman period.

The first walk in this chapter is along part of the **Ridgeway**, thought to be the oldest surviving road in Britain, taking you across the North Wessex Downs from just outside Swindon, via the Vale of the White Horse, to the pretty Oxfordshire village of Goring. It's designed as a two-day walk with an overnight stop at the *Court Hill Centre*, but if you want to do just one day, make it the first, which includes an abundance of extraordinary prehistoric monuments. The **North Wessex Downs** walk takes you to the highest point of the downs, Inkpen Hill, which is surmounted by a Neolithic burial mound, an Iron Age hillfort and a weird gibbet dating back to the seventeenth century. The third walk leads from Salisbury, via the remains of Old Sarum, up a lush river valley to **Stonehenge**, giving unforgettable long-range views of the imposing, ineffably mysterious monument. The final route in the chapter is a shortish **New Forest** walk, designed to take in the variety of landscapes that this wonderfully distinctive region offers, as well as a thousand-year-old pub.

Thanks to efficient (though pricey) **train services**, these places can be reached in just over an hour from central London. The exception is the New Forest, which takes 1hr 40min to get to – the walk is relatively short, to take account of the time it takes to get there. Fast trains for Swindon depart from **Paddington**, as do trains for Kintbury, for the North Wessex Downs walk. Services for Salisbury and the New Forest leave from **Waterloo** and call at Clapham Junction. The North Wessex Downs walk and Stonehenge are the easiest options for **drivers**.

THE RIDGEWAY

Foxhill to Wantage and Goring

Distance and difficulty day 1: 17.5km; day 2: 25km; strenuous.
Duration day 1: 4hr 20min; day 2: 6hr 15min.
Trains London Paddington to Swindon (every 20min; 1hr); return from Goring to London Paddington (every 15min; 1hr).
Map OS Landranger 174: *Newbury & Wantage*; OS Explorer 170: *Abingdon, Wantage & Vale of White Horse.*

The **Ridgeway**, a 136-kilometre path starting at Overton Hill in Wiltshire and ending at Ivinghoe Beacon in Buckinghamshire, formed part of an ancient **trading route** between southwest England and mainland Europe, which may have started on the Dorset coast and run up to Norfolk. The route has been used by traders, invaders and drovers for at least five thousand years, the proliferation of Neolithic and Bronze Age burial sites and Iron Age forts along the way attesting to its cultural and strategic importance. The Ridgeway was the scene of skirmishes between the Saxons, under Alfred the Great (see box, p.188), and the Vikings, who sought to use it to penetrate the kingdom of Wessex. Its primary purpose in the medieval period was as a drove road between Wales and the home counties. There probably wasn't one specific road here until the Enclosure Acts of 1750 – the modern Ridgeway is an amalgam of several smaller routes and originally people would have used the easiest and driest section available on the day.

The section of the Ridgeway covered here leads east from **Foxhill** to the **Vale of the White Horse**, passing some of England's most intriguing prehistoric sites including Wayland's Smithy, Uffington Castle and the White Horse itself. You can return to London via **Wantage** at the end of day one, or stay at the spectacular hostel just off the route and continue for a second day to the village of Goring, which sits in a gentle bend of the River Thames. If you only do one day of this walk, make sure it's the first.

Day one

17.5km

The first day of the walk is crammed with interest, from medieval field terraces to the cluster of prehistoric sights at the **Vale of the White Horse**. The pubs to the north of the Ridgeway at Ashbury, Woolstone and Kingston Lisle all make decent **lunch** stops, although as these all involve a 3km round-trip detour from the route, you might prefer to take a picnic lunch. Day one ends

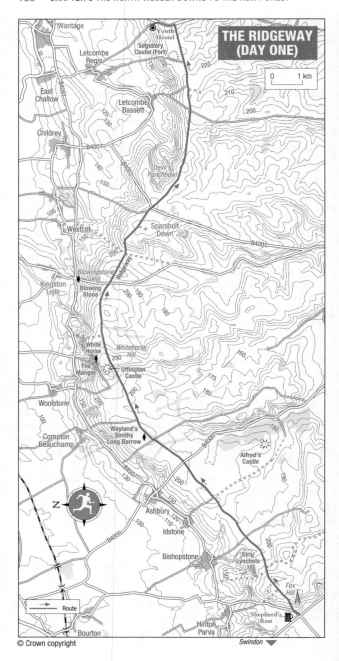

THE RIDGEWAY
(DAY ONE)

0   1 km

Wantage

Youth
Hostel

Segsbury
Castle (Fort)

Letcombe
Regis

Letcombe
Bassett

East
Challow

B4001

Childrey

B4001

Devil's
Punchbowl

Westcot

Sparsholt
Down

B4001

Ridgeway

Blowingstone
Hill

Blowing
Stone

Kingston
Lisle

White
Horse

Whitehorse
Hill

The
Manger

Uffington
Castle

Woolstone

Wayland's
Smithy
Long Barrow

Alfred's
Castle

Compton
Beauchamp

B4507

Ashbury

Idstone

Bishopstone

Strip
Lynchets

Fox
Hill

B4000

Shepherd's
Rest

Hinton
Parva

Bourton

Route

© Crown copyright

Swindon ▼

near **Wantage** – you can either get a taxi into town for the station if you want to end your walk, or stay at the **Court Hill Centre**, which lies just off the route.

Getting started

Walk straight ahead out of **Swindon station** and up Wellington Street to the **bus station**. From here, take bus #46, #48 or #48a to Foxhill (Mon–Fri hourly, Sat every 40min; 25min; ☎01793/428428); ask the driver to drop you at the *Shepherd's Rest* pub. A **taxi** (☎01793/536666 or 511199) to Foxhill will cost around £10.

Foxhill and the Strip Lynchets
5km

Get off the bus at **Foxhill** (there's a row of terraced cottages on the right) and, with the *Shepherd's Rest* on your left, head straight up the sealed minor road, signposted to the village of Hinton Parva. After 200m, follow a second sign, on the right, which signals the start of this stage of the **Ridgeway**. Head along the route, ignoring the public path that leads off to Charlbury Hill after around 750m. The path ascends quite steeply for 500m, over the brow of a hill, with the tumulus of **Lammy Down** visible to the right.

A worthwhile detour leads left for 200m down a path (marked with a bridleway sign) to the **Strip Lynchets**, a well-preserved example of the medieval system of field terracing. These grassy steps sit in a lovely valley, with glorious views ahead to the green swell of Uffington Castle and down to the village of Bishopstone.

Returning to the Ridgeway, you descend steadily for another three kilometres, crossing two minor roads, the first to Bishopstone and the second to Idstone. At the Idstone road, down to the right, is the small Iron Age fort of **Alfred's Castle**, where Alfred fought the Danes in 871. This piece of ground was developed earlier by the Romans and traces of what may have been a villa or temple have been excavated, along with a cache of ten babies' skeletons. Roman law did not permit burial within towns or forts, but babies under ten days old were exempt from this, as they were not classed as citizens.

Wayland's Smithy
1.5km

Returning to the Ridgeway, it's another 1.5km to the atmospheric Neolithic tomb of **Wayland's Smithy**; cross the road to Ashbury and walk through a strip of woodland; the tomb's tall sarsen stones can just be seen to the left in a stately circle of beech trees.

Wayland's Smithy, thought to be 5500 years old, originally comprised a wooden, tent-shaped chamber containing the remains

Alfred the Great

The first written mention of the Ridgeway is in the Anglo Saxon Chronicle, which describes Danish raiders sweeping along the route, from Ashdown to Scutchamer Knob. The chronicle was in part a record of the exploits of the scholar-king Alfred the Great, who almost certainly commissioned it. **Alfred's military** achievements are recalled in sites along the route of the Ridgeway, from the battle ground at Ashdown to the Blowing Stone (see p.190). Lying low during a lull between battles, this local lad, born in Wantage in 849, famously allowed himself to be scolded by a peasant woman for leaving her cakes to burn. He was venerated, in his time and even now, more than a thousand years later, both as a brilliant general and as a protector of the poor.

Alfred began his onslaught against the Danes during the reign of his brother Ethelred, culminating in the famous victory at the **Battle of Ashdown** in 871. The following year Ethelred died and Alfred became king of Wessex. Periods of peace alternated with renewed Danish attacks, until Alfred finally defeated the invaders once and for all in 897. One of his innovations as a tactician was the establishment of fortified burghs – grass-covered earthworks that are still a part of the landscape of the Ridgeway.

A thoughtful and inspired peacetime leader, Alfred used the lulls between conflicts to focus on civic reorganization. The monasteries, shattered by the Danes, were re-established as centres of learning, and Alfred founded schools in Oxford, even learning Latin himself in middle age and making translations of books of theology, history and philosophy, which he freely infused with his own thoughts, thus contributing to the earliest English literature.

of fourteen people. Around 3300 BC, a longer cruciform tomb was built on top of the old one, which was covered over with a mound of chalk and stone. The three stone chambers of the more recent tomb were excavated in the 1920s and eight bodies were found. The tomb acquired its name when the Saxons stumbled upon it and, ignorant of its real function, appropriated it for their god, Wayland the Smith; it was said that Wayland would shoe travellers' horses if they left a penny on the capstone of the tomb. You may see various offerings of flowers, grain, fruit and feathers around the tomb, left by New Age types.

The Vale of the White Horse

1.5km

Some 1.5km beyond Wayland's Smithy, the Ridgeway climbs a steepish hill to reach the **Vale of the White Horse**, a unique collection of prehistoric sights; at the brow of the hill turn left through the gate at the National Trust sign.

The landscape opens out to reveal the great circular earthwork of **Uffington Castle**, built between 300 BC and 43 AD and encircled by a bank and ditch, now eroded and grazed by sheep and scattered with field scabious, poppies, pyramidal orchids and cowslips. The "castle" – or, more accurately, fort – is roughly oval in shape and eight acres in extent. It had a single entrance to the northwest and its ramparts would have been faced with sarsen stone. One in a chain of such defensive structures, it's thought that Uffington Castle was built to protect travellers along the Ridgeway from attack from the north.

About 200m beyond the fort, the land tumbles vertiginously down to the undulating glacial valley called the **Manger**. Obscured by the steepness of the valley wall until you are almost upon it is the **White Horse** (legend is that the horse comes down off its hill at night to graze in the Manger). It was popularly thought that the 114-metre-long horse was cut into the turf to commemorate Alfred's victory over the Danes, but in fact it's much more ancient, being the oldest chalk figure in the country and dating back three thousand years. One of the many curious things about the horse is that its shape can only properly be seen from a distance because of the curve of the hill. Nearby signs feature a drawing of the horse, which will help you appreciate the figure's abstract beauty: it looks as if it was sketched by Picasso in a few deft strokes. The local legend which asserts that "while men sleep the horse climbs up the hill" is not as whimsical as it sounds; the upper edges of the chalk lines are gradually eroding and the lower edges silting up, causing the horse to edge up the hillside.

Fairs at Uffington Castle, the first record of which is in 1677, were held every seven years or so until 1857; thirty thousand

◄ The White Horse

people were said to have attended in 1780. These were celebratory occasions when the White Horse was "scoured", or cleaned; the maintenance of the horse was one of the conditions by which the lord of the manor held his land. Horse and ass races were a feature of the fair, as was the bizarre practice of sliding down the hill on a horse's jawbone, according to one eighteenth-century account.

Just below the horse is a small artificial hillock, **Dragon's Hill**, which, according to local legend, is where St George killed the dragon. Two oval mounds between the horse and the fort were excavated in 1857 and found to contain fifty Roman skeletons. Five of the bodies held coins between their teeth, to pay the ferry-man to carry them over the River Styx into the underworld.

The White Horse to the Blowing Stone
2.5km

Continue on the Ridgeway for 2.5km to the next minor road which crosses the route – to the left down the hill is the village of Kingstone Lisle. On the right, towards the bottom of the hill, you can detour off the route for 1.5km to the garden of a neat cottage that encloses the **Blowing Stone**, a rough block of sarsen that resembles a holey cheese (though it's quite a steep hill, so only make the detour if you're feeling energetic). The legend connected with the stone is that King Alfred blew into it to call the Saxons to fight the Danes. With some determination you can produce a strange booming sound by blowing into one of the holes in the stone; local advice is to blow a raspberry into it, covering the hole completely with your mouth – and try not to think of all the congealed saliva that you're adding to.

If you fancy a pub stop at this point, cross the B4507, which cuts across Blowingstone Hill, and carry straight on for 700m past the idyllic thatched cottages and country gardens of Kingston Lisle, bearing right at the junction for the *Blowing Stone Inn* (daily noon–3pm & 6–11pm; ☎ 01367/820288), a gentrified but pleasant pub which serves steaks, cod and chip and so on for under £10.

To Segsbury Castle and the Court Hill Centre
7km

Back on the Ridgeway, past long lines of gallops – fenced areas used for exercising race horses – the route ascends **Sparsholt Down**; you'll see a radio mast on the right-hand side and a farm and paddock where there's a **drinking-water tap**. Turn right onto the sealed road that crosses the **B4001** to Wantage; the Ridgeway resumes opposite the "give way" sign.

The grassy ground to the left of the Ridgeway falls dramatically away to form a smooth valley called the **Devil's Punchbowl**. After 1.5km, you cross a track that runs north to **Letcombe Bassett**, immortalized as Cresscombe in Thomas Hardy's *Jude the Obscure*.

Around 1.5km from here, a broad track to the left opposite some corrugated-iron farm buildings leads for 100m to another Iron Age relic, **Segsbury Castle**. It was, according to an eighteenth-century account, fronted by tall sarsen stones – these have since been removed and all you see now is a steep grassy mound. Nineteenth-century excavations uncovered human bones in a stone chamber, flint scrapers and pottery, plus what is thought to be a boss from a Saxon shield.

If you're doing both days of the walk, you can spend the night at the excellent **Court Hill Centre**: turn left onto the **A338**, past Redhouse Cottage, and go down the hill. It's a very attractive building, constructed from five disused barns and designed to exploit the superb views of the valley below. The dorms resemble wooden ship berths, and there's a sense of space and light throughout. If you want to end your walk here, a **taxi** (ⓣ01235/762035) from the *Court Hill Centre* to Wantage will cost around £5.

The *Court Hill Centre* (ⓣ01235/760253, ⓦwww.courthill.org.uk; £16.50 per person) has twin-bed rooms, family rooms and large dorms, as well as teepees for hire. Aim to arrive by 6pm, so you can order dinner (around a fiver), though you can arrange it by phone in advance. Breakfast is also available and there's a shop selling drinks and chocolate as well as packed lunches (order before 10.30pm the night before) – a good option if you don't want to detour away from the Ridgeway on day two.

Day two

25km

The second day of the walk is less exciting than the first, although the Saxon burial mound at **Scutchamer Knob** provides some atmosphere, and there's a good pub **lunch** detour to East Ilsley. The walk ends at the pretty conjoined villages of **Streatley** and **Goring**.

Getting started

7km

To return to the Ridgeway, take the path signed "to the Ridgeway" immediately opposite the hostel drive. After 200m, turn left onto the chalky farm track and then where the track bends left 100m further on, go straight ahead up the narrow grassy path. The path eventually

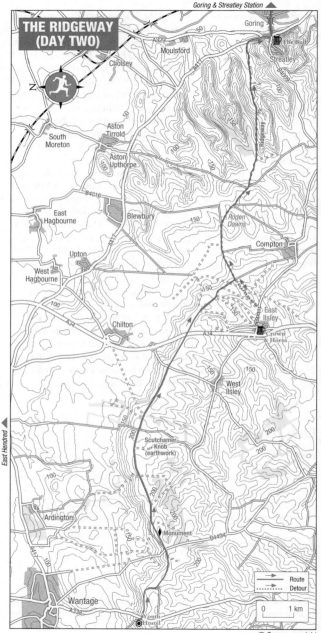

THE RIDGEWAY
(DAY TWO)

Goring & Streatley Station

Goring
The Bull
Streatley

Moulsford
A329
Cholsey

Aston
Tirrold

South
Moreton

Aston
Upthorpe

Ridgeway

Roden
Downs

Compton

East Hagbourne

Blewbury

Upton

West
Hagbourne

East
Ilsley
Crown
& Horns

Chilton

West
Ilsley

Scutchamer
Knob
(earthwork)

Ardington

Monument

B4494

Route
Detour

0   1 km

Wantage

Youth
Hostel

East Hendred

© Crown copyright

curves left to rejoin the Ridgeway (you'll see the wooden Ridgeway fingerpost on your left). Just over 1km from the road, the route divides into two wide paths – follow the one to the left. Cross the B4494 to Wantage, beyond which you'll come to a tall **monument** to the right of the route, erected by Baroness Wantage in 1901 in memory of her husband.

Scutchamer Knob towards Rodden Downs

6.5km

Three kilometres past the monument is the easy-to-miss **Scutchamer Knob** (it lies in a little copse off to the right, behind iron railings). A horseshoe-shaped mound of earth, Scutchamer Knob is thought to be the burial place of the Saxon king **Cwicchelm**, who died in 593 AD. Whatever the mound's original function, it's a restful spot, with views over the rolling fields to the south. Just south of here, off the Ridgeway, is one of several "**Starveall Farms**", the name perhaps an echo of an ancient famine. Other settlements along the route – Woolpack and Woolstone, for example – recall the area's wealth in wool and meat during the Middle Ages, when the Ridgeway was used as a drove road.

Cross the minor road to East Hendred. On the far side, you'll see lines of gallops in the field to the right – many racehorses are trained and stabled around here. The panorama also takes in one of the few signs of industrial England visible on the walk, **Didcot Power Station**, almost 10km away. When permission was given to build the power station, it was on condition that it was modified, with six cooling towers grouped in two groups of three rather than the usual eight grouped in two groups of four, supposedly to make it more attractive.

After 500m you cross another minor road, walking through a small car park; 1.5km from here the route dips under the busy **A34**.

Over Rodden Downs

5km

For a short stretch beyond the underpass the Ridgeway is paved; 2.5km beyond the underpass you reach a crossroads: bear left to stay on the Ridgeway. If you fancy a diversion for a **pub lunch**, take a right on the path to the village of **East Ilsley**, 1.5km distant – after just over a kilometre, turn right onto the path into the village that runs parallel to the road. The *Crown & Horns* is next to the *Swan*, which you can see as you approach. Sheep fairs were held at East Ilsley for hundreds of years – in the mid-eighteenth century around eighty thousand sheep were sold at its annual fair, and there were thirteen pubs to sustain the drovers and farmers.

The welcoming *Crown & Horns* (Mon–Sat 11am–11pm, Sun noon–
10.30pm; ☎01635/281545) in East Ilsley serves sturdy pub food
and real ales – there's outdoor seating in the stable yard.

Continuing along the Ridgeway, the route ascends **Rodden
Downs**. Bear right at the crossroads 2.5km beyond the East Ilsley
turn-off; the left-hand fork runs up to **Lowbury Hill** which is
said to be haunted, perhaps by the Roman woman who was found
buried here under an earth bank.

To Streatley and Goring

6.5km

After a long slow climb, the landscape opens out for the gradual
descent towards **Streatley**, with undulating fields to either side.
The path drops through a wooded avenue to a thatched cottage
and farm, then bears left. From this point the remainder of the
walk is on a sealed road.

Continue along the road past a row of red-brick terraced houses
and, at the "give way" sign, turn right onto the A417 to Streatley
and bear right again at the second "give way" sign. Carry on for
another 300m and you'll come to the handsome *Bull* **pub**, which
may be a very welcome sight at this stage. Opposite the pub, the
turning to the left leads down, past an attractive jumble of brick,
flint and thatched houses, towards the Thames. Just before you
cross the river, you could detour 50m to the left to **St Mary's**,
a pretty thirteenth-century church that was heavily restored
– though in an uncharacteristically plain way – by the Victorians.

A double-humped bridge takes you across the river to **Goring**.
Off to the right is the handsome Norman church of **St Thomas**.
The interior is in an attractive state of decay, with peeling paint
and metal braces straining round huge circular columns. To reach
Goring station, head straight up the hill and turn right after the
railway bridge.

THE NORTH WESSEX DOWNS

Kintbury to Inkpen and back

Distance and difficulty 16km; moderate–strenuous.
Duration 4hr.
Trains London Paddington to Kintbury (hourly; 1hr 15min); return from Kintbury to London Paddington (hourly; 1hr 15min).
Map OS Landranger 174: *Newbury & Wantage*; OS Explorer 158: *Newbury & Hungerford*.

The **North Wessex Downs** reach their highest point at **Inkpen Hill**, between Newbury and Hungerford, which is crowned by the remains of a vast Iron Age fort and a long barrow, still surmounted by a gibbet that was originally erected in the seventeenth century. The walk starts from the village of **Kintbury**, sitting snug in the valley of the Kennet, and goes across farmland to **Inkpen**, a ramblingly attractive village where the friendly *Swan* serves up fine organic pub **lunches**. From Inkpen it's a steep but short scramble up on to the ridge of the downs, where the sweeping views take in five counties. Paths and minor roads bring you in a circle back to Kintbury, where the *Dundas Arms*, sitting prettily on the river, is a great spot to wait for your train home.

Kintbury to The Swan

5km

From the station, head left towards the *Dundas Arms*. Cross the canal at **Kintbury Lock**, and then the river, where you'll see a weir up to the right. Go up the road, which curves to the right through the village. Just past the *Blue Ball* pub on the right, follow Wallington's Road to the left, a dead end that leads towards the St Cassian Centre, a Catholic youth retreat.

After 500m, at the gates of **St Cassian's**, take the signposted public footpath to the left, rather than the private road to the centre. After 200m you'll reach some dilapidated farm buildings. Follow the public footpath sign that points across the fields to the right, then cross the road 150m beyond and beyond that a concrete track. Carry on up the field, with St Cassian's to the left. Go through a patch of woodland for 250m to emerge into a field; head straight across the field, and turn right onto a minor road. Head down the drive that leads past **Balsdon Farm** (don't be deterred by the "private" signs – this isn't a bridleway, but it is a public footpath).

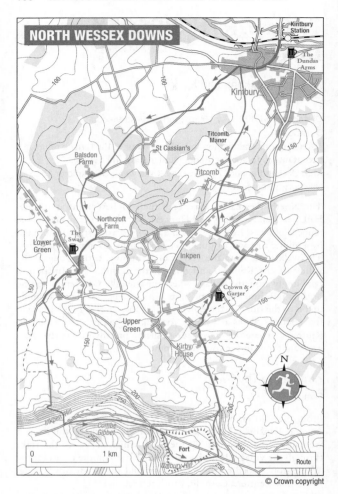

© Crown copyright

Beyond the farm are some signposts; follow the public footpath sign to the left, rather than the bridleway sign. Ahead you can see the ridge of the downs. After 100m, cross the plank bridge over a stream – another 600m further on, you'll see the pretty but dilapidated buildings of Northcroft Farm to the left. Where the path comes out on a minor road, turn right and follow the road for 500m until you get to a small, triangular green and a red phone box. This is the western edge of Inkpen, known as **Lower Green**.

Turn right past the grandiose mock-Georgian houses, untypical of this otherwise modest village, and right again to reach the seventeenth-century **Swan** pub.

The *Swan* (Mon–Sat 11am–11pm, Sun noon–10.30pm; ☎01488/668326) has nice terraced seating outside and the food is excellent, with local organic meat – try the sausages – plus plenty of veggie options and home-made puddings, which come with large dollops of organic clotted cream. There's an organic farm shop attached to the pub.

Inkpen Hill

5km

From the pub, go back up the road to the phone box and then along the road signed towards Combe and Ham. The road curves round to the right; after 250m you'll see thirteenth-century **Inkpen Church** a couple of hundred metres away to the left – continue following the road. Some 200m past the church, follow the public footpath sign pointing to the left and go along this track, which leads up to the long grassy ridge of the **downs** – the gibbet (see below) is visible on top of the hill ahead of you. Go through an avenue of trees for 400m, after which the path begins to climb the steep hill. After 100m, it's joined by a grassy track leading diagonally to the left up the hill. Don't turn left on the first path you reach at the top of the ridge (which leads down the ridge and away from the fort); instead, keep going for 50m or so until you reach a track enclosed by fences; turn left here.

Combe Gibbet long barrow, 600m further on, dates from around 3500 BC, which makes it even older than similar Wayland's Smithy on the nearby Ridgeway (see p.187). Little is known about the site, which has never been excavated, but as well as being a burial mound, its prominent position suggests it delineated the territory of the people who built it. The **gibbet** was first erected in 1676 to hang locals George Broomham and his mistress Dorothy Newman – the pair murdered George's wife and son, but were seen by the village idiot, "Mad Thomas". They were hanged from either side of the gibbet, which explains its unusual shape – most gibbets have just one arm. This is not the original gibbet: the structure has been replaced several times over the centuries. The first gibbet rotted away, the second was struck by lightning, and the third was blown over in a storm in 1949. The people of Inkpen, however, had by this time become so fond of the cheerful sight of a gibbet looming over their village that they clubbed together for a new one, which was made of oak and erected in 1950.

Carry on along the chalky track past the gibbet and the car park onto **Walbury Hill** – take the track to the right of the early Iron Age hillfort. Walk round the fort – the largest in the country, stretching for 700m.

Back to Kintbury

6km

A hundred metres beyond the fort, between it and the next car park, follow the signed public footpath to the left, which leads down the hill and to the left – follow it round to cross a stile and go through woodland, descending to a **minor road**. Turn left onto the road and continue 500m to a junction, then go straight ahead, following the signs to Inkpen. A kilometre beyond lies **Kirby House**, an elegantly proportioned Queen Anne country mansion, flanked by avenues of trees and stables.

Just past Kirby House, follow the sign on the right along the road to Kintbury. After 500m you come out at a junction; immediately to the right is the *Crown & Garter* – turn right and go past the pub, and then, after another 200m, past a row of white houses on the left and a silver-birch wood to the right. A hundred metres beyond the houses, take the public bridleway to the left, signed to "PO and Folly roads". This track passes a couple of farms, and then after 250m dips down into woodland and over a little bridge. Head up the hill out of the woods and onto a narrow track. Ignore the public bridleway sign to the left and go straight ahead, following the public footpath sign through what looks like a private garden, with a small gazebo to your right. At the end of the lawn you'll see a public footpath sign; follow this past a handful of houses on the outer edge of Inkpen.

Cross the road here, after which you soon leave the houses behind, heading downhill through a field. Go through the squeeze gate and down through another field. At the end of the field you emerge at a post with public footpath signs, which point back the way you came and to the left; go straight ahead here, down the road, ignoring the public footpath sign 200m further on to the right. Ahead, you can make out **Titcomb Manor**, but before you reach it go through the squeeze gate on the right and turn left. Halfway across the field, you come to a public footpath sign pointing right – follow it across the field to the wooden gate marked with public right of way signs. Cross the stile and go down the edge of the field and then follow the enclosed path. Go over the bridge and almost immediately turn left over another stile, then go through a tunnel of trees to emerge onto the High Street in Kintbury, opposite the *Blue Ball*. Turn right to get back to the **station**.

STONEHENGE

Salisbury to Stonehenge via Old Sarum

Distance and difficulty 16.5km; moderate–strenuous.
Duration 4hr 20min.
Trains London Waterloo to Salisbury (every 30min; 1hr 30min);
return from Salisbury to London Waterloo (every 30min; 1hr 30min).
Map OS Landranger 184: *Salisbury & The Plain*; OS Explorer 130:
Salisbury & Stonehenge.

This walk starts in the cathedral city of **Salisbury**, heading to
the circular ruins of the Norman city of **Old Sarum**, Salisbury's
predecessor, which was abandoned in the fourteenth century
due to water shortages. From Old Sarum, the route runs to the
handsome old village of Upper Woodford where the *Bridge Inn*
is a good place to stop for **lunch**. From here, country lanes and
footpaths lead through the lush Avon Valley and past increasingly
numerous tumuli – prehistoric burial mounds that dot the whole
area. Long, low **Normanton Down**, its summit crowned by a
line of tumuli, brings you onto downland and within sight of
Stonehenge – a stunning sight, however familiar it may be from
photographs. Check the times of the return bus from Stonehenge
before you set out and bear in mind that the complex closes early
in winter (see p.204).

Getting started

4km

From **Salisbury station**, bear left, following the sign to the city
centre. Go right onto Fisherton Street for 500m, crossing the river.
At the large stone market cross head left up Minster Street and then
straight ahead along Castle Street. Go under the railway bridge,
emerging at the Castle Roundabout; go through the underpass
beneath the roundabout – you come out into the centre – then turn
left through another underpass and then right up the steps.
   Some 250m beyond the underpass, take the road signed towards
Stratford Subcastle. From here, there's a bit of suburban sprawl
before the walk proper begins. Follow the Stratford Subcastle
road for just over a kilometre, with views of the downs emerging
as the houses give way to countryside. You'll see a footpath sign;
ignore this and carry on for another 100m where a track leads off
to the right, by a beautiful, long thatched cottage. Head straight
ahead up this track, which soon narrows to become a path. Gaps
in the hedgerow give occasional views of the downland and of the
high, bulky outline of Old Sarum. When you have nearly reached

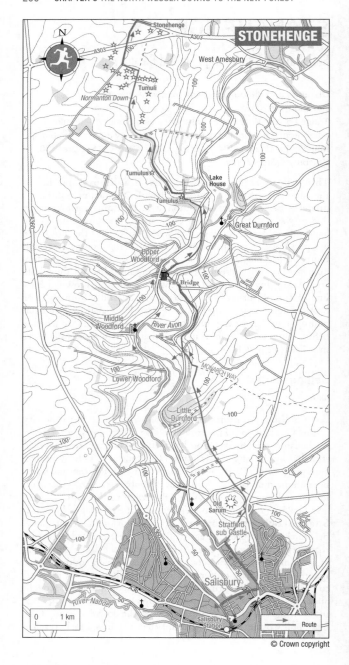

STONEHENGE

N

Stonehenge

A303

A303

West Amesbury

Tumuli

Normanton Down

Tumulus ☆

Lake House

Tumulus

Great Durnford

Upper Woodford

The Bridge

Middle Woodford

River Avon

Lower Woodford

MONARCH WAY

Little Durnford

Old Sarum

Stratford sub Castle

Salisbury

River Nadder

Salisbury Station

0   1 km

→   Route

© Crown copyright

the busy road ahead, turn left and cross the field to Old Sarum, through a wooden gate and into the site.

Old Sarum

1km

Cross a wooden bridge over the deep ditches of an Iron Age hill-fort to the remains of **Old Sarum**. The site, set within the remains of circular walls, is surprisingly compact, considering it once contained a Norman castle and garrison. There was also a substantial religious community attached to the Romanesque cathedral, the remains of which lie just outside the walls of Old Sarum – the outline of the foundations can be clearly seen in the grass.

Old Sarum is open daily: April–Sept 10am–5pm (July & Aug opens 9am); March & Oct 10am–4pm; Nov–Feb 11am–3pm; £3 (EH).

The site was originally an Iron Age hillfort, resettled by Saxons and then the Normans; the bishopric of Sherbourne was moved to the site in the 1070s and the cathedral was built soon after. Old Sarum suffered water shortages though, and its exposed position on Salisbury Plain must have made it a windswept and inhospitable place in winter. In 1220, the clergy, following conflict with the town's other occupants, appealed to the pope for permission to relocate to New Sarum (which subsequently became known as Salisbury). Sarum Cathedral was destroyed in 1331 to provide building material for the new town, and the old town gradually emptied, although the notorious "rotton borough" of Old Sarum returned two MPs until 1833, William Pitt being one of the proud incumbents.

You get very little sense of Old Sarum's past from the scant ruins of the buildings: all that remains are low walls and grass-covered mounds. However, there are tremendous views north to **Salisbury Plain** and south to Salisbury itself and the soaring spire of its cathedral.

Across country to Upper Woodford

5km

From the entrance to Old Sarum, head back down the drive and follow it round to the left. After 100m the drive curves round to the right, but instead of following it go straight ahead through two wooden gates, following the **bridleway** sign. Follow the path down the hill to cross a minor road.

Continue straight ahead for 1km, past a red-brick semi-detached house, followed by a patch of woodland on your left. Ignore the avenue of lime trees on the left leading to Little Durnford 600m further on, and continue straight ahead for another 800m, past a thatched cottage and through cornfields. The grassy track peters out at the end of a field, joining a narrow and overgrown path marked by a blue arrow – follow this to the left through woodland until you come to a post with a bridleway sign. Don't go through the metal gate ahead; instead, turn left and head down through the trees. The path winds round to the right, running along the valley wall; there's a fence on your left, beyond which the land drops down to lush farmland. The path emerges at **Salterton Farm**. Turn right onto the tarred road at the farm, then immediately right again, onto the bridleway track. At the wooden bench turn left over the stile, across a field and, via a metal gate, through woodland for 1km. Joining the tarred road again, turn right and follow it for another kilometre, as it meanders past mansions and cottages to emerge at the *Bridge Inn* in Upper Woodford.

Upper Woodford

2km

The riverside *Bridge Inn* is a good stop for **lunch** or a pint. Turn left out of the pub, and after 200m, opposite Boreland House, take the gravel path on the right marked with a green public footpath sign. Follow the path as it curves round to the left; go straight ahead instead of towards the house down to the right and, at the point where the track curves up to the left, take the path directly in front of you. This is a very pretty stretch, lined with ash, beech and poplar trees, with the **River Avon** down to the right and cornfields to the left. After 800m you come to a bridge over the Avon; ignore this and continue along the path.

The *Bridge Inn* (Mon–Sat 11am–3pm & 6–11pm, Sun noon–10.30pm; ☎ 01722/782323) serves Hop Back ales and good fresh food. There's a games room and an attractive riverside garden.

The Normanton Down Barrows

3km

The path emerges at a minor road; cross this and go through the gate ahead of you, where you'll see public footpath signs (the distinct mound of a tumulus can be seen just off the path and down to the right). Carry on straight ahead up the field, keeping its boundary and the wood to your immediate left; down the hill to the right you'll see Lake House, a graceful Jacobean manor that's home to Sting and his wife Trudi Styler.

Continue down the path to reach a stile to the right of a metal gate – cross this and head down the path. Once through the

Stonehenge and the druids

Modern fascination with the **druids**, fuelled by lurid tales of sacrifice and magic rites, can be dated to the Renaissance and the rebirth of interest in the Classical world. Descriptions of the druids come from Classical writers such as Pliny, Tacitus and Julius Caesar – Caesar wrote that the druids "know much about the stars and celestial motions, and about the size of the earth and the universe, and about the essential nature of things, and about the powers and authority of the immortal gods; and these things they teach to their pupils".

There are no physical descriptions of druids, but it is probably because of the connection with Roman writers that, in the popular imagination, they come clad in white, toga-like garments. All that's known for certain about them is that they formed a class of priests, practised a religion dictated by nature and the seasons, and that they performed animal and human sacrifices.

Seventeenth- and eighteenth-century antiquarians such as **John Aubrey** and **William Stukeley** seized on these Classical descriptions – it was they who made the speculative connection between the druids and the building of Stonehenge, even though Classical descriptions of druidic rites place them firmly in the natural world, amongst groves and springs, suggesting that they would have had little interest in fashioning the enormous megaliths of Stonehenge.

Subsequent events further clouded the real identity of the druids. William Stukeley is thought to have founded the **First Order of Druids** in Primrose Hill in London in 1717, a quasi-mystical order that also took inspiration from freemasonry. This was supplanted by the **Ancient Order of Druids**, which continued through the nineteenth century and into the twentieth – Winston Churchill was a member, hosting a gathering of "druids" at Blenheim Palace in 1908.

Exactly when the first **summer solstice** celebrations were held at Stonehenge is unclear, but by 1900 the then owner of Stonehenge, Sir Edward Antrobus, was so alarmed by the numbers attending the rites that he had the site fenced in and imposed an entry fee – the druids were outraged and refused to pay. The annual celebrations continued, though, and eventually took on a less ritualistic and more celebratory character; by the 1970s, the masonic form of druidism had been replaced by hippy-influenced neo-paganism. Clashes between the police and summer-solstice worshippers became an annual occurrence, reaching a climax at the "Battle of the Beanfield" in 1985, when seven hundred people were arrested. The six-kilometre exclusion zone that operated after the riots was relaxed in 1999, and access is now permitted on the solstice.

woodland, go straight down the field, then turn left on the chalky road, following the sign to Stonehenge. At **Springbottom Farm**, turn left past the big barn. The track then splits – take the right-hand fork.

There's a long ascent of the hill ahead, up the wide grassy path; if you're beginning to flag, you'll be revived by the extraordinary first sight of **Stonehenge**, the focal point of endless downland. One of the strange properties of the stones is the way their proportions appear to change: from this distance they appear elongated and hugely tall, like a megalithic Manhattan; a little nearer and they seem rather squat; while when you're up as close as you're permitted to get they are broodingly large.

The ridge commanding this spectacular view is capped by the **Normanton Down Barrows**, a line of low mounds to your left and right, which lie on private farmland and aren't accessible to the public. The barrows stretch for a kilometre and include the early Bronze Age **Bush Barrow**, where the most significant finds were uncovered – it contained the grave of a tall, stout man who was buried with artefacts to carry to the afterlife, including a bronze axe, a spearhead and a dagger.

Stonehenge

1.5km

Just beyond the Normanton Down Barrows, turn left through a field for 300m, then turn right towards the A303. Cross the A303 (no easy feat), follow the track ahead of you for 500m, then turn right up the A344. Although the megaliths loom to your right, you need to cross the road to the left to the hideously ugly but mercifully submerged **ticket office** and gift shop; an underpass, daubed with murals depicting hairy Stone Age types, leads under the road and up into the site.

Stonehenge is pinned between the thunderingly busy A303 and the A344; it's a tribute to the special qualities of the place that any atmosphere survives the roar of traffic and touristy tat – one advantage of the first distant view of Stonehenge is that the A303 is for the moment tucked into a fold of the downs, though as you continue it becomes all too evident. Plans to bury the roads have been in the offing for years, but arguments continue over what type of tunnelling to use.

Stonehenge is open daily: mid-March to May & Sept to mid-Oct 9.30am–6pm; June–Aug 9am–7pm; mid-Oct to mid-March 9.30am–4pm; £6.50 (the entrance fee includes a rather waffling audioguide) (NT & EH).

The site

The exact function and significance of Stonehenge – and the way in which it was built – have been the source of endless speculation over the centuries; it has been attributed to Romans, Danes, druids and even extra-terrestrials. The site contains the ruins of stone monuments and earth structures dating from between 3000 and 1000 BC. Its earliest features are a circular **bank and ditch** and the **Heel Stone**, an irregular upright megalith that sits just to the northeast of the ditch. Inside the ditch a circle of 56 pits was found, filled with a mixture of earth and human ash.

But it's the central section of the complex, constructed around 2000 BC, which makes Stonehenge unique. This is where the huge **trilithons** – two uprights linked by a capstone – stand. These sarsen stones were transported from the Marlborough Downs, around thirty kilometres away, and were then smoothed and shaped with a swelling in the middle, designed to counter perspectival distortions (a technique later employed by the builders of the Parthenon). A circle of 25 trilithons was formed, with a horseshoe of trilithons in the middle of the circle – the capstones were fastened to each other with tongue-and-groove joints and to the upright stones with mortice-and-tenon joints. There is an earlier, uncompleted circle of smaller stones amongst the trilithons – these are bluestones from Preseli in Wales, three hundred kilometres distant. There is a theory that they were carried here naturally as a result of glacial activity, but it's more likely that they were dragged here or brought on rafts. The stones were carefully laid out, oriented towards the northeast for the **midsummer** sunrise and the midwinter sunset; if you were to stand at the centre of the horseshoe at dawn on midsummer's day, you'd see the sun rising directly above the Heel Stone. The precise nature of this alignment suggests that Stonehenge may have been used as an observatory or time-measuring device.

Buses leave for Salisbury from the car park near the ticket office (8 daily; 30min; £3.50; ☎ 01722/336855). A **taxi** (call ☎ 01722/505050 or 423000) to Salisbury station will cost around £15.

THE NEW FOREST

Lymington to Brockenhurst

Distance and difficulty 11km; easy.
Duration 2hr 45 min.
Trains London Waterloo to Lymington Town (hourly; 1hr 38min); return from Brockenhurst to London Waterloo (every 30min; 1hr 30min).
Map OS Landranger 196: *The Solent & Isle of Wight*; OS Explorer 22: *New Forest*.

Despite its name, the **New Forest** isn't just made up of woodland – the name actually describes an area of some 230 square kilometres that was (and still is, to a certain extent) governed by an ancient system of forest law. Along with tracts of medieval woodland, the forest also covers large areas of gorse-covered heath and bogs, all rich in plant, insect and, especially, animal life. Wherever you go you'll see the sweet-looking but occasionally vicious **ponies** for which the area is famous – they're said to be descendants of Spanish ponies from Armada vessels that were wrecked on the coast – while the woods are home to large populations of red, roe, fallow and tiny sika **deer**, as well as badgers and foxes, and otters can be spotted in the Lymington River. The spring **flowers** in the woods are wonderful too: violets, primroses and wood anemones, followed by swathes of bluebells.

This walk takes in a variety of New Forest landscapes, from the boggy banks of the **Lymington River**, a haven for migratory birds, to stretches of dense ancient **woodland**. You can also detour from the village of **Pilley** – where a thousand-year-old pub provides lunch – onto the open expanses of **Beaulieu Heath** (but don't attempt this if conditions are wet, as you're likely to end up knee-deep in boggy water).

Getting started

2.5km

Leaving **Lymington Town station**, turn right onto Waterloo Road, then go right again at the T-junction at the end of the road to cross the railway line and the estuary of the Lymington River; on the far side of the bridge, turn left onto the road for Beaulieu. After 100m, where the Beaulieu road curves round to the right, go straight ahead, up the minor road. Continue along this road for 900m then, where the road curves to the right, follow the bridleway sign into the **Lymington Reed Beds Nature Reserve**. Once in the reserve, the path leads initially through woodland and then through more open boggy land along the right bank of the Lymington River. You can often see wild ponies splashing through

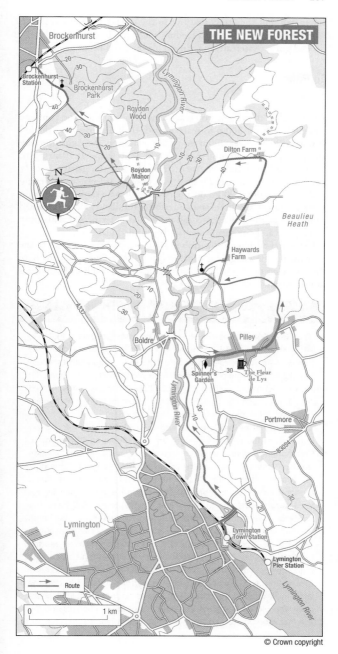

THE NEW FOREST

Brockenhurst

Brockenhurst
Station

Brockenhurst
Park

Royden
Wood

Lymington River

Dilton Farm

Royden
Manor

Beaulieu
Heath

N

Haywards
Farm

Boldre

Pilley

Spinner's
Garden

The Fleur
de Lys

Lymington River

Portmore

Lymington

Lymington
Town Station

Lymington
Pier Station

Lymington River

→ Route

0   1 km

© Crown copyright

the marsh, but the otters that live in the reserve are more reticent. The entire reserve is also a feeding place for birds such as black-headed gulls, oystercatchers, ringed plovers, and Brent geese.

To Pilley

1.5km

At the end of the reserve you reach a gate – go through and continue straight ahead for 300m to reach a road, then turn right up the hill towards Pilley. After 200m you'll see a sign on the right pointing to **Spinner's Garden** (mid-April to mid-Sept Tues–Sat 10am–5pm; £2.50; mid-Sept to mid-April; free, though the garden is only partly open); it's worth a visit if you have an interest in gardening and is only another 200m off the road. Built on a slope overlooking the river valley, this luxuriant and exotic woodland garden is planted with azaleas, rhododendrons and magnolias, interspersed with curly ferns, irises and rare shrubs such as the purple Judas Tree.

The thatched *Fleur de Lys* **pub** is 300m beyond the turn-off to the garden, on the straggling outskirts of **Pilley**. They claim to have been serving up drinks since 1096, and you'll see a list of landlords at the entrance, dating back to 1498.

The laws of the New Forest

The **New Forest** was named by William the Conqueror in 1079, when he established it as his personal hunting ground. He and his son, William Rufus, ruled over their land with an iron hand, imposing violent penalties on poachers, from mutilation to execution. The locals must have breathed a sigh of relief when nasty Rufus, named for his rosy features, was killed in the forest in 1100 in a "hunting accident" (most probably a political assassination).

The **Charter of the Forest**, drawn up in 1217, modified forest law in favour of the inhabitants, who are still known as **Commoners**. Commoners' rights, framed in arcane medieval language, include "turbary" (the right to cut peat or turf as fuel); "estovers" (the right to collect firewood); and "mast" (the right to turn pigs out during a period known as "pannage"). This system is maintained by the **Verderers Court**, one of the oldest judicial courts in Britain. The Verderers were originally charged with implementing the harsh Norman laws, but in 1877 the largely defunct court was reinvented, and it now upholds the rights of Commoners and oversees the health and welfare of the forest animals. They meet ten times a year in the seventeenth-century **Verderer's Hall** in Lyndhurst, where the Crown Stirrup is also preserved – in Norman times, any dog too large to fit through the stirrup was lamed so that it couldn't chase deer. The eleven Verderers appoint six **Agisters**, who manage the five thousand ponies and cattle that roam the forest.

The *Fleur de Lys* (Tues–Sat 11am–3pm & 6–11pm, Sun noon–3pm; ☏01590/672158) has pretensions to being a gastro pub and has lost much of its old character, but it serves local ales and has a small garden at the back.

Coming out of the pub, turn right and head up the road through the village. You pass the Working Men's Club on your left and the "Pilley" sign, and cross a cattlegrid. Walk for 300m along the main road until it bends sharply right, where you take the little paved path to the left. After 100m you reach a "no parking" sign on the left and after a further 50m there's a footpath sign on the right. Follow this across the field, along the slightly ridged grassy path, to reach a line of trees on the far side of the field, then turn left immediately as you pass them (unless you want to make a detour onto **Beaulieu Heath**, in which case turn right).

To Roydon Wood

6km

You'll see two footpaths ahead – a bridleway on the left and a footpath over a stile to the right. Take the latter and go diagonally through the woods until, after 50m, you emerge at the bottom right-hand side of a clearing. Head towards the top left-hand side of the clearing, from where a path leads through the trees and then straight ahead across the fields for 700m. You come out onto a crossroads – go down the paved road to the right for 200m to the Norman and medieval **Church of St John the Baptist**. Unusually, the church, which sits on a mound, is in an isolated position away from any village – it's thought to have been built on the site of a prehistoric place of worship. The writer and illustrator **William Gilpin** was rector here in the late eighteenth century and wrote scathingly about the "indolent race" of foresters who marred the serenity of the New Forest by "forest pilfer... deer stealing, poaching or purloining timber".

From the church, follow the footpath sign towards the car park, where you'll see a yellow arrow on the fence post ahead of you, pointing forwards. This path emerges after 200m at **Haywards Farm**; turn left onto the gravel road and continue ahead for another 600m. Approaching Dilton Farm, which you'll see ahead of you, take the track that curves round to the left, marked with a blue bridleway sign, rather than going straight ahead to the farm.

You're now in **Roydon Wood Nature Reserve**, an area of broadleaf woodland, some of it ancient and undisturbed. Just over a kilometre into the wood you come to a junction, with bridleway signs pointing to the left and right – turn left and head down the hill to cross the wooden bridge over the Lymington River. On the

Beaulieu Heath

Beaulieu Heath is a great open expanse, its fourteen-kilometre circumference framed by woodland. The thin soil supports a meagre covering of heather and gorse, but the boggy areas are rich in rare plant and insect life. Even on a short detour you can get a real sense of isolation, but bear in mind that the paths across it are unmarked and faint, and can easily be confused with tracks made by the pint-sized ponies. The lack of clearly definable tracks makes it impossible to describe a route here – if you do want to venture out onto the heath, arm yourself with OS Explorer 22: *New Forest*.

right is **Roydon Manor**, a seventeenth-century brick mansion, thought to have been a chapel of the Knights Templar.

The path comes out onto a track. Turn right here following the bridleway sign, which leads after 200m to a red-brick cottage. Turn left up the hill for 100m then follow the wiggly bridleway ahead of you, rather than continuing along the track, which curves to the left. The track continues through the woods for 700m, dipping down and then climbing steeply before coming out of the trees along the field edge to the right into Brockenhurst Park and then joining a minor road.

Brockenhurst

1km

Turn right along the road and walk 200m to reach the **Church of St Nicholas**, the oldest church in the New Forest – Christians have worshipped on this site since the eighth century. Some Saxon herringbone stonework survives in the south wall of the nave, though the building is mainly Norman, with an eighteenth-century brick tower and Victorian additions. The dark shaggy yew tree next to the church is at least a thousand years old. A hundred casualties of World War I are buried in the graveyard, among them 93 New Zealanders, one Australian and three Indians, brought from French battlefields to be treated at Brockenhurst Hospital. Don't miss the curious grave of local snake-catcher **"Brusher" Mills**, depicting a bearded Brusher with the tools of his trade – a forked stick and sack. Brusher lived in a hut in the forest and took up snake-catching in the 1880s; some of his snakes were sent to London Zoo to feed the birds of prey, while others were used to make ointments. Brusher once emptied a bag of snakes onto the floor of his regular, the *Railway Inn* in Brockenhurst (now called the *Snake Catcher*), to help clear a path to the bar.

To reach **Brockenhurst station**, carry on down the road beyond the church for 300m – it's across the busy road.

7

The Thames Valley

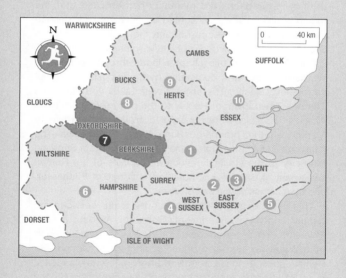

Windsor Great Park
A circular walk in
the Great Park.............................. 213

The Thames Towpath
and the Chiltern Way
Henley to Marlow via
Hambleden 219

Roman Silchester
Stratfield Mortimer to Bramley
via Calleva 224

Perhaps the most marked characteristic of the **Thames Valley** is – as it has been for centuries – affluence. The stretch of the river immediately to the west of London has long provided an escape from the capital for those wealthy enough to enjoy such privilege: the Romans built villas along the river's fertile banks, and it later became a rural escape route for the monarchy who, from Henry II onwards, have generally preferred Windsor Castle as their principal place of residence. The area was again favoured during the Victorian era, when wealthy industrialists built Neoclassical villas along the river banks; it was also much frequented by day-tripping Londoners – nearly seven thousand people took the train to Henley to enjoy the 1888 regatta. The towns and villages of the Thames Valley comprise what is still the most prized part of London's commuter belt, lending parts of the area an exclusive and sometimes snobbish air. More positively, the not-in-my-back-yard mentality has ensured that the region remains largely unblighted by development, despite its proximity to the metropolis, and the countryside around Silchester and Hambleden is beautifully unspoilt.

The first walk in this chapter leads through expansive **Windsor Great Park**, dominated by the imposing profile of its medieval castle. The second walk takes you along the **Thames Towpath** from Henley to the picturesque Chilterns village of Hambleden for lunch, and on via wooded hills to Marlow, another prosperous little Thames-side town. The final route lies to the south of the river, running from Stratfield Mortimer to the strikingly evocative remains of the Roman settlement of Calleva, just outside the village of **Silchester**, and then across country to Bramley.

This is an easy area to access by **train**: services are regular and relatively efficient. Trains for Windsor & Eton Riverside, the departure point for the Windsor walk, depart from **Waterloo**, and also from Paddington via Slough. For Henley, services leave from **Paddington**. Trains also leave from Paddington for Stratfield Mortimer, the stop for the Silchester walk. The Windsor walk is a good option for **drivers** – the Henley one is the trickiest, as there are no direct trains from Marlow to Henley.

WINDSOR GREAT PARK

A circular walk in the Great Park

Distance and difficulty 20km; moderate.

Duration 5hr.

Trains London Waterloo to Windsor & Eton Riverside (every 30min; 50min) or London Paddington to Windsor & Eton Riverside (every 30min; 40min); return from Windsor & Eton Riverside to London Waterloo (every 30min; 50min) or London Paddington (every 30min; 45min).

Map OS Landranger 175: *Reading & Windsor*; OS Explorer 160: *Windsor and Weybridge*.

Windsor Great Park, measuring some 24km in circumference, is too extensive to be a park in the ordinary sense of the word, and while there are some formal gardens and graceful avenues of trees, large sections remain wooded and relatively wild, and parts are given over to farmland. Giant oaks and beeches flourish, some standing solitary and some in thick clusters – several of the oaks date back to the Norman conquest. Medieval Windsor Castle, one of the major seats of the royal family, is superbly theatrical, if slightly Disneyfied, while the grace-and-favour houses scattered throughout the park certainly give you a sense of how the other half live – if you enjoy seeing the upper classes at play, the sight of the polo ground might provide some amusement. The best **time to visit** is late May and early June, when the rhododendrons and azaleas are in bloom; the park is open daily from dawn till dusk and is free to enter. **Lunch,** snacks and cakes can be bought at the Savill Building in the heart of the park, and you can round things off with a pint at the atmospheric *Two Brewers* just outside the gates.

Parts of the castle are open to the public, though these aren't described in detail here, as you're unlikely to be able to visit the castle and do this longish walk in one day.

Getting started

0.5km

Exit **Windsor & Eton Riverside station** and turn right towards Windsor town centre, then take the first left towards the information office and the **castle**, which you'll see rising up on the left-hand side. Continue up the hill and round the flanks of the castle, then head straight up the High Street, following signs for the **Long Walk**. At the end of the main street, turn slightly to the left up Park Street. You'll see the rose-covered *Two Brewers* pub on

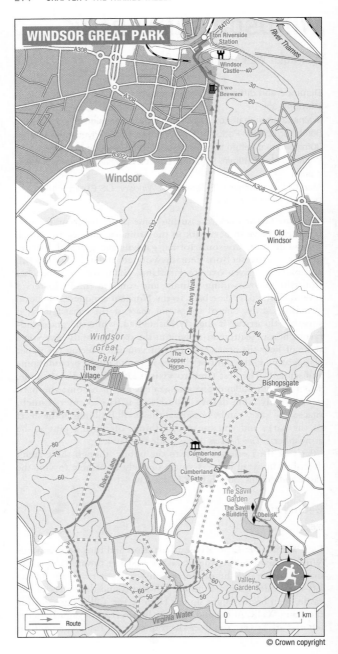

WINDSOR GREAT PARK

Eton Riverside Station

River Thames

Windsor Castle

Two Brewers

Windsor

Old Windsor

The Long Walk

Windsor Great Park

The Copper Horse

The Village

Bishopsgate

Cumberland Lodge

Duke's Lane

Cumberland Gate

The Savill Garden

The Savill Building

Obelisk

Valley Gardens

Virginia Water

N

Route

0   1 km

© Crown copyright

the left; go through the gates just beyond and into the park, then turn right for the Long Walk.

The Long Walk and Savill Garden

6.5km

The **Long Walk**, laid out in the time of Charles II and William III, runs in a straight sweep, lined with plane and horse chestnut trees and bookended by Windsor Castle and a bombastic copper statue of George III on horseback, known as the **Copper Horse**. The walk crosses Albert Road (the A308), but is otherwise uninterrupted, except for the gate you pass through to enter the deer park. At the end of the long paved path, climb up the little mound to the Copper Horse; behind it go straight ahead, following the wide grassy path that runs through a metal gate and then between hedgerows, curving round to the left and entering a small patch of oak woodland.

Head through the woodland to emerge onto a paved road. Turn left and almost immediately right, following the signs to handsome **Cumberland Lodge**, built in the time of Oliver Cromwell and named for the odious Duke of Cumberland (see p.217). It's now a conference centre, set up with royal approval to facilitate discussion about the Commonwealth from a Christian perspective. Just before you get to the lodge, take the path that curves round it to the left. At the gates to the lodge, turn left and, where the drive splits, take the right-hand fork. Some 150m further on, turn right at the crossroad onto the paved path. You pass some tile-hung cottages before coming to an orange-brick gatehouse, **Cumberland Gate**.

▼ The Long Walk and Windsor Castle

The castle and the park: some background

Windsor Castle (daily March–Oct 9.45am–5.15pm; Nov–Feb 9.45am–4.15pm; £14.20; Ⓦ www.royal.gov.uk) lies at the north-eastern edge of Windsor on a low mound, which gives it a commanding position above the town and park. William the Conqueror acquired the surrounding forest for hunting and established the castle as an important residence of the English sovereigns, which it remains today. The castle's first round tower was built by Henry III around 1272, but Edward III reconstructed it in about 1344 as a meeting place for the newly established Knights of the Garter. Subsequent additions were made over the centuries until the 1820s, when over-zealous restoration by George IV diminished the castle's presence, giving it a toy-town look that chimes with the heavily heritage-bound atmosphere of Windsor itself. The Chapel of St George within the castle walls, however, is one of the finest examples of Perpendicular architecture in England, and ranks second only to Westminster Abbey as a royal mausoleum.

Since the time of William the Conqueror, the castle has played an important role in English history. Most dramatically, it was seized in 1642 by the **Parliamentary army** under Colonel Venn, who desecrated the chapel and killed the park's deer. Charles I was imprisoned in the castle in 1648 and later taken from there to Whitehall, where he was executed. His body was returned to Windsor in a coffin and was buried without ceremony.

The most significant event in the castle's recent history was the **fire** during the queen's "annus horribilis" of 1992, which gutted many of the State Apartments; the royals were inadequately insured, so the queen was obliged to fork out for half the £50 million repair bill, the nation having expressed its reluctance to shoulder the entire burden.

The **park** itself was enclosed for the hunting of boar and deer in the thirteenth century. In 1580, Lord Burleigh ordered the planting of trees within the park to replenish timber stocks following the war with Spain. His successor Charles II planted the **Long Walk**, which links the castle and the park, in 1680. George III was confined at Windsor during his "madness", diagnosed in the twentieth century as a rare metabolic disorder; he famously jumped from his carriage to address an oak tree as the King of Prussia. The unstable monarch, known as Farmer George, was responsible for introducing agriculture to the park – farming and forestry interests were later developed by Prince Albert, and remain a significant part of the park's profile. More whimsically, the park is said to have been haunted for the last thousand years by **Herne the Hunter**, who wears stag antlers and rides a black stallion with a pack of black hounds at his feet; he appears when there is trouble ahead, then gallops through the park and melts into the air.

Go through the gate and turn immediately left onto the paved path, along the polo ground, passing a beautiful dove-grey Georgian house on the left, festooned with clematis and roses, and go through walkways of rhododendrons and azaleas. Continue to follow the signs along the sinuous path leading towards Savill Garden – you'll see the walled gardens on the right-hand side and a huge greenhouse. The path curves round to the right; follow it for another 250m to the entrance to the Savill Building. Constructed using four hundred larch trees and one hundred oaks from the park itself, the 90-metre long building is topped by a wonderfully organic wavy roof. Via the building you can access the **Savill Garden** (daily: March–Oct 10am–6pm; Nov–Feb 10am–4.30pm; £7), a woodland garden, begun in the 1930s, which incorporates herbaceous borders, rose gardens, peat beds and a bog garden, as well as umpteen rhododendrons and azaleas.

> The award-winning Savill Building houses an airy canteen-style café which serves up organic juices, tea, coffee, slabs of cake, pasties and sandwiches (opening hours as per the Savill Garden).

Valley Gardens

5km

To continue the walk, take a right out of the Savill Building. After 150m you'll see a huge **obelisk** on the right-hand side, raised by George II for his son, William, Duke of Cumberland. This overblown monument recalls the commander who became known as "the butcher" for his grotesquely cruel treatment of soldiers and civilians following the Battle of Culloden in 1746. Follow the paved path, to the left as you face the Obelisk; the **Obelisk Pond** lies on the right, surrounded by sweet chestnuts and rhododendrons and edged by yellow irises.

Some 200m beyond the pond, you come to a junction. Turn right into a birch wood and continue until you emerge at the bottom of the polo field, then carry on for 500m along the polo field, keeping it to your right and passing the stands. The path splits; take the left-hand fork past the information board and head down the path into the **Valley Gardens**, which comprise flowering trees, shrubs and hardy plants. The path then forks – take the right-hand fork downhill and, after 200m, turn left onto the road. Cross **Virginia Water** and take the road that curves left, following it for 1.5km. Just before you reach the little pink gatehouse at Blacknest Gate, there's a riding track to the right-hand side which, though churned by hooves, saves you walking on the road. Follow the track through the wood for 1.5km.

Duke's Lane

3km

Turn right where the path joins the paved **Duke's Lane**. From this point, you are back in quietly dramatic open parkland. You reach a red-brick cottage called "The Hollies" on the right – go straight ahead at the junction here. The road is crossed by a couple of other narrower roads; keep going straight on and you'll eventually see Windsor Castle ahead, with the Copper Horse to the right. At the T-junction at the end of Duke's Lane, turn right; after 600m you reach the turning on the left on the path you came up earlier, opposite the right-hand turning for Cumberland Lodge. Take this left turn to return to the foot of the mound surmounted by the Copper Horse.

Back to Windsor

5km

From here, rejoin the **Long Walk** to head back up to Windsor. Towards evening, the great trees lining the walk throw long shadows, the deer are more in evidence, and the imposing asymmetry of Windsor Castle forms a fine backdrop. You may see huge herds of deer crossing the road ahead of you at dusk – they will be keen to avoid you, but be sure to keep your distance in the rutting season in the autumn, and stay away from does with their young. Just out of the gates of the park, on the right, the welcoming *Two Brewers* is an excellent place to stop for a pint before you head home.

THE THAMES TOWPATH AND THE CHILTERN WAY

Henley to Marlow via Hambleden

Distance and difficulty 14.5km; moderate.
Duration 3hr 40min.
Trains London Paddington to Henley (hourly; 55min); return from Marlow to Maidenhead (hourly; 20min), Maidenhead to London Paddington (every 20min; 40min).
Map OS Landranger 175: *Reading & Windsor*; OS Explorer 171 and 172: *Chiltern Hills West* and *Chiltern Hills East*.

This satisfying walk runs between the affluent Thames towns of **Henley** and **Marlow**, passing through the Chilterns village of **Hambleden** en route, which makes a good stop for a pub lunch. The route from Henley runs along the east bank of the **Thames**, past rowing clubs housed in neat pavilions and elegant villas with wooden boathouses. The crowds of dog-walkers and families thin out as you walk further north up the Thames, until the only sounds are the thwack of swans' wings on the water and the shouts of the rowing coaches who cycle up and down the path, bellowing at rowers in the passing racing boats. At **Hambleden Lock** you cross the Thames over a roaring weir to **Mill's End**. From here the route leaves the river and runs across meadows to the unspoilt little village of **Hambleden**. Beyond Hambleden, a steep climb takes you into the Chilterns, after which the route – now following the **Chiltern Way** – levels out, taking you across farmland and downs and through two dense stretches of woodland: **Homefield** and **Davenport woods**. From there you descend, via minor roads, into **Marlow**.

From Marlow you need to buy a single ticket to Maidenhead, where you connect with the Henley–London service.

Getting started

4.5km

Coming out of **Henley station**, turn right and walk for 50m towards the *Imperial Hotel*. Turn right at the hotel and head down to the river, then turn left towards the eighteenth-century *Angel* pub; if you fancy a cuppa before you start, try the *Henley Tearooms*, on the left on the way to the pub. At the *Angel*, cross the bridge then turn left, following the Thames Towpath sign towards Hambleden Lock.

The **Thames Towpath** runs down the wide and grassy east bank of the river. This is where crowds gather for the **Henley Regatta**,

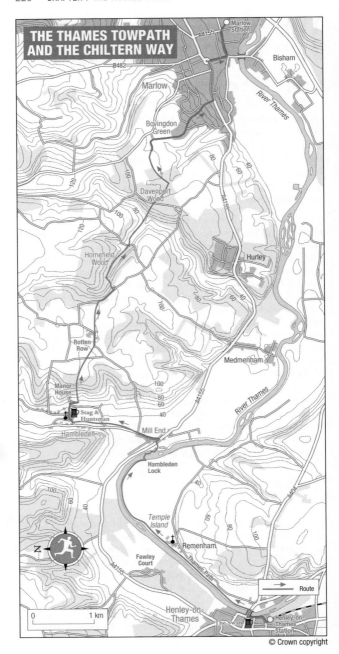

THE THAMES TOWPATH
AND THE CHILTERN WAY

Marlow Station

Bisham

Marlow

Bovingdon
Green

Davenport
Wood

Homefield
Wood

Hurley

Rotten
Row

Medmenham

Manor
House

Stag &
Huntsman

Mill End

Hambleden

Hambleden
Lock

River Thames

Temple
Island

Remenham

Fawley
Court

Thames Path

Henley-on-
Thames

The Swan

Henley-on-
Thames
Station

Route

0   1 km

© Crown copyright

which runs from the last Wednesday in June to the first week in July. The regatta's first incarnation was as the Oxford and Cambridge boat race, which ran between Hambleden Lock and Henley Bridge in 1829, but which was soon moved to London; Henley Regatta itself was established in 1839. A major fixture in the British social and sporting calendar, the regatta's principal attraction these days is not so much the racing itself but the spectacle of legions of drunken posh people mooning each other and falling into the river.

Less than 2km beyond Henley, just off the route to the right, you'll see a church and a cluster of houses that comprise the village of **Remenham** – to the left across the river you can glimpse red-brick **Fawley**, designed by Christopher Wren in 1684; James Wyatt made additions to the house in the 1770s, at which time Capability Brown designed the gardens. Just over 500m beyond the house, **Temple Island** is home to a little white temple, designed by James Wyatt as the fishing lodge for Fawley Court; it now marks the start of the Henley Regatta course. Some 700m beyond Temple Island, on the opposite bank, stands the village of **Greenlands**, home to a gleaming white Neoclassical mansion built by the newsagent W.H. Smith in 1853. Smith is buried in Hambleden churchyard (see below).

Seven hundred metres beyond Greenlands is **Hambleden Lock**: follow the public footpath sign to cross it. The path leads for 300m along the weir, through the middle of the river, with the water thundering down to the right.

Mill End to Hambleden

1.5km

On the north side of the river is the tiny settlement of **Mill End**. There has been a mill here since at least 1086; the present mill, a substantial but plain clapboard building with a slate roof, only stopped operating in 1952. Go past the mill and the cluster of attractive cottages beyond and on to the road. Turn right here, then left almost immediately after, following the road sign to Hambleden. At the right-hand turning for the minor road to Rotten Row, 300m further on, follow the signed **public footpath**, which runs through the fields parallel to the road you've been on. Ahead are gentle rolling hills, topped by woodland; Hambleden's **Manor House** (see p.222) can be seen up to your right, while ahead are the orange-tiled roofs and square grey church tower of the village itself. After 500m the path emerges onto a little track; turn right and continue for a few metres, then take the signed public footpath on the left, which runs for another 500m through meadows to the village.

You come out at a tiny arched bridge over the stream that edges **Hambleden**, a neat little village of red-brick and flint houses surrounded by profuse cottage gardens. Go straight ahead through the village to the mainly Norman **Church of St Mary the Virgin**. Inside, don't miss the alabaster and marble memorial to Cope and

Martha D'Oyley (died 1633 and 1618 respectively) and their five sons and five daughters. Two of the sons wear Royalist garb; the rest wear Puritan outfits. The children who predeceased their father hold skulls, a macabre touch intensified by the masterful depiction of each member of the family – it's thought they are actual, rather than idealized, portraits.

Continue along the road through the village to reach the **pub**.

....

The friendly and bustling *Stag & Huntsman* pub (Mon 11am–3pm & 6–11.30pm, Sun noon–3pm & 7–10.30pm; ☎01491/571227) serves good bar food, real ale on handpump and farm cider. There's a large garden at the back, though it gets packed on sunny days.

....

The Chiltern Way to Marlow

6km

From Hambleden, the route ascends into the Chilterns, picking up the **Chiltern Way**, which you follow for most of the return route to the outskirts of Marlow. Go through the pub car park, then left up the field to emerge near the Manor House. Turn right onto the track here, then left up the skinny path that leads steeply through a field, passing the **Manor House** on the left. The house's plain brick Georgian facade conceals an early seventeenth-century interior; Charles I stayed here in 1646 during his flight from Oxford to St Albans, just prior to his imprisonment. At the top of the hill, continue along the path through the woods for 400m. When you're nearly through the wood, follow the Chiltern Way into a field.

Red kites

Keep an eye on the sky on this walk, as you may be lucky enough to see **red kites** soaring above you. These marvellous birds, with a mighty wingspan of 1.5m, are identified by their deeply forked tails and russet colour, though the wings also have a patch of white and the jagged wing tips are black. They emit a harsh mewing sound.

The birds died out in Britain in the nineteenth century, with the exception of Wales where a few pairs struggled on. They were successfully reintroduced to the Chilterns by the RSPB in the 1990s and there are now thought to be up to two hundred breeding pairs in the area, though sadly some of the birds are being poisoned by gamekeepers. In fact they pose little threat to lambs and other livestock, as they mainly feed on carrion, as well as worms, young birds and the odd small mammal.

Four hundred metres beyond the woodland, the path comes out onto a track; go straight ahead towards the flint farm buildings that comprise the hamlet of **Rotten Row**. After 200m you come onto the curve of a road; turn left towards the buildings of Rotten Row, passing the farm on your left and a pond on the right. Go straight ahead, following the Chiltern Way sign into the field, crossing a couple of stiles and a second field. At the end of this field cross the stile and, just inside the woods, turn right onto a minor road. Ignore the public footpath sign to the left after 150m and carry on down the road for another 200m to reach a second public footpath sign on the left, with Woodside House to the left.

The path leads into the beech woods, skirting round the edge of **Homefield Hall**. The path is a little faint here – it descends the hill, via a small stile, to join a track after 250m; turn right here and continue through **Homefield Wood**, a National Trust nature reserve. After 650m you come out onto a minor road; turn right along the road for a few metres, then go left, following the Chiltern Way signs. Carry on for 500m across the grassy downland till you reach **Davenport Wood**. Go straight ahead, following the Chiltern Way signs and climbing steeply up the hill – the path is rather faint, but bear in mind that 200m into the wood you need to cross the road that runs through it. Once across the road, the path continues straight ahead, though again it's rather indistinct – the white arrows painted on the trees every 50m or so should keep you on course. Carry on through the woods, following both the Chiltern Way signs and the white arrows. After 600m you emerge from the woods, with some orange-brick houses ahead of you.

Into Marlow

2.5km

You come out at the village of **Bovingdon Green** – rather than crossing the green, turn right past the row of red-brick cottages. Walk down the minor road for just over a kilometre, with villas and cottages lining the road. The road, signed after 600m as **Spinfield Lane**, leads downhill into **Marlow** and joins a main road at the bottom of the hill. Turn left, and look out on the left for a white villa with pointy Gothick windows. Percy Shelley and his wife Mary lived here from 1817 to 1818 – it was here that Mary, at the tender age of 21, wrote *Frankenstein*.

Some 650m beyond the point where you turned left along the main road, you reach a roundabout. Turn right here, following the signs to the station, down Marlow's busy High Street, which is lined with Georgian and Victorian buildings. At the end of the street, turn left onto Station Road at the roundabout and carry on for 650m; **Marlow station** is on the right, just beyond the *Marlow Donkey* pub.

ROMAN SILCHESTER

Stratfield Mortimer to Bramley via Calleva

Distance and difficulty 13km; moderate.
Duration 3hr 15min.
Trains Paddington to Mortimer via Reading (hourly; 1hr); return from Bramley to Paddington via Reading (every 30min; 1hr).
Map OS Landranger 175: *Reading & Windsor*; OS Explorer 159: *Reading*.

This pretty and satisfying walk runs along footpaths and country lanes from the hamlet of **Stratfield Mortimer** to the picturesque remains of the Roman town of **Calleva** – a stately ring of defensive walls and a well-preserved amphitheatre, one of only sixteen built in Roman Britain. There's a convenient if slightly mediocre **lunch** stop at the *Calleva Arms* in the nearby village of **Silchester**, though in good weather you might prefer to have a picnic at Calleva itself, where there are plenty of scenic spots. From the ruins, the route leads across country to the station at **Bramley**.

Along Foundry Brook

1.5km

From **Mortimer station**, turn left down Station Road; when you come to the junction at the end of the road, turn left again. Continue up this road for 200m, then turn left at the green metal "byway" sign and follow the path past the church.

Beyond the church, at the end of the track, turn right, keeping **Foundry Brook** to your right. After 500m there's a junction – cross over Foundry Brook using the metal bridge and then continue

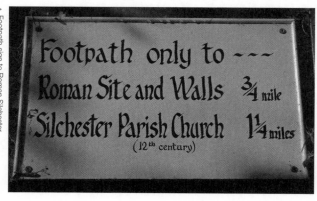

▲ Footpath sign to Roman Silchester

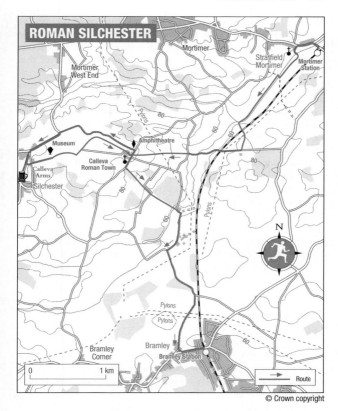

© Crown copyright

along the path on the other side of the brook. Walk along the brook for a kilometre, until you see a small wooden stile on the left. Cross the stile and go across the field to the brook (there isn't a proper path at this point), turn right and continue along the field with the brook immediately to your left. At the end of the field, cross the wooden stile with the yellow sign, then carry on over the small stream. At the end of the next field there's another stile with yellow signs, marking a public right of way; cross this and go over the bridge over Foudry Brook – it's at the point where the railway line, power lines and brook almost converge.

To Calleva and Silchester

5km

Ascend the gentle slope away from the brook and cross the metal bridge over the railway line. Head over the field, keeping the line of the hedge to your right. The footpath emerges onto a narrow tarred road, with an attractive red-brick cottage ahead; turn right, over the railway bridge, and follow the road, lined with damson and apple trees, for 800m until it comes to a T-junction. Head straight across the junction and into the field beyond, following a wide track that leads across the field, rejoining the tarmac opposite a red-brick house. You'll see a red postbox on the right and, beyond that, a wooden gate that leads to the amphitheatre (see opposite).

If you don't want to go to the pub in Silchester you can start exploring the amphitheatre and walls here, or visit the museum (see below) – for the latter, follow the directions for the pub given below but turn left where you see the signs for the museum.

If you want to carry on to **Silchester** and the *Calleva Arms* before visiting Calleva, continue up Wall Lane, then turn left at the end, following the sign for Silchester. After 800m the road branches into three – take the middle route. Entering the village, you'll see the **pub** to the right of the road.

. . . .

The *Calleva Arms* (Mon–Fri 11am–3pm & 5.30–11pm, Sat & Sun 11am–11pm; ☎ 0118/970 0305) is beautifully sited on a green and has an attractive beer garden, but the food is nothing special.

. . . .

Calleva museum and site

2.5km

From the pub, retrace your steps for 600m, then follow the wooden sign to the right to the excellent **Calleva Museum** (9am–dusk; free). Housed in a green, shed-like building, the museum uses interpretive panels and artists' impressions of Calleva to trace the history of the site from its beginnings as a pre-Roman tribal centre.

From the museum, turn left to follow the road to the Roman walls. You'll pass red-brick cottages on the left-hand side, and cross a wooden stile. Ignore the little stile to the left, and continue down the narrow path, then pass through the wooden gate to take the **Roman Town Trail** that circles round the walls, which are punctuated by lofty oak and ash trees.

From the top of the walls you can appreciate the scope and symmetry of the site, as well as its tactical significance – it occupies high ground, with sweeping views to the south and east. The **walls** themselves, striped in flint and mortar, stand as high as 4.5m in some places, their expensive materials reflecting Calleva's importance. A number of gateways stud the 2.5-kilometre circumference; a pair of human skulls were found outside the north gate, which guarded the route towards Dorchester-on-Thames – it's thought that severed heads on poles stood grisly guard on either side.

Having circled the northern part of the walls, you'll see some flint and wood farm buildings and the church to your right. Follow the

The life and death of Calleva

No one knows why **Calleva** was abandoned when the Romans withdrew from Britain at the beginning of the fifth century, unlike similar towns such as Winchester and Canterbury. Whatever the reasons, the fact that the site was never developed means that its layout remains spectacularly intact. The walls describe an irregular hexagon and were built in the third century when, like many Western European towns, Calleva must have felt the threat of barbarian invasion. Traces of Roman roads radiate out from the main gates; these would have cut through thick forest to link the town with Winchester, London and other lesser settlements.

At the heart of the town lay the **forum**, a great open square lined with two-storey colonnaded public buildings and shops; it was here that the town's principal roads converged. Along the forum's west side was the **basilica**, an aisled hall, thought to have been 25m high and constructed using marble from Italy – it was here that taxes were collected and justice was meted out. Just southeast of the forum sat a small fourth-century **church**, built after 313 AD, when Christianity was no longer a proscribed religion. The town's other major buildings included an elaborate bathhouse with an exercise court, three temples and an official guesthouse.

There were only around eighty houses of any significance at Calleva, their scant number and modest though graceful mosaics and frescoes suggesting that the town was not populous or extravagantly wealthy. Calleva served as the market town for the surrounding area, and there was some commercial activity: metal-working, pottery-making, glass- and lead-production, carpentry, milling and brewing.

There is some evidence – such as the apparently deliberate filling up of the town's wells with rubble – to suggest that Calleva was systematically evacuated and then destroyed, perhaps because of the political rise of Dorchester-on-Thames in the post-Roman period.

path that leads to the left, down from the walls – which are particularly impressive at this point – to a wooden stile and gate. Another stile with a plank bridge leads up to the road; turn right towards the amphitheatre, which is tucked in the trees beyond a wooden fence.

The amphitheatre

Built in 55–75 AD in earth and timber, and rebuilt in stone in the third century, Calleva's **amphitheatre**, ringed with oak, silver birch, holly and ash, lacks the grandeur of those in mainland Europe, though it's still a dramatic-looking place, with steeply raked concave walls and an oval arena. Public entertainments took place here on holidays and festivals and are thought to have featured riding displays, animal hunts and wild beast shows rather than gladiatorial contests.

St Mary the Virgin Church

Head out of the amphitheatre through the wooden gates, following the curve of the road, with a red letter box to the left and Manor Farmhouse to the right, to reach **St Mary the Virgin Church**, a charming thirteenth-century building with a low bell tower, partly built using stone from Calleva; a column from one of the Roman temples lies just to the west of the church. Inside the church, look for the slender effigy of **Eleanor Baynard**, wearing a wimple, with a dog at her feet and two winged angels at her head. Baynard was a wealthy resident of Silchester who obtained permission to worship at a private oratory in her house in 1348, the first year of the Black Death. (The proliferation of mid-fourteenth-century names in the list of clergy in the church reflects the dreadful toll taken by the Black Death.) It is thought that Eleanor may have commissioned the remodelling of the church – the south aisle was rebuilt to accommodate large Gothic windows with intricate tracery.

Across country to Bramley

4km

Opposite the driveway to St Mary's, go up the wooden steps through the hedgerow; turn right into the field, and head down towards the line of trees. At the bottom of the field, turn left and follow the path round the field. When you get to the far corner, go straight ahead; you'll see a wooden sign telling you to keep dogs on a lead, and white arrows painted on the trees. Head straight on to where the path dips slightly into a field, curve round the field to the right, and then go straight ahead. At this point the path broadens out, becoming wide and grassy, and joins a little track at the end of the field.

Turn left and continue for a few metres, then go right over a stile, with a copse on the left. Head up the field and keep the fence to the left; go over the stile straight ahead (ignoring the one to the right) and cross a concrete bridge – carry on until you reach another stile to the left which leads onto the road, with a red-brick house on the left-hand side.

Follow the road as it curves round to the right – ignore the left-hand turn to the pub. After 750m you come to a T-junction: take the left-hand route to Bramley. Some 800m further on, take the turning on the right, just before the red-brick railway bridge. Heading down the road you'll see tall pylons marching towards an electricity substation to the right of the road. Entering the village of **Bramley**, look out for the quirky barn to the left, resting on stone toadstools that protect its contents from rodents. Just beyond the barn, turn left towards Bramley train station; the *Bramley Inn* is on the left-hand side and the station just beyond to the right.

8

The Chilterns and Blenheim

The Misbourne Valley
Amersham to Chalfont St Giles
and back... 231

The Northern Chilterns
Wendover to Chequers
via Coombe Hill.............................. 236

Ivinghoe Beacon
Tring to Aldbury 243

Around Blenheim Palace
Long Hanborough to Blenheim
Palace and North Leigh
Roman Villa..................................... 250

lanking London's northwestern edges, the **Chiltern Hills** are part of an extensive range of chalk uplands that run from Wiltshire in the west all the way to Yorkshire in the north. The Chilterns are the most dramatic part of these hills within easy reach of London, rising on their western side to a high, steeply shelving escarpment offering panoramic views west and backed by the characteristic beech woodlands that thrive in the chalky soil. Beyond the escarpment, the gentle Oxfordshire countryside undulates away towards the Cotswolds, providing the setting for **Blenheim Palace**, one of the greatest of all English stately homes.

The first of the walks in this chapter heads out from the commuter town of Amersham, through the Chilterns via the attractive **Misbourne Valley**, to the village of Chalfont St Giles. The second walk starts in Wendover and leads west to the Chilterns' highest viewpoint, Coombe Hill, before descending into the **Chequers Estate**, the prime minister's country retreat. The third walk follows the Ridgeway trail from Tring to **Ivinghoe Beacon**, the second highest of the Chilterns' viewpoints, before looping back through beech woods to Tring. Beyond the Chilterns, in the heart of the Oxfordshire countryside, the last of the walks in this chapter makes a circuit of the **Blenheim Estate**, and also includes a detour to the Roman villa remains at North Leigh.

The Chiltern walks are easily and cheaply reached from **Marylebone** train station; the walk from Amersham can be reached by tube (Metropolitan Line) and is covered on a zone 1–6 Travelcard (though you'll need to ask for a special free extension ticket that covers this station). Blenheim is a little more expensive to reach; trains depart from **Paddington** station. All four walks in this chapter are circular and therefore convenient if you're **driving**.

THE MISBOURNE VALLEY

Amersham to Chalfont St Giles and back

Distance and difficulty 16km; moderate.
Duration 4hr.
Trains Marylebone to Amersham either by overground train (every
30min; 30min) or tube (Metropolitan Line); return from Amersham to
Marylebone (every 30min; 30min).
Map OS Landranger 165 and 175: *Aylesbury & Leighton Buzzard*;
and *Reading & Windsor*; OS Explorer 172: *Chiltern Hills East*.

This easily accessible walk, reached from London by either train
or tube, leads from Amersham to Chalfont St Giles and back
again, following the **Misbourne Valley** as it cuts through the
Chilterns. Starting at the station in **Amersham-on-the-Hill**,
the route begins by descending into the pretty medieval country
town of **Amersham**. Past Amersham, the walk follows a ridge of
the Chilterns above the Misbourne Valley into **Chalfont St Giles**.
Centred on an attractive village green, Chalfont boasts the cottage
(now a museum) that John Milton lived in while he completed
Paradise Lost, as well as plenty of pubs for **lunch** – the best is the
Fox & Hounds. The **return route** back to Amersham again follows
the River Misbourne, but this time along the valley floor, offering
a fresh perspective on the chalky surrounding hills.

Getting started

1km

Turn left out of the train station into **Amersham-on-the-Hill**
and head down to the junction by Twist in the Tale childrens'
bookshop. Turn left onto the main road (A416), heading under the
railway bridge and downhill towards Amersham Old Town.
   Some 200m beyond the bridge and just before Parsonage Place,
a short row of houses set back from the main road, take the
well-marked public footpath into **Parsonage Wood**. Keeping
close to the easterly edges of the wood, the track rises sharply
for the first 50m or so, then levels off as it heads through the
heart of the wood. From between the beech trees you can catch
glimpses across the valley of the farmland and wooded hilltops
through which the walk will take you. Take the left-hand path
where there's an option, for roughly 300m.

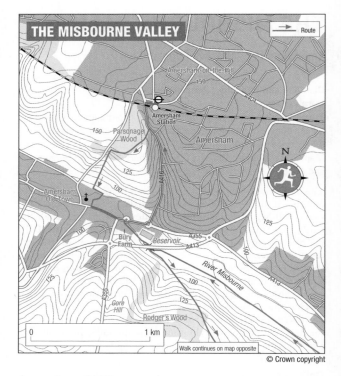

© Crown copyright

Amersham Old Town

0.5km

When you emerge from the woods, bear left and head downhill on a tarred path and over grassland to **Amersham Old Town**, which sits on the banks of the River Misbourne, its centre marked by the tower of St Mary's parish church. At the bottom of the hill, past allotments on the right, the track ends at a T-junction before a high red-brick wall; to your left is the old **cemetery**. Take the footpath that leads to the left, then, a few metres further on, cross the **River Misbourne** – little more than a babbling brook at this point – via the tiny stone bridge to your right. This brings you to **St Mary's Church**. Though the original church dates from the thirteenth century, much of what you see today – including the flint facing, the stair-turret and much of the interior – are part of a heavy-handed late-Victorian restoration; it's a handsome building, nonetheless, in an attractive setting at the heart of the old town.

Turn left into the churchyard, 100m from the bridge, and follow the path through to the aptly named **Broadway**, the old town's main drag. Here, tiny timber-framed and brick-fronted

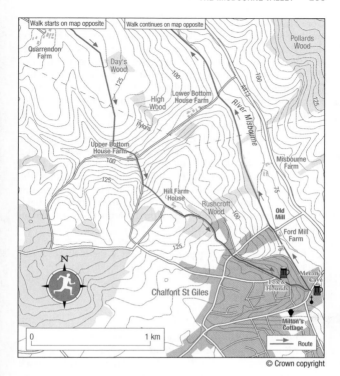

Walk starts on map opposite   Walk continues on map opposite

Quarrendon Farm

Pollards Wood

Day's Wood

High Wood

Lower Bottom House Farm

River Misbourne

Ryons

Upper Bottom House Farm

Misbourne Farm

Hill Farm House

Rushcroft Wood

Old Mill

Ford Mill Farm

N

Chalfont St Giles

Merlin's Cave

Fox & Hounds

Milton's Cottage

0 ———————————— 1 km

→ Route

© Crown copyright

seventeenth-century cottages line the wide main street. Just to your right, at the end of Broadway, is the red-brick **Market Hall**, topped by a wooden bell-turret and with a plaque recounting some of the town's history.

Turn left and follow Broadway for 200m, heading out of town to the roundabout by Tesco. Just beyond the roundabout, a few metres along London Road West and just before **Bury Cottage**, on the opposite side of the road, turn right into **Bury Farm**. The public footpath sign is partly lost in the trees. Bear left to head behind Bury Cottage and over a stile into a field between a sewage works to your left and the A413 to your right.

Amersham to Upper Bottom House Farm

3.5km

At the far side of the field, head through the tunnel under the A413 and up into farmland. In the hedgerow on the right, 50m or so from the tunnel, is a stile; cross this and head through two fields and over another stile, climbing steadily and aiming for the left-hand side of **Rodger's Wood**, which runs along the brow of

Gore Hill, overlooking the valley. At the edge of the wood, cross another stile and take the path on the opposite side, which cuts through the woods to reach a second stile after 100m, at the edge of a field. Cross this stile and head diagonally across the field to the end of the hedgerow on your right, over the access road to **Quarrendon Farm**, and on, following the hedgerows along the edge of the fields towards Day's Wood, a small copse 300m ahead. There are superb views from here back across the valley floor to Amersham and further west into the heart of the Chilterns.

Just before **Day's Wood**, cross a stile in the hedgerow to your right and go into the field. Follow the edge of the field, keeping the wood on your left, until you get to another field with a pylon in it. Cross the field diagonally, aiming a little to the left of the pylon. Hidden in the hedgerow opposite is another stile; cross this and continue downhill to the far right-hand corner of this field, then left along the hedgerow with **Upper Bottom House Farm** on the other side of it to your right.

At the end of the hedgerow the path drops down into the farm itself. Walk past the buildings, turning right at the small road. Just before the farmhouse itself head left, uphill on a dirt track.

Chalfont St Giles

3km

Keeping the hedgerow to your right, head up the track away from Upper Bottom House Farm for 200m, then turn left onto a minor track just before an enclosed area of woodland. Follow this track – it gets increasingly overgrown – uphill until you reach a white sign with four pointers: follow the one for **Chalfont St Giles** which takes you past Hill House Farm and through Rushcroft Wood. You emerge on Mill Lane, at the edge of the village. Cross this and head straight on down Dodds Lane, which becomes Silver Hill and leads after 750m to the attractive little High Street and village green, surrounded by seventeenth-century timber- and brick-built cottages. Behind High Street, the village's heavily restored medieval flint church rises above the houses.

The best pub option is the *Fox & Hounds* (daily 11am–2.30pm & 6–11pm; ☏ 01494/872151) on Silver Hill. Right on the village green, *Merlin's Cave* (Mon noon–12.30am, Tues–Sun 8am–12.30am; ☏ 01494/875101) serves good, if predictable, pub-grub. To the right of *Merlin's Cave*, also overlooking the green, there's a decent deli.

What brings most visitors to Chalfont St Giles is **Milton's Cottage** (March–Oct Tues–Sun 10am–1pm & 2–6pm; £4), in which the poet John Milton sought refuge from plague-stricken London in 1665 as a guest of Thomas Ellwood. Milton completed

Paradise Lost here, and it was during the same stay that Ellwood suggested to him the idea of *Paradise Regained*. The red-brick and tiled cottage now contains a modest little **museum** devoted to Milton's life and works, including first editions of his poems. The house is a few hundred metres uphill from the village green, on Dean Way, the continuation of the High Street.

Chalfont St Giles and Lower Bottom House Farm

2.5km

The route back to Amersham is easy to follow. From the village green, take the public footpath, Stratton Chase Drive, just to the right of **Silver Hill**, the road you came down to reach High Street. At the end of this lane, 300m from High Street, the track continues straight on into woodland. Where the route forks, take the narrower right-hand path, along a field and past some cottages to a road. Opposite you is the Old Mill. The road, **Mill Lane**, crosses the River Misbourne a few metres to the right here; often little more than a trickle in the drier summer months, the river can be a deluge in winter.

Just to the left of the mill, you can rejoin the public footpath at the waymarkers. Again, the track heads through the trees, their branches here arching over the path to make a shady avenue, dappled with light, for the next kilometre or so. The River Misbourne flows some 500m to your right – you'll catch glimpses of it intermittently for the rest of the walk, though you'll see little of it at this stage – and there are views across the Misbourne Valley and over to Pollards Wood on the hillside opposite.

Lower Bottom House Farm to Amersham train station

5.5km

The path through the avenue of trees ends at a stile. Head over it into a field and from here continue straight ahead, along easily followed paths, crossing fields and stiles for a little over 4km.

With the wooded hills east of Amersham rising above you to the right and the hills along which you walked earlier looming up to the left, this is a much more enclosed route than the walk out to Chalfont St Giles. The going is much easier, too, as the path not only follows the flat valley floor, but also largely crosses pasture rather than arable land.

Several fields and numerous stiles later you reach the tunnel under the A413, which leads out to the field before Bury Farm; head back through the farm and down its drive to London Road West. From here, just to the left of **Bury Cottage**, you can retrace your steps back via Amersham Old Town to return to Amersham station.

THE NORTHERN CHILTERNS

Wendover to Chequers via Coombe Hill

Distance and difficulty 15km; moderate.
Duration 3hr 45min.
Trains Marylebone to Wendover (1–2 hourly; 45min); return from Wendover to Marylebone (1–2 hourly; 45min).
Map OS Landranger 165: *Aylesbury & Leighton Buzzard*; OS Explorer 181: *Chiltern Hills North*.

This varied and beautiful circular route begins and ends at **Wendover**, a small medieval market town that sits in a gap in the Chilterns. From Wendover, the walk joins the **Ridgeway**, which climbs up onto **Coombe Hill**, the highest viewpoint in the Chilterns, before looping around the **Chequers Estate**, the prime minister's country retreat. Beyond Chequers, the route heads into the village of **Great Kimble**, where the *Bernard Arms* makes for an excellent **lunchtime** break. The return route to Wendover takes you along public footpaths through the rich agricultural land of the **Vale of Aylesbury**.

Getting started

0.5km

The walk begins at **Wendover station**, though it's worth making time to look around the town itself before setting off on the walk – the High Street is lined with picturesque timber-framed houses and grander Georgian mansions. To begin the walk, turn right out of the station and head up to the main road; turn right onto this and head out of Wendover via the road bridge over the busy A413 and on past a row of terraced cottages. After a couple of hundred metres you reach a bend in the road; on the left-hand side of the road there's a large brown sign for Bacombe Hill by two waymarked tracks. Take the right-hand track, waymarked as part of the **Ridgeway** (see p.185; signs show a white acorn on a brown post). A few metres beyond, bear left onto a side track, still following the Ridgeway signs, and head uphill along a steep and muddy path.

Bacombe Hill and Coombe Hill

2km

The path climbs steeply for 300m, then rises gently along the northern flank of **Bacombe Hill** to reach the summit of **Coombe**

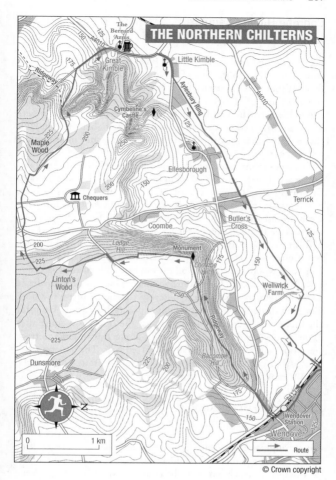

THE NORTHERN CHILTERNS

The Bernard Arms

Great Kimble

Little Kimble

Cymbeline's Castle

Maple Wood

Ridgeway

Aylesbury Ring

Chequers

Ellesborough

Terrick

Coombe

Butler's Cross

Lodge Hill

Monument

Coombe Hill

Linton's Wood

Wellwick Farm

Dunsmore

Ridgeway

Bacombe Hill

N

0   1 km

Wendover Station

Wendover

→ Route

© Crown copyright

Hill, 2km beyond. The track is well signposted, and there are superb views north and west over the Vale of Aylesbury and back across Wendover.

Just before the summit of Coombe Hill, beyond a small thicket of trees, you pass through a kissing gate and the view opens up to reveal the **Boer War monument**, which tops the hill and dominates the skyline for miles around. Built in 1904 and topped by a gilded sculpture representing an eternal flame, it was erected to honour the dead of the Royal Bucks Hussars. The monument stands in a 106-acre National Trust site that was gifted in 1918 by Arthur Hamilton, who also gave the Chequers Estate to the nation.

Coombe Hill to Chequers

2.5km

From Coombe Hill, head for the Ridgeway waymarker by the row of trees just to the left of the monument as you approach it from Wendover. Continue for a few hundred metres along the western flank of the hill. The hillside falls away steeply to your right down to the hamlet of **Coombe**; beyond, the Chequers Estate begins to come into view in the lee of angular Beacon Hill, the red-brick chimney tops of its Elizabethan manor house visible above the trees.

The track continues gently downhill for 500m. Eventually you reach a metal gate – go straight ahead into the beech wood, following the Ridgeway sign. The gate marks the southern boundary of the National Trust property and takes you along the Chilterns escarpment, here called **Lodge Hill**, for 250m to reach a quiet lane through the woodland opposite a handsome red-brick and flint cottage. Turn right and follow the lane downhill for a few metres to an access road on the left into **Lodge Hill Farm**, set in a small woodland clearing on the opposite side of the road.

Walk down this track for 10m and then cross the stile in the fence to your right to regain the Ridgeway through **Linton's Wood**. The path through the woods is faint at points, but just look out for the numerous Ridgeway signs amongst the trees. You come after 700m to a wide dirt track; turn right along this to emerge from the woods after 400m at a bend in a tarred lane. The gate opposite marks the southeast corner of the Chequers Estate – hence the CCTV cameras that watch over it.

Chequers to Great Kimble

3km

Go through the gate and into the estate itself – there are fine views from here up to the mid-sixteenth-century manor house of **Chequers**, which has been the country retreat of British prime ministers since the early twentieth century. Lloyd George was the first prime minister to make use of the house, while Winston Churchill often retreated here during the air raids of World War II, delivering some of his most famous broadcasts from the house. It's regularly used by incumbent prime ministers, both as a retreat from the day-to-day wrangles of political life, and for hosting visiting heads of state (see box opposite).

The house (along with a £100,000 endowment) was given to the nation in 1921 by **Arthur Hamilton** on condition that it be used as the country retreat of the incumbent prime minister. Born in Britain, but half-American, the well-connected and ambitious Hamilton had previously enjoyed a glittering military career, becoming a close friend of Teddy Roosevelt along the way, and later being elected Conservative MP for Fareham and the First Lord of the Admiralty. In recognition of his services – and possibly a little influenced by his generous donations to the state – the British government elevated him to the status of Viscount Lee of Fareham in 1922.

Records show that there has been a settlement on the site since Roman times, though nothing remains of these early buildings. The current house dates from the mid-sixteenth century and, despite the addition of some Gothic features in the nineteenth century, it retains a largely Elizabethan appearance – all red brick, leaded windows and soaring chimneys. Remember, though, that this is a private estate and stick to the public footpath, which heads west, over the main drive and on to a gate. Go through the gate, across the drive just north of the lodge houses, then through two more gates and into a field.

The track climbs gently for 400m through the field towards **Maple Wood**. At the edge of the wood, turn right and follow

Gins and tonic: Boris Yeltsin at Chequers

During its time as the British prime minister's retreat, Chequers has played host to dignitaries from around the world. Perhaps the most popular anecdote about a VIP visit concerns the then Russian president, **Boris Yeltsin**, who stayed at Chequers in the mid-1990s. After a series of lengthy meetings with the Russian premier, prime minister John Major suggested that they go for a walk to get some fresh air. And so the two world leaders, their wives and a large entourage of diplomats and security officers set out across the Buckinghamshire countryside.

Within a few hundred metres, however, it became apparent that the Russian president was not one of life's great walkers, and he began to look decidedly grumpy as they climbed up to the brow of a hill. At the top, Major presented Yeltsin with three choices: walk back over the fields to Chequers – to which Yeltsin grunted; climb down the hill to the waiting cars and be driven back to the estate – another grunt; or walk on to the old-fashioned English pub, the *Bernard Arms*, in the village of Great Kimble. At this final suggestion, Yeltsin perked up considerably, shouting gleefully, "Gins and tonic! Gins and tonic!" Arriving in Great Kimble, however, they found that the pub was shut. Yeltsin started hammering on the door, yelling, "Open up! This is the president of Russia!" To which the dry reply came from inside: "Oh yes? And I'm the Kaiser." When the pub was finally opened, Major ordered a pint, while Yeltsin asked for a bottle of vodka, only to be refused such a large measure by the nonplussed barmaid. A diplomatic incident was avoided when the Russian president agreed to drink his vodka a glass at a time – like everyone else.

the track for about 500m to reach another gate – there are superb views from the wood back across the valley floor to Chequers and beyond to the monument on top of Coombe Hill. At another gate, turn left and away from Chequers, heading uphill across a field, over the brow of the hill and down to another gate. Pass through this and head on down the track.

After 100m the track opens up onto a wide field, the boundary of the Chequers Estate, marked to your right by a low fence. Take the right-hand footpath off the **Ridgeway** and head along the fence, towards the woods on the far side of the field. At the end of the field, turn left along the fence for 100m. A metal kissing gate in the corner of the field takes you onto the **North Bucks Way**: turn right here down the hill. The track heads to a tarred lane and leads after a couple of hundred metres to a T-junction with the A4010. Turn right here and head uphill into **Great Kimble** – little more than a church, a row of Victorian cottages and a pub – the *Bernard Arms* sits 150m from the lane, just beyond St Nicholas's church, and makes a good spot for **lunch**.

. . . .

The *Bernard Arms* (Mon–Fri noon–3pm & 5–10.30pm, Sat noon–10.30pm, Sun noon–7pm; ☎01844/346172) has an attractive secluded garden and serves excellent lunches, including a few tasty vegetarian options, plus good seasonal salads, soups and stews.

. . . .

Great Kimble to Ellesborough: the Aylesbury Ring

2.5km

From the pub, continue along the A4010 towards Little Kimble. After 500m, turn right down **Ellesborough Road**, passing **Little Kimble's** village church, **All Saints**, which boasts some of the finest medieval wall paintings in the county; they feature the martyrdom of St Margaret, and you can also make out St James in his wide pilgrim's hat, St Christopher bearing Christ on his shoulder and the elegant figure of St George. Continue past the church straight on towards Ellesborough; ignore the green public footpath sign to the left just beyond the church.

About 500m beyond the turn-off from the A4010, on the edge of Little Kimble and, confusingly, at the village limit **sign for Ellesborough** (though this village lies a further 1km up the road), turn left. Cross the stile next to a modern house, following the black sign (it's a little lost in the hedge), to the **Aylesbury Ring** – this is still a dedicated public footpath, although you might feel as if you're trespassing since the footpath has been incorporated into the house's lawn. After a few metres, the footpath bends round to the right, continuing between the older properties at the edge of Little Kimble.

After 100m, at the end of this short track between the houses, cross over a stile and out into farmland, and continue straight on. Almost immediately, Ellesborough's church comes into view, an impressive Victorian flint and brick pile with an imposing stair-turret tower, sitting proudly on a small hill at the roadside a few hundred metres off to your right. To the right of the church rises the man-made mound nicknamed **Cymbeline's Mount** – the motte of a small medieval castle.

Ellesborough to Wellwick Farm

2.5km

The track here leads across the rich arable farmland of the **Vale of Aylesbury**; to your right, the Chiltern escarpment rises steeply above the villages – Little Kimble, Ellesborough and Butler's Cross – strung out along the Ellesborough Road, itself a good 500m beyond and above the public footpath. Follow the public footpath, passing below the church and crossing three stiles to come out after 800m at the end of a lane by the thatched Springs Cottage. Head straight on along the lane, which marks the southern boundary of Ellesborough; where it bends round to go up to the main road, pick up the trail to the left of the houses and go straight ahead, between two fields. Crossing over three more stiles, the path passes through fields and paddocks to come out after around 500m at the busy road into **Butler's Cross**.

Turn left, cross the road just beyond Somerfield Cottages and pick up the path on the far side at a metal gate. The track continues east, passing over two more stiles and through a gate before climbing gently for 500m to the brow of a hill, then heads gently downhill again, over three more stiles towards a small copse another 700m further on. The copse hides the splendid Elizabethan red-brick and flint **Wellwick Farm** from view until you're almost at the house. There are good views of the house as you follow the path, close by its northern facade and on around the easterly side through a gate into a field. From here, follow the waymarkers up into the farmyard, crossing a stile en route.

Wellwick Farm to Wendover station

2km

Head out of the farmyard, straight over the access road and into the next field, then follow the waymarkers across the field. Just before the hedgerow begins, turn left, passing over the stile and heading straight on towards the bridge – a farmyard track over the A413 – a few hundred metres further on. Cross three more stiles on the track, after which you'll come out in a field just before the **bridge**. There's a public footpath straight to the bridge, though this is not always respected by the farmer who owns this land, and you may well find it ploughed and muddy in winter and difficult to pass when planted in summer. If so, head round the edge of the field to get to the bridge.

On the far side of the bridge, turn right at the public footpath sign and follow the narrow track, which leads behind houses to emerge on a quiet access road after 200m; this leads to a small industrial estate. **Wendover station** is just under 500m along this road from here.

IVINGHOE BEACON

Tring to Aldbury

Distance and difficulty 13.5km; moderate.
Duration 3hr 20min.
Trains Euston to Tring (Mon–Sat every 30min, Sun hourly; 40min);
return from Tring to Euston (Mon–Sat every 30min, Sun hourly;
40min).
Map OS Landranger 165: *Aylesbury & Leighton Buzzard*; OS
Explorer 181: *Chiltern Hills North*.

This superb circular walk leads from **Tring station** in
Hertfordshire and up onto the Chiltern escarpment. The first half
of the route follows the **Ridgeway Long-Distance Footpath**
(see p.185), a 136-kilometre hilltop track that begins in Wiltshire
and ends at **Ivinghoe Beacon**, one of the highest points in the
Chiltern Hills. Passing through beech woodland and over chalk
uplands, the walk gives fine views over the Vale of Aylesbury,
a patchwork of farmland dotted with small villages and towns.
From Ivinghoe Beacon, the route leads back through the woods
of the extensive **Ashridge Estate**, once the seat of the dukes of
Bridgewater and now home to a network of public footpaths and
a handily placed **tearoom**. Beyond the **Bridgewater Monument**,
which dominates the hillside hereabouts, the route drops down
into the handsome village of **Aldbury**, with half-timbered
cottages and a duck pond. From Aldbury, it's a short walk back to
Tring station.

For lunch take a **picnic** – there are lots of good picnic spots,
not least Ivinghoe Beacon itself – or eat at the National Trust
tearooms by the Bridgewater Monument. There's a good **pub**,
The Greyhound Inn in Aldbury, located close to the end of
the walk.

Getting started

0.5km

From **Tring station**, turn right onto Station Road and walk
along it for 300m, passing a turning off to your left. At a bend
in the road, turn left, following the fingerpost for the Ridgeway
up the access road to **Westland Farm**. This short concrete road
leads after 100m past the entrance to the farm to a metal gate in
the hedgerow, where you reach the **Ridgeway Long-Distance
Footpath**.

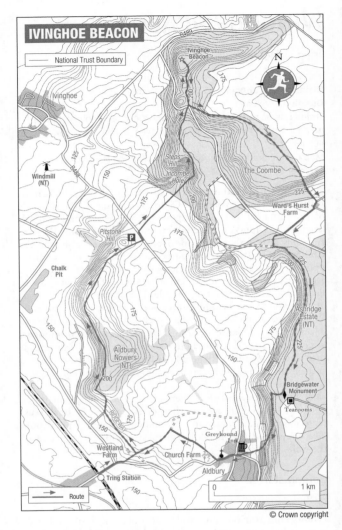

IVINGHOE BEACON

—— National Trust Boundary

© Crown copyright

Through Aldbury Nowers

1.5km

Turn left onto the Ridgeway and follow it gently uphill through an avenue of hawthorns behind Westland Farm. After 600m you come to an intersection with another public footpath; turn right, following the fingerpost signs for the Ridgeway along the steep track up into **Aldbury Nowers**, a mature beech wood on the chalky upland above Tring. A few metres into the wood, turn left off the main track at the next Ridgeway fingerpost and head up a series of dirt steps. At the top of the steps, the path veers off to the left and briefly heads out of the trees, giving great views across the rich farmland of the **Vale of Aylesbury**. Within a few metres you begin to climb quite steeply into the woods again. At the top of this rise, the track, which is clear and wide at this point, bears right and heads through the heart of the woodland along the edge of the Chiltern escarpment.

From here there are views out across the valley; a patchwork of fields dotted with small settlements and farm buildings. The dominant feature, however, is what looks like a large reservoir a few kilometres to the northwest. This is actually a disused **chalk pit**, beyond which lies the (also disused) Pitstone Cement Works, for which the chalk pit was dug. The gentle walk through Aldbury Nowers ends at a wooden kissing gate after just under 1km; beyond lies open chalk upland, with the summit of Pitstone Hill rising steeply to your right and the Chiltern escarpment dropping steeply down to your left.

Pitstone Hill

1.5km

Follow the Ridgeway signs straight on along the wide grassy track that follows the edge of the escarpment, just below **Pitstone Hill**, and then winds its way up to the summit, following **Grim's Ditch**, one of many ancient earthworks in the area that may have acted as land boundaries. At the top of the hill (head for the blue and yellow waymarkers in front of the hawthorn bush ahead), the views to the east across the Ashridge Estate and ahead to Ivinghoe Beacon open up, with the Chiltern escarpment rising with dramatic suddenness out of the flat farmland.

A couple of kilometres away in the valley below, in fields between the disused chalk pit and the villages of Pitstone and Ivinghoe, stands **Pitstone Windmill**, a traditional, seventeenth-century post mill which is one of the oldest of its type in Britain. Post mills were built around a central post that could be turned round to allow the sails to catch the wind – an essential feature for a working mill in what could otherwise be a windless spot.

The wide grassy path at the top of the hill leads along the ridge for 800m before dropping down steeply, flanking the edge of some fields on your right; continue straight on, following the fingerpost by a stile to your right then a blue waymarker just to the right of the mound, to come out at a wooden kissing gate by a telegraph pole.

Incombe Hole and Steps Hill

1.7km

The gate leads through to a picnic area at the edge of a car park. A few metres beyond here, a lane heads left to right towards Pitstone and Ivinghoe villages. Cross the lane and turn left to follow it up to the Ridgeway fingerpost a few metres further on at a metal kissing gate opposite the entrance to the car park. Go through this and continue straight on along the wide track through farmland. The bowl of Incombe Hole (see below) lies straight ahead; beyond it, along the rippling folds of the escarpment are, in turn, **Steps Hill** and **Ivinghoe Beacon**.

This glacial valley is at its most dramatic here: to either side flat farmland stretches out along the valley floor; ahead, the escarpment rises steeply, the Ridgeway heading straight on and up the escarpment by **Incombe Hole**. A dramatic depression in the escarpment, the "hole" is a good example of a so-called "dry valley", formed by ice melt in the frozen limestone of the escarpment at the end of the last ice age. Follow the track up the escarpment and round the edge of Incombe Hole to a gate and stile 700m or so from the valley bottom (ignore the yellow waymarker off to the right at the bend).

Following the waymarkers, continue along a track to the left of the gate and stile and head into the hawthorn thicket ahead; the way through the thicket is clear and well marked, and brings you out after around 100m to the grassy side of **Steps Hill**. Head downhill for a further hundred metres, keeping close to the barbed-wire fence to your right and go out of the field through the kissing gate. The route leads up to the right and over scrubland for 300m before heading downhill to a bend in a road (Beacon Road) that runs round the base of Ivinghoe Beacon.

Ivinghoe Beacon

1km

Cross the road, on the far side of which you'll find the junction of three waymarked public footpaths. Go left here and up the final 500-metre ascent to the top of **Ivinghoe Beacon**. The last few metres are a steep scramble, but worth it for the panoramic views: south and west across the Chilterns and the Vale of Aylesbury respectively, north towards Buckingham and the Midlands, and east along Gallows Hill towards Whipsnade and the Dunstable Downs.

Ivinghoe Beacon marks the northern end of the Ridgeway Long-Distance Footpath, though the ancient trail is thought to have once continued down off the escarpment and on towards East Anglia. Standing 223m high, the hill takes its name from the beacons that were periodically lit here, part of an early warning system against potential invasion, from Roman times through the Spanish Armada to World War II. Ivinghoe Beacon was also the site of one of Britain's earliest **hillforts**; metalwork and pottery finds from its summit indicate that it was occupied from as early as the eighth or seventh century BC, and you can still make out parts of the enclosure and fortifications – including the ditches and mounds that bounded the fort – at the summit.

Through The Coombe
2.3km

From the beacon, retrace your steps back down to the three way-marked public footpaths by Beacon Road and go right. After a few metres this path leads to a gate at the edge of sheep-farming land. You're now on the **Icknield Way**, another famous long-distance footpath, which you follow for the next couple of kilometres. Head down across the field to a gate 150m further on; go through the gate and continue straight on.

After 400m you reach another gate, leading into the field to your right. Take the lower of two paths that lead away from the stile and around the side of the hill before you – a few metres from the stile you'll spot a yellow waymarker in the distance pointing towards a beech wood. This is **The Coombe**, an outlying part of the Ashridge Estate. The track through it is easy to follow for the first 600m, after which you come to the edge of a well-established fir plantation, with rows of giant firs stretching on ahead of you. The track, marked by a yellow waymarker at this point, is just to the left of the row of firs directly in front of you. Follow the path as it zigzags between the rows of trees to emerge after 300m at the edge of the woodland.

Follow the yellow waymarker at this point, heading straight on along the edge of the woods and then up the steep, wooded bank that rises a few metres ahead of you. The initial sharp climb is followed by a steady ascent to a gate at the far (southerly) end of The Coombe, just before **Ward's Hurst Farm**. Go through the gate and continue along the edge of the field beyond it for 30m, to come out into the farmyard. The route leaves the Icknield Way at this point; turn right, following the public footpath signs, and go through the farmyard and down the drive back to **Beacon Road**.

The Bridgewater Monument
2km

Cross Beacon Road and head into the beech woods at the public footpath sign opposite. The path heads into the heart of the National Trust-managed **Ashridge Estate**, the former estate

of the dukes of Bridgewater. A few metres on from Beacon Road, turn right onto a wide dirt track and follow this round for 300m in a long, gradual curve as it heads down through the woodland to a crossroads. Turn left here (ignoring the yellow waymarkers straight on down a minor track), following the main track along the chalky ridge through the heart of the estate; you'll soon start to see official waymarkers for the **Ashridge Estate Boundary Trail** every few hundred metres.

The trail follows a ridge of the Chilterns for 1.5km, giving good views out across the valley towards Aldbury Nowers, passing a bijou log cabin and crossing a wooden bridge over a dry ditch (part of an ancient earthworks) before coming out at the **Bridgewater Monument**. It's owned by the National Trust; you can climb to the top (April–Oct Sat & Sun noon–5pm; £1.20) for great views out across the surrounding countryside. The monument – a Doric column topped by a square plinth and copper bowl – was erected in 1837 in honour of Francis, third duke of Bridgewater, the "father of inland navigation". The duke, inspired by the navigational waterways he'd seen in France, commissioned the building of a canal at his coal mine in Worsley, northwest of Manchester, in the late 1760s. Though not the country's first canal (the Sankey Brook Navigation Canal in St Helen's claims that title), the **Bridgewater Canal** was the prototype for the man-made waterways that crisscrossed the country by the early nineteenth century.

The National Trust tearooms in front of the monument (Tues–Sun noon–4 or 5pm, also Mon in summer) serve soups, sandwiches and jacket potatoes, as well as afternoon teas.

Aldbury to Tring station
3km

Head straight across the clearing and follow the bridleway beyond the disabled car park outside the tearooms, waymarked as part of the **Hertfordshire Way**, a 265-kilometre, circular long-distance footpath round the county. The path leads downhill, ever more steeply, through a cutting in the chalky hillside to come out after just under 1km in the village of **Aldbury**. Turn right along the lane and head down to the handsome village green, complete with a reed-lined duck pond and village stocks, and surrounded by half-timbered Tudor cottages, a tiny village post office, a medieval church and the welcoming *Greyhound Inn*.

To return to Tring station, head straight along Station Road past the church. Just beyond the churchyard, and before a bend in the road, turn right and head through a kissing gate. The path leads through a gate and across a paddock behind the farm buildings of **Church Farm**. A few metres ahead you come to another kissing gate by the line of buildings to your left. Go through this and turn right, exiting the paddock onto a dirt track that runs behind the farmyard buildings and beside a hedgerow to reach two metal gates, either side of a farm track; go through these and carry straight on between fields to a wooden kissing gate, some 750m beyond the farm. Here, the path meets a bridleway, just before a golf course; turn left onto the bridleway and follow it downhill for 600m to a metal gate and down some steps to return to the **Ridgeway**, just by Westland Farm.

From here, retrace your steps: go straight on, through the metal gate on the opposite side of the Ridgeway track and down the concrete road, past the gate into **Westland Farm**, to the lane (Station Road). Turn right and follow this lane back to **Tring station**, 300m further on.

AROUND BLENHEIM PALACE

Long Hanborough to Blenheim Palace and North Leigh Roman Villa

Distance and difficulty 11.5km, plus 7km detour; moderate.
Duration 2hr 45min plus 1hr 45min for detour.
Trains London Paddington to Hanborough (Mon–Sat hourly, Sun every 2hr; 1hr 15min); return from Hanborough to London Paddington (Mon–Sat hourly, Sun every 2hr; 1hr 15min).
Map OS Landranger 164: *Oxford*; OS Explorer 180: *Oxford*.

This walk runs from the Oxfordshire village of **Bladon**, where Winston Churchill is buried, to his birthplace, the Baroque masterpiece **Blenheim Palace**. The route initially skirts the park and runs to the genteel and fantastically pretty small town of **Woodstock**. The pub food on offer there isn't great – if you want **lunch** it's better to buy a picnic at the excellent deli in Woodstock or head for the café in the palace grounds.

Beyond the palace, the route curves through open parkland designed by Capability Brown. Having left the palace grounds, you can either return via country lanes to the station at Long Hanborough, or make a circular **detour** across glorious country to the modest Romano-British remains of **North Leigh Roman Villa** (you're unlikely to have time to make the detour if you do the Blenheim Palace tour, unless you get an early start).

To Woodstock

4km

From Hanborough **station**, turn right onto the busy A4095. Though you'll see entrances to the park on your left, these are either restricted to local residents or private, so you need to stick to the main road at this point. After 1.5km you come to the village of **Bladon**; the churchyard where **Winston Churchill** is buried is to the right, up a flight of steps. The surprisingly simple grave lies just beyond the entrance to the church.

Some 750m beyond Bladon you come to a small, triangular green on the left with a road leading up to a gatehouse. To the right of this road, under a big horse chestnut tree, is a **footpath** sign; follow this across a stile, then go up the faint grassy path that skirts the park – the park wall lies to the left. Continue across the field until you come to some farm buildings on the left, then cross the stile ahead to reach the A44. Turn left along the A44

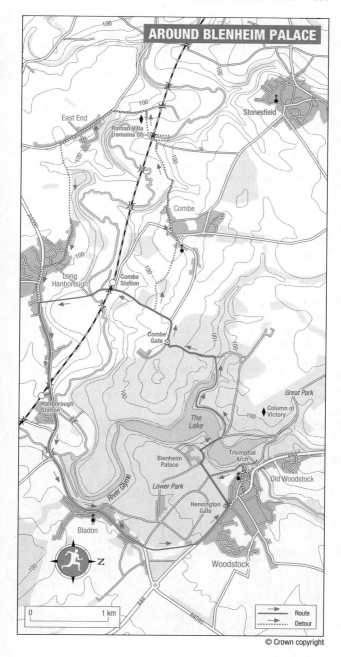

AROUND BLENHEIM PALACE

East End

Roman Villa
(remains of)

Stonesfield

Combe

Long
Hanborough

Combe
Station

Combe
Gate

Hanborough
Station

Great Park

Column of
Victory

The Lake

Triumphal
Arch

Blenheim
Palace

Old Woodstock

Lower Park

Hensington
Gate

River Glyme

Bladon

Woodstock

N

| 0 | 1 km |

Route

Detour

© Crown copyright

for 700m, then take a left to reach **Hensington Gate** (daily 9am–dusk; £2.50, or free with palace ticket which you can buy here), then continue to the bridge in front of the palace (see p.254) to pick up the continuation of the walk. Alternatively, to get to Woodstock, just carry on down the busy road for another few metres. To access the palace grounds from here, go past Hampers deli and take the first left onto Market Street. Head past the *Bear Hotel* and, at the road's end, you reach the **Triumphal Arch**, the dramatic entry point for the park.

. . . .

Hampers deli at 31–33 Oxford St in Woodstock is a great place to buy a picnic, with organic bread, local cheeses, meats and good bottled beer for sale. Another option for lunch is the café in the palace grounds.

. . . .

Blenheim Palace grounds

4.5km

The Triumphal Arch leads into the **palace grounds** (9am–dusk; £2.50, or free with palace ticket). Follow the curving path to the left to reach the palace itself (see p.254), then cross **Vanbrugh's bridge** – which was conceived to resemble a Roman aqueduct – over the vast artificial lake designed by Capability Brown. In an echo of the victorious note sounded by the palace itself, Capability planted the park's trees so that they represented the formation of the battalions of soldiers at the Battle of Blenheim. The view is dominated by a **statue** of the first Duke of Marlborough, who poses fetchingly in a toga atop the tall Column of Victory.

▲ Blenheim Palace

Some 100m beyond the bridge, go through the wooden gate to the left and follow the path, which now runs through woodland, skirting the lake, for 1.5km, until you come out at a T-junction under a stand of tall beeches – this is at the point where the lake peters out. Turn left along the track and soon after go left through the gate or over the stile and then follow the grassy path to the right which runs uphill, curving past some fir trees. You then join a tarred path; turn left onto that and carry on up the hill. Finally, on the right, there's a turning to **Combe Gate**; you'll see the gate-house through the trees.

Blenheim to Long Hanborough
3km

Turn right out of Combe Gate onto the narrow country lane and then left at the next junction, following the sign to Long Hanborough. If you want to take the **detour** to North Leigh Roman Villa (see below), turn right into the meadow after 250m, following the green footpath sign to Combe.

Missing out the detour, carry on down the road to **Combe station**. You may be able to get a train from here back to London, but the service is limited. To get to Hanborough station, follow the road under the railway line and continue for 200m, crossing the bridge across the River Evenlode. Just over the bridge, follow the footpath sign that points directly ahead of you (don't turn left onto the track here, as the route has become overgrown). The path leads across a field for 500m, eventually emerging at the A4095. Turn left and follow the road for 1.5km to **Hanborough station**.

Detour to North Leigh Roman Villa
7km

The detour to **North Leigh Roman Villa** makes a moderately strenuous but enjoyable cross-country circuit. Though the remains of the villa aren't exactly breathtaking, it's fun to discover them as you tramp across a field, and the church at **Combe** with its medieval wall paintings is well worth a look.

Across country to Combe
1km

The **public footpath** leading off the road to Combe station runs for 250m to a clump of woodland – skirt the woodland, keeping it to your right, then turn right into the field: follow the yellow arrow, and take the path across the field. This is a gorgeous part of the walk, with a thatched cottage to the right and the tower of Combe's church ahead.

Blenheim Palace

Altho' the building was to be calculated for and adapted to a private habitation, yet it ought at the same time, to be considered both as a Royall and a National Monument and care taken in the design, and the execution, that it might have the qualitys proper to such a monument, vitz, Beauty, Magnificence and Duration.

John Vanbrugh, architect of Blenheim Palace

When John Churchill, first Duke of Marlborough, defeated the French at the Battle of Blenheim on the Danube in 1704, his reward from a grateful nation was the royal estate at Woodstock, and a staggering £240,000 (worth £25 million today) with which to build a suitable home. The result was the remarkable **Blenheim Palace** (mid-Feb to Oct daily 10.30am–5.30pm; Nov to mid-Dec Wed–Sun 10.30am–5.30pm; £16.50 palace, park and gardens, £9.50 park and gardens; ⓦ www.blenheimpalace.com), built by John Vanbrugh assisted by Nicholas Hawksmoor. The palace was conceived in a spirit of celebration and triumph, and the humiliation of the French and their king is trumpeted by many subtle and not-so-subtle devices. The gateways to the stable courtyards feature carvings depicting the Lion of England attacking the Cock of France; a bust of Louis XIV stuck on the south front of Blenheim, "like a head on a stake", as the duke described it; while in the palace rooms a portrait of the French king is flanked by tapestries depicting the battle, with English soldiers charging towards their victim from either side.

The triumphalism is tempered by a strong theatrical element, evident in the arcaded lines of the building and in the stage-like central courtyard, a strangely blank space that seems to be awaiting some drama – this quality may stem from the fact that Vanbrugh was also a well-known playwright. Certain features of the building are whimsical and high-spirited, notably the fanciful pinnacles and turrets that run along the rooftop and lighten the sculptural symmetry of the palace.

Vanbrugh's genius went unappreciated in his time. The Duchess of Marlborough would have preferred Christopher Wren, but the duke – who had been impressed by Vanbrugh's designs for Castle Howard – overruled her. The duchess was openly hostile to Vanbrugh and it was left to Hawksmoor to act as diplomat. Money ran short, the duchess accused Vanburgh of mismanagement and he finally left, deeply offended, taking Hawksmoor with him. The building was then completed under the direction of the duchess, who watered down many of the original designs, which were by general consensus considered overly flamboyant and even vulgar. When Vanbrugh tried to visit the palace in 1725, a year before his death, he was refused entry.

continued opposite

If you tour the palace, you may feel just a little sympathy for the duchess, who had wanted "a clean sweet house and garden be it ever so small". The scale of the interior is emphatically undomestic; the palace is built entirely on one floor, with hugely high ceilings (three of them sculpted in stucco and gold leaf by Hawksmoor). The rooms were originally conceived to run into each other, providing sweeping vistas that, however visually dramatic, must have been a little overwhelming to actually live in. Subsequent restructuring – some carried out during World War II when the palace was the home of MI5 – has closed off several corridors.

The path leads straight across two fields towards the church and comes out at the village playing field, just opposite **St Laurence's Church**. This is a handsome fourteenth-century parish church whose unusually wide nave is decorated with fifteenth-century **wall paintings**. These were painted over following the Reformation and only uncovered in 1892. Though the figures are painted rather crudely, with heavy outlines, the scenes are lively and inventive and the scheme as a whole must have been strikingly colourful. The most substantial tableau is over the chancel arch and would have sent an unequivocal message to the medieval congregation. It depicts the Last Judgement, with Christ seated on a rainbow, the blessed floating up serenely from their graves to his right and, to his left, the damned being poked down into the open mouth of hell by red demons. Other paintings show the Crucifixion, set in a border of stylized clouds, to the left of the chancel arch; a much damaged St Christopher, on the south wall, with a shark, an otter, fish and a mermaid frolicking in the river around him; and, to the right of the chancel arch, the touching fragments of an Annunciation scene, with just the eyes and wing tip of the Angel remaining, and the hand of God floating above. Apart from the paintings, look out for the medieval **stained glass** and the **pulpit**, decorated with blind tracery.

Combe to North Leigh Roman Villa
2km

Coming out of the church, turn left into **Combe** to reach the village green and pub, then turn left along the green and follow the road signposted to Long Hanborough. Turn right immediately after the renovated chapel and carry on up the road called West End, continuing straight ahead, past Chatterpie Lane.

From here, continue straight on for 750m, past Higher Westfield Farm and downhill, past the sewage works, to **Lower Westfield Farm**. Go over the stile just beyond the farm buildings; the track leads across and down the field – turn right along the stream through the gate, and then take a left over the bridge. Turn left immediately after the bridge, with the stream on your left, and carry on till you pass under the railway bridge. Just beyond the bridge, head across the field to the right; you can see the buildings of North Leigh Roman Villa from here. Cross a stile to go along the field, with the villa to your left; go through the gap in the hedge to reach the villa ruins.

North Leigh Roman Villa

North Leigh Roman Villa is one of many such remains that dot the area, its extent marked by low foundation walls. A modern structure has been built to protect the partially intact **mosaic floor**; the door is generally locked, but you can see the floor through a large viewing window.

The very term "Roman villa" is rather misleading; by the fourth century, when this villa's buildings reached their most developed form, such houses would have been built and lived in by Britons. Although these villas featured Roman-style courtyards and bath-houses, they were otherwise so adapted to a colder climate that they resembled later manor houses rather than continental Roman villas. Like a manor house, this villa was essentially a farm, but did feature luxury items such as the mosaic floor itself. This, rather prosaically, would have been ordered from one of seven factories in Cirencester – buyers chose a design from plans issued by the factory, and the floor would have been constructed there, rather than in situ at the villa. Slabs of mosaic floor were wrapped in straw and transported to the site by bullock cart, and the slabs were then laid, the skill being to disguise the joins between them. The interlocking geometric decoration that edges the floor was for good luck, a charm protecting anyone who stood within it.

To Long Hanborough via East End
4km

From the villa, take the main track up the hill and turn left, heading up to a minor road, where you turn left again. The road leads through the pretty, straggling village of **East End**. Walk right through the village, ignoring the first footpath sign on the left-hand side, then turn left at the second path, 100m further on, marked with a blue bridleway sign. The path runs for around 750m, dipping down the field and then up past woodland before joining the minor road into Long Hanborough; carry on straight ahead for 750m. At the junction, go straight ahead till the road joins the A4095. Here, turn left and follow the road for 1.5km – **Hanborough station** is on the right.

9

St Albans to Bedfordshire

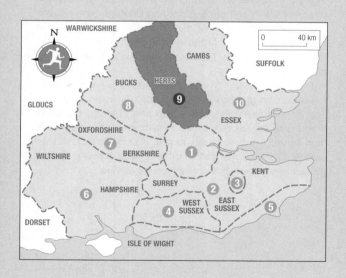

The Lea Valley Way
Harpenden via Wheathampstead
to Oppidum..................................... 259

St Albans and around
St Albans via Verulamium
to Gorhambury............................... 265

Woburn Estate
Aspley Guise to Woburn Village..... 273

The affluent and densely populated county of **Hertfordshire** provides the setting for the first two walks in this chapter, both set on or near the course of **Watling Street**, the great Roman Road that once ran from Londinium (London) to Deva (Chester), and both liberally dotted with the remains of previous eras, from Roman villas to Belgic earthworks. The first walk begins and ends in **Harpenden**, a stop north of St Albans on the railway line from London, following the Lea Valley Way to nearby Wheathampstead, on whose eastern limits are the massive earthworks of Oppidum. The second leads from the medieval market town of **St Albans**, through Roman Verulamium to the manor houses of the Gorhambury Estate. Further north is Bedfordshire's chief attraction, the **Woburn Estate**, with an impressive stately home and England's largest safari park.

St Albans and Harpenden are both connected to **King's Cross Thameslink** by fast and frequent **train** services. The walk to Woburn begins on a branch line between Bletchley (services from Euston) and Bedford (King's Cross Thameslink). Most King's Cross Thameslink services call at West Hampstead, while those from Euston usually call at Harrow & Wealdstone. Tickets are surprisingly good value for all routes.

The St Albans and Wheathampstead walks are both close to London, so good choices if you don't fancy an early start. The Woburn walk will take the best part of a day, especially if you plan to visit the abbey itself or make the additional loop around the park, so aim to start walking by no later than around 11am. All the walks in this chapter follow a circular route, making them convenient if you're **driving**.

THE LEA VALLEY WAY

Harpenden via Wheathampstead to Oppidum

Distance and difficulty 15.5km; moderate.
Duration 3hr 50min.
Trains King's Cross Thameslink to Harpenden (every 5–10min; 30–45min); return from Harpenden to King's Cross Thameslink (every 5–10min; 30–45min).
Map OS Landranger 166: *Luton & Hertford*; OS Explorer 182: *St Albans & Hatfield*.

This varied walk starts from the pleasant commuter town of **Harpenden** and heads along the **Lea Valley Way** – an 80-kilometre walk that follows the **River Lea** (or Lee, as it's sometimes spelt) from its source north of Luton to the River Thames. The route passes through the handsome medieval village of **Wheathampstead**, named for the wheat that was harvested and milled there for over a millennium. Beyond Wheathampstead the walk heads through the massive earth-works, known as the **Devil's Dyke**, that once protected the Celtic settlement of **Oppidum**, then continues southwest into **Nomansland Common** and on to nearby **Amwell**, where the *Elephant & Castle* pub makes a great stop for **lunch**, though it doesn't open on Sundays; an alternative is the *Wicked Lady*, just outside Wheathampstead. From Amwell, the route continues north to rejoin the Lea Valley Way and head back into Harpenden.

Getting started

2km

Turn right out of Harpenden **train station** and head down the station drive to the main road; turn right here, go through the tunnel under the railway and uphill along Station Road (the B652). Continue along this busy thoroughfare for just over 1km to reach the **River Lea** at a bend in the road, with grassy slopes running down to the river at a series of weirs, a popular spot with the feel of a village green. Take the path from Marquis Lane down the right-hand side of a hawthorn hedge, which leads to the river, then turn right, following the near side of the river, passing the weirs by a children's playground and following the dirt track along the riverbank.

After 300m you come out at a lane. Turn right here and continue 100m to reach a left-hand turn into a lane in front of the *Marquis of Granby* pub. Houses line the right-hand side of the

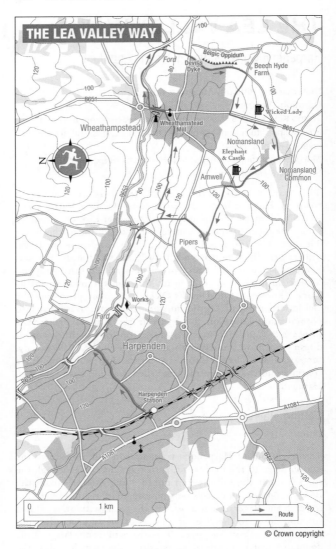

THE LEA VALLEY WAY

© Crown copyright

lane; to the left, fields lead down to the river. After just over 200m you pass under a bridge at the entrance to a small sewage works (don't worry: things will improve shortly). Take the steps on your left up onto the track over the lane, then turn right, following the **Lea Valley Way** signs, which lead you out of town and into open countryside.

Into Wheathampstead

3km

The well-maintained track continues east out of Harpenden, with views across the shallow **Lea Valley**, the river meandering below you along the valley floor. To your right, Piggotshill Wood stands on the hillside, while below it the greens of a golf course run down to the public footpath. A kilometre or so from Harpenden, you reach the hamlet of **Leasey Bridge**. Turn right and walk 50m along the lane to **Little Croft**, a modern bungalow; the public footpath, clearly waymarked from the verge of the lane, leads up the bungalow's driveway to a metal kissing gate in the hedgerow to the right. Go through this to come out into a paddock behind the housing, then head diagonally across the field to reach a kissing gate in the far corner. Keeping the hedgerow close to your right, continue uphill to reach a third kissing gate 100m further on, just to the right of a large barn. Remember this point for later on, since you'll return here towards the end of the walk.

Go through the gate and turn left onto the track in front of the barn, following the Lea Valley Way signs along a dirt track that leads left then right, at first following the boundaries of the neighbouring paddocks for 250m, then heading along a hawthorn hedge out into farmed land. The path is 20m above the valley floor at this point, giving good views over the surrounding countryside and scattered farm buildings, and over to Gustard Wood, which stands on the hillside on the far side of the valley. Some 600m further on, go through the wooden kissing gate in the hedgerow ahead and straight on across the field on the opposite side towards the modern development that marks the western edge of Wheathampstead.

Wheathampstead

0.5km

The attractive medieval town of **Wheathampstead** was developed – and named – as a result of local wheat production, for which this part of Hertfordshire was well known prior to the Industrial Revolution; there was a working mill on the river here as early as 1086. It's now a commuter town, as demonstrated by the rash of modern housing developments which mar its outskirts, though the old high street preserves an attractive clutch of half-timbered and brick cottages.

The public footpath along the Lea Valley leads into town via a short alley through a functional 1970s housing estate. At the end of the alley, turn left and head down to a T-junction (there are generic yellow waymarkers on the lampposts), then turn right for 100m to Church Street. Turn left to reach a T-junction with Wheathampstead's High Street. Just to your left is the village church, **St Helen's**, on Bury Green. Built in the late fourteenth

century, the flint church is topped by an unusual lead-clad broach
spire, which begins like a pyramidal roof and culminates in an
octagonal spire – a Victorian addition, built in imitation of an
earlier medieval one.

Turn left onto the High Street, a particularly attractive spot,
lined with whitewashed medieval cottages, and head downhill for
200m to return to the banks of the River Lea. Straddling the river
is **Wheathampstead Mill**, a rambling brick structure dating from
the sixteenth century which remained in operation until the early
twentieth century; it's now home to craft shops.

Towards Devil's Dyke

1.5km

Cross the river and take the first turning right into a modern
housing estate at the edge of the village. Follow the waymarkers,
which take you out of the estate after 100m and over a rough
track, leading straight on past an area of bulrushes. For the next
kilometre the track runs a few metres above the riverbank before
ending at a wooden kissing gate by the **Cory-Wright Way**,
Wheathampstead's bypass road.

Go through the gate, turn right and head down the track that
runs parallel to the road. After 150m you reach a wider track. Turn
right and follow this down to the river and over the ford just before
Marford Farm (there's a footbridge, useful if the river is in spate and
you don't want to get your feet wet). Follow the lane for 300m up to
a main road, then cross the road and carry straight on, up Dyke Lane,
following waymarkers for the **Hertfordshire Way**, a long-distance
footpath that makes a 265-kilometre circuit of the county.

Devil's Dyke to Amwell

3km

Just 200m from the main road, a wrought-iron gate to your left
flanked by red-brick gateposts marks the northern end of **Devil's
Dyke**. This is the western defensive ditch of **Oppidum**, the earliest capital of the Belgic Catuvellauni tribe. The 100-acre site, now
farmland, was first excavated in the 1930s, and again in the 1970s;
all the finds are now on display at the Verulamium Museum in
St Albans. Go through the gate and walk through the dyke itself,
whose massive fortifications are still an impressive sight: a tree-
filled dell up to twelve metres deep, forty metres wide and half
a kilometre long. The dyke is one of two remaining earthworks
bounding the site; the second, **The Slad**, lies 600m to the east – it's
just as impressive, but unfortunately lies on private land.

At the far end of Devil's Dyke, you come out at the edge of some
fields. Bear right along the field and at the end go through the narrow

Catuvellaunian Britain

A hundred years before the arrival of the Romans, Britain was invaded by the **Catuvellauni** (meaning "expert warriors"), an aggressive warrior tribe from Belgium who, by the first century BC, had gained control of much of southern Britain, making **Oppidum** (and later Verlamion, outside St Albans) their capital. The Catuvellauni also had a hand in events on the Continent, making raids back across the English Channel and assisting their kinsfolk, the Gauls, who were holding back the Roman armies in northern Europe.

Julius Caesar considered the Catuvellauni's influence in Gaul to be so significant that he launched an expedition across the English Channel and reputedly killed their king, Cassivallaunus, at Oppidum in 54 BC. With the Belgic tribe weakened, the Romans were able to seize Gaul and prepare their plans for an invasion of Britain – though in the event this was not to occur for a further century. The Catuvellauni were still a significant threat to the invading Roman army, however, so much so that one of the earliest fortifications in the area was within sight of the then Catuvellaunian capital, Verlamion, just outside present-day St Albans. (For more on this, see box on p.269.)

gap on the right, back onto Dyke Lane. Turn left along the lane and continue for 200m to the public footpath signs opposite the entrance to Beech Hyde Farm. Turn right here, taking the track across open fields back towards Wheathampstead. Some 300m from the lane, the track runs behind houses to come out after 200m at the main road into the village from the south.

Go straight across this and turn left, following the public footpath signs downhill towards **Nomansland Common**, which you reach after 800m, emerging opposite the *Wicked Lady* pub/restaurant, which is over-gentrified but provides an alternative to the *Elephant & Castle* (see p.264) for **lunch**. The common's unusual name derives from an ecclesiastical squabble in the fifteenth century, when the monasteries of St Albans and Westminster both claimed it as part of their territory. After twenty years of wrangling, a jury ordered that both parishes should share it as grazing land – hence the moniker of No Man's Land, which the common retains to this day.

Opposite the *Wicked Lady*, a small access road leads off to your right to some cricket huts. Cross straight over this and onto the edge of the cricket pitch, following the line of benches straight on. At the third bench, bear right and head towards the trees bordering the northwest corner of the cricket pitch. Here, a gap in the trees marks the start of a track – the gap is clear enough, though the track itself is a little hard to spot at the very edge of the wood; you should soon pick it up, though, behind the gnarled old tree dead ahead of you.

The track runs west for 500m before emerging at a lane. Turn right here and head uphill through **Nomansland village** – little more than a hamlet of half-timbered houses at the edge of the common – and on uphill towards **Amwell** village. At the southern limits of Amwell, 500m on from the common in a fork in the road, stands the *Elephant & Castle* **pub**.

The *Elephant & Castle* (Mon–Fri noon–2.30pm & 5.30–11pm, Saturday noon–11pm, Sunday noon–10.30pm; ☏ 01582/832175) is a lovely old pub, with a large inglenook fireplace, stripped-back brickwork, wood panelling and tiled floors.

Amwell to the Lea Valley Way

2km

Take the left fork at the *Elephant & Castle*, following the signs for Down Green, and continue 150m up this lane, then turn left at the public footpath sign opposite Weaver's Cottage, up a short series of steps to a track that runs straight on, along the edge of a golf course. The views across the Hertfordshire countryside open up here, with the hamlet of Ayres End, nestling 1km south on a wooded hillside, the only settlement in view that interrupts the undulating folds of the valley. At the end of the golf course, head straight on through a gap in the hedge, and continue on along the waymarked path through the middle of fields and towards the buildings of **Pipers Stud Farm**, which flank the track to the left, for 150m until you reach Pipers Lane. Turn right onto the lane, past a clutch of large 1930s houses, heavily influenced by the Arts & Crafts movement – the first and smallest of the houses, the half-timbered and red-tiled **Pipers Croft**, is a typical example.

After 500m the lane ends at a T-junction with the main Harpenden Road. Cross straight over the road and carry on into a field beyond the hedgerow. Go diagonally across the field, heading down to the left to the large barn. Go past the barn to the metal kissing gate and a fingerpost sign, to rejoin the path you were on earlier in the walk.

Back to Harpenden station

3.5km

Retrace your steps from here, going back through the metal kissing gate down to Leasey Bridge, then along the track that flanks the southern bank of the River Lea into Harpenden. Turn right by the *Marquis of Granby* pub, then left, following the riverside track to come out at the weirs by the children's playground. Go along the pavement by the hawthorn hedge and up Station Road, from the bend by *The Dolphin* pub, to return to **Harpenden station**.

ST ALBANS AND AROUND

St Albans via Verulamium to Gorhambury

Distance and difficulty 15km; easy.
Duration 3hr 45min.
Trains King's Cross Thameslink to St Albans (every 15–20min;
20–30min); return from St Albans to King's Cross Thameslink (every
15–20min; 20–30min).
Map OS Landranger 166: *Luton & Hertford*; OS Explorer 182:
St Albans & Hatfield.

Starting in the cathedral city of **St Albans**, this gentle circular walk is crammed with historical and architectural interest. It leads through the remains of Roman **Verulamium** to **Watling Street**, the great Roman road that ran from London to Chester. Leaving the old Roman city, the walk then continues out through the surrounding countryside to the village of **Gorhambury**, whose fine Georgian country house stands next to the picturesque Tudor ruins of an earlier manor. Beyond Gorhambury, there's a conveniently located pub, the *Holly Bush*, which makes an excellent lunch stop. Earlier in the walk there's the venerable **Ye Olde Fighting Cocks** in St Albans, and a couple of great **pubs** offering good grub in St Michael's, on the far side of Verulamium Park.

Note that the lane leading up to Gorhambury from Verulamium is a **permissive path** through private land rather than a public right of way, and is closed on 1 June each year, and on Saturdays from September to January.

◄ Cathedral of St Alban

Getting started

1km

From the northbound platform at St Albans **train station** (the one you arrive at from London), head straight through the ticket barrier across the small car park and out to the main road. Turn left up **Victoria Street**, passing Trinity Reformed Church at the

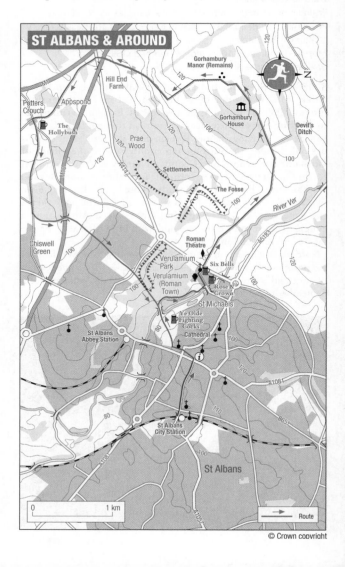

© Crown copyright

crossroads on your right and a mishmash of bland twentieth-century office blocks and diminutive Victorian workers' cottages beyond, then follow the road as it climbs steeply towards the centre of affluent St Albans. At the top of the hill, the heart of the city is marked by the early nineteenth-century **town hall**, whose confident main facade, consisting of a giant first-floor portico punctuated by four fluted Ionic columns, overlooks the town's wide principal drag, St Peter's Street.

From the town hall to the cathedral
0.5km

St Albans is at its bustling best on a Saturday, when the area in front of the town hall and the streets around it are filled with **market stalls** selling everything from fruit and veg to antiques. Victoria Street ends at a T-junction with St Peter's Street at the side of the town hall. Cross St Peter's Street and head left past the town hall, taking the road that leads downhill on its far side. You're now in the heart of medieval St Albans, with its ancient brick-and-flint and half-timbered buildings (most now converted into shops) and the cheery pubs of Market Place. Between them stands the city's fifteenth-century **Curfew Tower**, complete with its original bell.

Head down pedestrianized French Row, to the right of the tower, to reach busy George Street. On the opposite side of George Street, just to the left of the pedestrian crossing, there's a narrow alley; head through this and down the flagstoned path towards the cathedral, then follow the path around the east end of the cathedral (left and then right) to the entrance on its south side. Overlooking grassy lawns sloping down to the River Ver, the **Cathedral of St Alban** is named for the first Christian martyr in Britain, a Roman convert who was executed here in 209 AD. The vast flint and brick building is largely Norman in origin, though there has been an abbey on this site since Saxon times. Materials from the Saxon abbey were reused to build the Norman cathedral, but what is most telling about the materials used in the construction of the cathedral is their similarity to those in the ruins of Verulamium; like much of the city that grew up outside the ruins of the Roman city, raw materials – flint and brick – were taken from the earlier site and recycled here.

Inside, it's the sheer size of the building that impresses: the cathedral has the longest medieval nave in the country. The rounded Norman arches and pillars are, again, clearly built from Roman brick (though those to the south are later additions, elaborate Decorated structures that replace the earlier Norman ones, which collapsed in a storm in 1323). Behind the high altar lies the **tomb of St Alban** – its pedestal is a nineteenth-century reconstruction, since the shrine was all but destroyed during the Dissolution. For more on St Alban, see the box on p.269.

....
The cathedral is open daily from 8am to 5.45pm.
....

Verulamium Park

1km

From the main entrance to the cathedral in the south transept, take the path that heads diagonally downhill across the lawns to the banks of the River Ver. At the bottom of the path, on the river-bank, is **Ye Olde Fighting Cocks** pub, which claims to be the oldest pub in Britain. Whether or not it is (a dozen other places across the country make the same claim), the pretty, higgledy-piggledy inn has been here since at least 1600 and once hosted Oliver Cromwell – cock-fighting took place in the bar area in the early 1800s. In summer you can sit out on benches by the river. A few metres beyond, a red-brick footbridge spans the river and leads you into Verulamium Park.

Verulamium Park, complete with two ornamental lakes and a host of ducks and geese, occupies the southern half of the site of the walled Roman town of Verulamium (see box opposite) – the River Ver marked the city's eastern boundary. You'll see the extensive remains of various other parts of the city throughout the walk. Bear right immediately beyond the bridge and follow the path that leads between the Ver on your right and the ornamental lakes on your left; from here you can see a small stretch of Roman wall on the far side of the lake.

Through St Michael's

0.3km

Follow the path that heads straight through the park and out onto the high street of **St Michael's**, a small eighteenth-century village that has now been absorbed into the city's outlying suburbs. Bear left and head up past the ancient timbered *Rose & Crown* and *Six Bells* pubs, both of which serve **lunch** and have small beer gardens (the former's is more appealing). The street rises gradually uphill then bears right.

A small road continues up to the left. Detour up here to reach the excellent **Verulamium Museum** (Mon–Sat 10am–5.30pm, Sun 2–5.30pm; £3.30). This well-put-together museum offers a fascinating insight into life in Roman Britain, with computer-generated "walk-throughs" of the Roman town and plenty of other gadgets and gizmos to entertain the lay person, as well as trays of finds for the more archeologically minded. The highlight is the collection of five remarkably complete floor mosaics; these were a status symbol in middle-class Roman society. The mosaics were all unearthed locally and date from around 200 AD.

The Roman Theatre

0.2km

Continuing up St Michael's Street from the turn-off to Verulamium Museum brings you after 50m to a T-junction with the busy A4147. Cross to the far side and head down the private road opposite, past a lodge house, following signs for the **Roman Theatre**. The remains of the theatre (daily 10am–4/5pm; £2) sit in the field to the right of this private road; tickets are sold at the small booth 50m from the main road. The theatre stood on

Roman Verulamium and St Alban

Following the fall of southern Britain to the advancing Roman armies in 43 AD, the invaders quickly established a fort on the banks of the River Ver, in the present-day suburb of St Michael's. The Romans were attracted not only by the site's strategic location, but also by its symbolic significance, since it stood just northeast of the former Belgic town **Verlamion**, capital of the Catuvellauni, a tribe which Julius Caesar had quashed a century earlier (see box, p.263). Within five years, the original fort had begun to expand into a prosperous Roman town, and **Verulamium**, as the new settlement became known, quickly developed into an important trading post on the London–Chester and Colchester–Silchester Roman roads. Despite being sacked by **Boudicca** in 79 AD and razed by fire in 155 AD, Verulamium remained an important Roman town until the fourth century, when it was finally abandoned by the retreating Roman armies. Some Roman civilians stayed on, however, and the remains of a middle-class villa dating from this time stands to the north of the city walls in the grounds of Gorhambury.

During the Roman period, the new religion of **Christianity** began to grow in popularity, despite being outlawed by Rome; in 209 AD, **Alban**, a Roman convert from Verulamium, became the first Christian martyr in England. The site of Alban's execution, on the hillside overlooking the town to the northeast, developed into a shrine during Roman times, then later a church and an abbey after the Romans had left. The religious buildings were made from materials pilfered from the abandoned town at the foot of the hill. The abbey was massively extended by the Norman abbot, **Paul of Caen**, in 1077, and the present-day cathedral has changed little since that time.

By 948 AD, records show that market traders were allowed to set up stalls just outside the abbey precinct, marking the beginning of the market town that grew up on the hill around the shrine to St Alban, from which it took its name. Like the abbey, the town buildings were largely made from reclaimed bricks from the Roman site, something that is particularly noticeable in the heart of the medieval city, where flint and brick houses predominate.

Watling Street, the main axis of the Roman town, and several tiers of the original building are clearly visible, though the columns on the stage are modern replicas, added to give a sense of scale to the ruins. You can also take a look at several Roman workshops, currently under excavation just south of the theatre.

Through Gorhambury Park

5km

The gate beyond the ticket booth marks the start of Gorhambury Walk, which leads up through **Gorhambury Park** to Gorhambury House. Initially taking the course of the tree-lined road ahead, the walk follows the route of **Watling Street**, the Roman road that ran from London via Verulamium to the great Roman city of Deva (now Chester) on the Welsh border; there's little in the way of evidence of the Roman road here today, though its course is clearly marked on Ordnance Survey maps. These also show the surrounding countryside to be dotted with Roman and pre-Roman remains – these include small temples, Roman fortifications protecting Verulamium ("The Fosse" on the maps), a post-Verulamium Roman villa (a short way north of the track) and **Verlamion**, a first-century BC stronghold of the Catuvellauni, a Belgic tribe who dominated the southeast prior to the Roman invasions (it's up in Prae Wood to your left). Unfortunately, all of these lie in the private grounds off the track, so you can't visit them.

Gorhambury Walk is open daily from 8am to 6pm, except from September to January, when it's closed on Saturdays. Dogs must be kept on leads.

It's the walk's rural attractions – and great views back to the city and cathedral – that are the principal appeal hereabouts. Beyond the Roman Theatre, fields run down to the **River Ver**, while Prae Wood blankets the hillside above the excavated site, and ahead Maynes Farm stands at a bend in the road. After around 1.5km, the road begins to climb uphill and away from the course of Watling Street, which formerly ran on through the fields to your right – though it's marked on the Ordnance Survey maps, there's nothing to see of the Roman road here today. On the rise to the left, elegant Gorhambury House (see below) appears through a break in the trees. Follow the drive as it sweeps up past **Nash Lodge** (once part of the Gorhambury estate, but now a private home) and onto the final gravel approach to Gorhambury House.

Continue up the gravel approach, then follow the path round behind **Gorhambury House** and past the stables and paddock. Built in the late eighteenth century, the house's creamy white facade is made from Portland stone, fronted by a Corinthian portico. The house takes its name from Geoffrey de Gorham, the Abbot of St Albans from 1119 to 1146, who had had the first manor house built here on what was then abbey land. Gorhambury House is open one day a week in summer (May–Sept Thurs 2–5pm); exhibits include family portraits, handmade carpets and Chippendale furniture – interesting enough, though you're really not missing too much if it's not open when you're passing.

Beyond the house, the path snakes past modern estate buildings before turning a corner and giving you your first view of the romantic ruins of old **Gorhambury Manor**, an unexpected sight, since you're almost on top of the remains before you see them. The estate was sold off following the dissolution of the monasteries, and a generation later fell into the hands of Sir Nicholas Bacon, father of philosopher Francis and Lord Keeper of the Great Seal to Elizabeth I. In 1563–68 Bacon senior constructed the house whose ruins you now see, reusing remains from Verulamium and the abbey buildings at St Albans. Sir Francis Bacon inherited the estate when his father died, but with no heir of his own to pass the property on to, he gave Gorhambury to his secretary, who later sold it to the Grimston family. The Grimstons later commissioned new Gorhambury House after the family outgrew the Tudor manor, abandoning it in 1784 and pulling down the old house to create a romantic ruin. The remains – the crumbling porch and part of the red-brick and flint hall – are today managed by English Heritage (free access). An inscription over the entrance commemorates the fact that it was built in the tenth year of Elizabeth I's reign; though following her first visit to the house, she complained that it wasn't big enough, forcing Sir Nicholas to have the building extended.

From old Gorhambury House, the drive heads downhill, past **Temple Cottage**, which has a portico echoing that of the big house and is named after a Roman temple that once stood nearby, and then past Stud Farm and some cottages before reaching a gate that marks the end of the private road. Head straight on up the public road, past Hill End Farm and through an underpass beneath the M10 to return to the busy A4147.

To Potters Crouch

1.5km

After the bucolic surroundings of the last 5km, the noise of these busy roads comes as a brief but unwelcome intrusion. There are **buses** (every 10–15min) back into St Albans from the stop just to the left of you as you reach the main road, but the **walk** back through the country lanes on the opposite side of the A4147 is pleasant enough, once you've put the roads behind you after around 500m.

Cross the main road and head down **Appspond Lane**, which flanks the M1 motorway for a few hundred metres before veering away and heading past the clutch of half a dozen whitewashed cottages that constitute the hamlet of **Appspond** and continue on into the small village of **Potters Crouch**, 1.5km from the A4147. The village is typical of the local architecture, with black weatherboarded houses with red-tiled roofs. The lane ends at a T-junction; turn left here and head through the village to *The Holly Bush* pub; at the pub follow Rugged Hall Lane off to the right, passing Potters Crouch East Farm, complete with duck pond.

The Holly Bush (Mon–Sat noon–2.30pm & 6–11pm, Sun noon–2.30pm &7–10pm; ☎01727/851792) is located in a wisteria-covered cottage with a pretty lawn at the back. It boasts an atmospheric interior and serves hearty and well-priced pub grub.

Back to St Albans

5.5km

Just under 1km from Potters Crouch you pass **Park Wood** on your left. Beyond it, a waymarked path leads through a gate off to the left. Head up this for 500m, flanking the side of the wood at the edges of Westfield's Farm, to reach a footbridge over the M10 motorway, just beyond a phone mast. On the far side of the motorway, a well-maintained track heads left and then downhill across a field to the modern sprawl of St Albans. The track cuts left and then up through a 1970s housing estate to come out after 1km at a pedestrian crossing on **King Harry Lane**. Cross the lane to reach the path directly opposite, which leads down and over a wooden footbridge across the ditch fortifications to the city of Verulamium.

You are now at the southwest corner of Verulamium Park, equivalent to the southwest corner of the Roman city and boasting the impressive remains of the brick and flint **Roman wall**, which flanks the modern footpath all the way down to the lawns above the park's ornamental lakes. Near the bottom of this path, you pass the remains of the **London Gate**, Verulamium's main southern entrance, where Watling Street ran into the city.

Carry straight on down the path and past the ornamental lakes to reach the bridge by *Ye Olde Fighting Cocks* and retrace your steps back up past the cathedral, through the town centre and down Victoria Street to **St Albans train station**.

WOBURN ESTATE

Aspley Guise to Woburn Village

Distance and difficulty 15km; moderate.
Duration 3 hr 15min.
Trains Euston to Bletchley (every 30min; 50min–1hr), then Bletchley to Aspley Guise (Mon–Sat 1 hourly; 15min); alternatively, St Pancras to Bedford (hourly; 30min) or King's Cross Thameslink to Bedford (every 15min; 1hr), then Bedford to Aspley Guise (Mon–Sat 1 hourly; 30min). Return from Aspley Guise to Bletchley (Mon–Sat hourly; 15min), then Bletchley to Euston (every 50min; 50min–1hr); alternatively Aspley guise to Bedford (Mon–Sat hourly; 30min), then Bedford to St Pancreas (hourly; 30min) or Bedford to King's Cross Thameslink (every 15min; 1hr). There are no services to or from Aspley Guise on Sundays.
Map OS Landranger 153 and 165: *Bedford and Huntington* and *Aylesbury & Leighton Buzzard*; OS Explorer 192: *Buckingham & Milton Keynes*.

Starting in the village of **Aspley Guise**, this circular walk takes you through the **Woburn Estate**, seat of the dukes of Bedford since the seventeenth century and now home to **Woburn Safari Park** – the country's largest – as well as the stately family home, **Woburn Abbey**, named for the monastery that once stood here. The walk loops round the safari park before heading to the estate's **deer park** and past the abbey itself. From the abbey, it's a short walk out to the attractive, largely Georgian village of **Woburn**, which has several good **pubs** – the pretty, whitewashed and thatched *Royal Oak* is the most conveniently located. The walk back to Aspley Guise takes you through farmland and along lanes to the medieval heart of the village.

Getting started

1km

From **Aspley Guise station**, head up the lane (across the level crossing if you're coming from Bletchley; or turn left straight off the platform if you're coming from Bedford) into Aspley Guise. The heart of the village itself lies 1km ahead, beyond the wooded hill. A hundred metres from the station, the road begins to snake up the side of this hill, passing bungalows and whitewashed Victorian workers' cottages and heading up to the village's medieval church, whose Perpendicular tower peeps up above the trees on the brow of the hill. **St Botolph's** was heavily restored by the Victorians – in fact the whole south aisle was

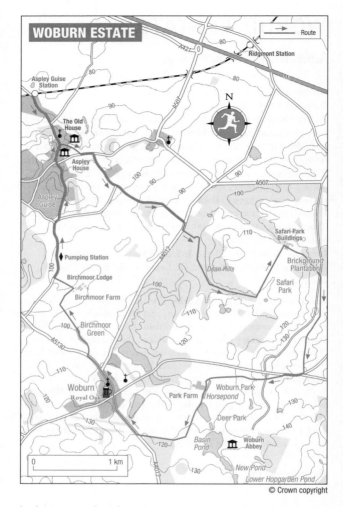

© Crown copyright

built in 1855 – but the exterior restoration, at least, was sympathetic to the medieval period.

A few metres beyond the church, at a bend in the road just before a high red-brick wall, turn left, following the public footpath signs onto a dirt track that leads gently downhill to Bedford Road. The track flanks the northern wall of eighteenth-century **Aspley House**, giving views across formal gardens of the elegant red-brick exterior. To your left is a small meadow, swathed with snowdrops and daffodils in spring.

Aspley Guise to the Woburn Estate

2km

The dirt track ends at another kissing gate at the Bedford Road. Turn left here, cross the road at the central reservation a few metres on, then continue along the far side of the road, passing the Tudor half-timbered and thatched **Park** and **Valentine cottages**. Just beyond the cottages, turn right onto **Mount Pleasant**, a quiet lane that leads up past *The Wheatsheaf* pub (hot and cold bar snacks) and rows of terraced brick cottages and larger Georgian houses to the village limits, where Mount Pleasant becomes **Horsepool Lane**. This runs gently downhill between fields and past a small copse before reaching a cluster of gabled red-brick houses at a T-junction on the A4012, 1.5km beyond *The Wheatsheaf*.

Woburn Safari Park

2.5km

A few metres to the right, on the opposite side of the road, is one of the entrances to **Woburn Safari Park**. Go through the metal gates at the entrance to the park. The road through the park soon splits – take the right-hand fork.

The road runs below wooded **Dean Hills**, which rise to your left, while rhododendrons border the roadside. Some 700m along the access road, just before a bend, turn left along a grassy waymarked track that follows the bottom of the hills; the track runs parallel to the road, 50m or so to the left of the **Leisure Area** (you'll see a children's adventure playground through the trees to your right). Of more interest to walkers is the animal life you'll

▲ Woburn Abbey

see all around: you'll often see rabbits on the wooded hillside, as well as some of the thousands of deer that live on the estate here.

Follow the grassy track for 600m. Just before the access road opposite some functional-looking maintenance buildings turn left, following the waymarked track uphill through the woods that cover the flanks of Dean Hills. At the top of the hill, a wooden gate leads out of the trees and onto the top of the hills. Below to your right you'll get your first view of the **safari park** itself.

The path continues along the hilltop for 700m, giving uninterrupted views into the park. You're pretty much guaranteed to see elephants, zebras, tigers, lions or rhinos, all of which live in the enclosures here: it's an unforgettably surreal sight to see stately Asian elephants ambling through the Bedfordshire countryside. This section of track ends at a large wooden kissing gate by Crawleyheath Farm, right by the **main entrance** to the park. Turn right and go through the farm, past a red telephone box and over the main approach to the park, flanked by two lion sculptures, then head for the metal gates in the fence opposite at the boundary of Brickground Plantation, a wooded hill that rises above the entrance to the Safari Park.

On to Woburn Abbey

4km

Through the gates of **Brickground Plantation** turn right for a few metres towards the "no entry" sign by the maintenance hut and then bear left on this private access route, up the wide dirt track into the trees.

At the top of the hill you come to a road, just to the right of a large whitewashed cottage and a gated entrance at the edge of Woburn's Deer Park. Head over the double stiles to the left of the cattle grid and then go straight on, following the footpath that

Woburn's deer

Home to ten species of **deer** – including the Père David, a species from China that the estate saved from extinction – Woburn is the largest deer sanctuary in the country in terms of number and types of species, although to the lay person they all look pretty much alike. If you're interested, distinguishing features include: a white throat (Axis or Chital deer); an absence of antlers (Chinese water deer); unusual colouring (fallow deer, which can be anything from white to black); tusks as well as antlers (Muntjac); a black stripe down the spine plus an unusually long tail (Père David); a winter mane (Rusa stags); large white patch on the rump (Manchurian sika); or bat-shaped ears (swamp deer). In addition to the species already mentioned, the park is also home to the red deer, the only one of the ten that is native to Britain.

runs along the left side of the road. The path heads straight along the high ground for 500m or so. You can see across to Dean Hills here, beyond the safari park, but next to nothing of the park itself.

Just beyond a tiny pond by a small white "No Pedestrian Access" sign, the waymarkers begin to lead you left, away from the access road and downhill towards the red-brick chimney-tops of houses just outside the estate, beyond another access gate. At the gate, turn right and head uphill, following the waymarkers on the far side of the road. Some 200m from the gate, at the end of the first steep rise, the waymarkers begin to lead you away from the road, over an access road to the farm buildings on your left, and straight uphill to the right of **Whitnoe Orchard Pond.**

You soon come to another access road; cross straight over this and on down the grassy path through a dip in the verge opposite to head into the heart of the estate's **deer park**.

Head straight across the deer park towards the mock-Tudor pavilion, complete with moat, just to the right of Horse Pond. On the far side of Horse Pond, turn left to head along the access road to Woburn Abbey itself, with Horse Pond on your left and the stable blocks to your right, and continue past **Cowmans Cottage**. You'll see Woburn Abbey away to your left.

Woburn Abbey, a grandiose Georgian pile, is home to the dukes of Bedford and takes its name from the twelfth-century Cistercian abbey that originally stood here. Overlooking a series of ornamental lakes, the west range (which is the one you first see) is its most impressive aspect: two and a half storeys high, with giant Ionic columns and faced with creamy white stone.

The estate was given to Sir John Russell, Earl of Bedford, in 1547 in recognition of his diplomatic missions for Henry VIII, though it didn't become the family home until 1619 or achieve its current form until 1747, when Henry Flitcroft was commissioned by the fourth duke to build the west range. Inside, Flitcroft's lavish staterooms are lined with paintings by artists including Gainsborough, Van Dyck and Reynolds. The **grounds** were landscaped in 1802, by Henry Repton who introduced the series of ornamental ponds that now stand before the house.

Woburn Abbey is open mid-March to Oct daily 11am–5.30pm (last entry 4pm); £10.50; ⓣ01525/290666, ⓦwww.woburnabbey.co.uk.

Woburn village

1km

The track leads beneath **Shoulder of Mutton** Pond. Carry straight on, passing a small brick maintenance hut on your right, to reach the edge of a wooded area and a large metal kissing gate. Go through the kissing gate and head down the dirt track between fields to your right and woods to your left, both bounded by high wire fencing. After 200m you reach another high kissing gate to the right of the red-sandstone **Ivy Lodge**.

Beyond this second kissing gate, turn right and follow the footpath alongside the A4012 for a few hundred metres into **Woburn village**. This beautiful, well-to-do place has a predominantly Georgian character (much of the village was destroyed by fire in 1720 and rebuilt in the style of the day), with tiny cottages lining the wide streets through which drovers once took their sheep to the thrice-weekly market.

As well as boutiques and restaurants there are several **pubs**: the first you come to is the whitewashed and thatched *Royal Oak* on George Street (as the A4012 is known as it enters the village).

Back to Aspley Guise station

4.5km

To walk back to Aspley Guise station, head straight through the village along the A4012, passing tiny **Market Place**, just beyond a crossroads. Ignore the first (main) right-hand turn just outside the village and take the second (minor) road 200m further on. Follow this road straight on through the tiny hamlet of **Birchmoor Green**, 100m beyond the turn-off, and then along the dirt track where the road ends, just beyond the village up towards a red-brick farmhouse to **Birchmoor Farm**.

At the hedgerow parallel with the farm buildings, turn right onto another waymarked path that takes you up to the entrance to the farmhouse, then sharp left down its drive towards Birchmoor Lodge. Here, you come out onto narrow Aspley Lane: turn right and follow the lane for 800m, passing a Victorian pumping station and a left-hand turn towards Woburn Sands. From this point on there are white fingerposts directing you uphill into Aspley Guise, which you'll reach after 1km. Cross the main road and head up the road leading off to the right of the tiny village square; after 500m you'll reach St Botolph's church; continue straight on to **Aspley Guise station**.

10

Essex, Cambridge and the Fens

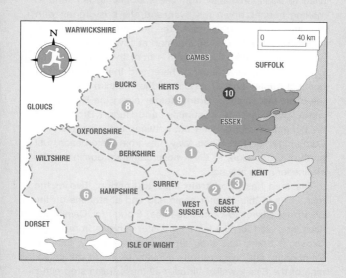

Along the River Stort

Bishop's Stortford to
Sawbridgeworth............................ 281

Uttlesford

Newport to Saffron Walden
via Audley End 286

Along the Cam

Cambridge to Grantchester 292

The Fens

Waterbeach to Ely......................... 298

Due north of London, the enticing university town of **Cambridge** is a well-established day-trip from the city – less crowded and less commercial than Oxford, the place retains an archaic, unhurried charm and the stately beauty of its college buildings takes some beating. By contrast, the rural fringes of Essex, to the south of Cambridge, and the flat fenlands to its north, are relatively little visited. This is a shame, since despite its brash reputation, **Essex** remains one of the least built-up of the home counties, and still boasts handsome market towns set in acres of unspoilt countryside. North of Cambridge, the **fenlands** provide a strong contrast with the walks in the rest of this chapter, offering a landscape that is harsh but strangely beautiful, with vast, perfectly flat fields of rich, peat-black soil, framed by immense skies.

The first of the walks in this chapter goes from Bishop's Stortford to Sawbridgeworth along the **River Stort**, once used to transport barley from the surrounding farmland to malting houses down the river, and still busy today with pleasure boats. Further north, the second walk heads out to **Saffron Walden**, a Saxon market town that made its name – and much of its wealth – from the saffron crocus that once grew in abundance here, and the nearby stately home of **Audley End**. From Cambridge, the third walk makes the short trip south to **Grantchester** along the River Cam, where punters head in summer and Rupert Brooke and his bohemian chums hung out between the wars. North of Cambridge, the Fen Rivers Way runs from Waterbeach, just north of Cambridge, to **Ely**, whose cathedral dominates the skyline for miles around.

The area has good **train** links to London. Two of the four walks in this chapter begin and end at stations on the **Liverpool Street** to Cambridge line, though for Cambridge itself (and also for Ely) there are faster services from **King's Cross**. It takes less than an hour to reach Ely, less for Cambridge, and thirty to forty minutes to get to the beginning of the Essex walks. Virtually all these trains stop either at Finsbury Park (from King's Cross) or Tottenham Hale (Liverpool Street).

ALONG THE RIVER STORT

Bishop's Stortford to Sawbridgeworth

Distance and difficulty 8.5km; moderate.
Duration 2hr 10min.
Trains Liverpool Street to Bishop's Stortford (every 30min; 35–55min); return from Sawbridgeworth to Liverpool Street (1–2 hourly; 40–50min).
Map OS Landranger 167: *Chelmsford*; OS Explorer 195 and 194: *Braintree & Saffron Walden* and *Hertford & Bishop's Stortford*.

Starting at the handsome market town of **Bishop's Stortford**, midway between London and Cambridge, this gentle walk follows the **River Stort** as it meanders its way south via picturesque lock houses and through lush pastureland and reed-filled floodplains to the impressive eighteenth-century maltings at **Sawbridgeworth**. The scenery is not dramatic, but the iris- and willow-lined banks of the river, punctuated by colourful canal boats, make for a quietly bucolic landscape (unfortunately the quiet is periodically shattered by planes from nearby Stansted Airport). Now a wealthy commuter town, Sawbridgeworth maintained a steady prosperity on the back of the brewing industry right up until the late nineteenth century. Fittingly, given its history, the town claims to have more pubs per capita than anywhere else in the country, meaning that there are plenty of choices for **lunch or a drink**.

Now plied by pleasure boats, the river was an important waterway during the Industrial Revolution, used chiefly to transport barley from local farms to malt houses along the riverbanks; Bishop's Stortford was once a major centre for brewing.

Getting started

0.75km

Take the main exit out of **Bishop's Stortford station** and follow the slip road up to a T-junction. Turn right here and cross the bridge over the railway, and then turn right again onto the busy A1060, following the rail tracks for a few hundred metres up to a roundabout. Bear right here along the minor road that crosses back over the railway and loops down past the *Tanners Arms* pub to the **River Stort**.

A low-arched bridge crosses the Stort – take the riverside path that leads off to the left, just beyond the bridge. After 100m, just beyond the railway bridge you come to a wooden footbridge over a **weir** – the first of many weirs along the navigable river, which help control the levels of water in it, siphoning excess volume into backwaters, reed beds, marshes or floodplains.

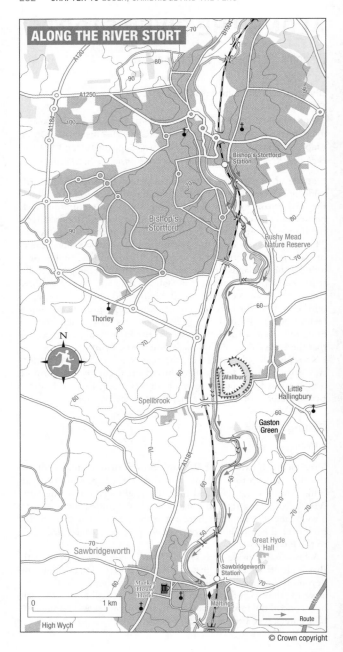

ALONG THE RIVER STORT

Bishop's Stortford Station

Bishop's Stortford

Rushy Mead Nature Reserve

Thorley

N

Wallbury

Little Hallingbury

Spellbrook

Gaston Green

Sawbridgeworth

Great Hyde Hall

Market House Hotel

Sawbridgeworth Station

Maltings

High Wych

0   1 km

→ Route

© Crown copyright

Southmill Lock to Twyford Lock

1.75km

A few metres beyond the weir is the first of the five locks that dot the walk: **Southmill Lock**. Now used exclusively by pleasure boats, these traditional locks, with their well-kept lock houses, form an attractive feature of the river. Cross the lock gates to the left bank of the river (which you continue to follow for the remainder of the walk). About 500m beyond here, a sign to the left of the path marks the first of two entrances to the **Rushy Mead Nature Reserve**, an 11.5-acre conservation area which protects part of the Stort flood-plain. The reserve covers three different wetland habitats – open water, reed and sedge beds – and has a host of aquatic wildlife, including reed warblers, snipes and willow tits; information boards throughout the reserve explain which types of plant and wildlife you can expect to see. It's possible to make a complete circuit of Rushy Mead – little more than 500m – and pick up the walk a few hundred metres further along the river.

Though it's hard to believe it from the pastoral scenery in the near distance, the bulk of Bishop's Stortford lies less than 500m off to the right of the river. It's not until the next lock – **Twyford** – a few hundred metres further on, that the town is truly left behind.

At Twyford Lock, cross the minor road to rejoin the tow-path, through a kissing gate a little to your left on the far side of the road. Passing by pastureland, the path soon rejoins the left riverbank.

Past Wallbury to Tednambury Lock

3km

Beyond Twyford Lock, the river runs through open countryside, where horses are paddocked and cattle graze. A little under 2km further on it passes a white bridge, from where a path leads up towards the northern flank of **Wallbury**, a Celtic hillfort that rises above the east bank of the river. Little is known about the original inhabitants of Wallbury, though Iron Age pottery has been recovered from the 30-acre site. The oval-shaped fort was defended by double ramparts and ditches; the original entrance can still be seen on the east side; today, the defences are heavily wooded and it's difficult to make out much of the original earthworks apart from the moat-like ditches that lie immediately below the towpath to your left. Some 500m after the white bridge is a third lock: **Spellbrook**. Cross the little road here, and continue down the riverside path.

Around 500m beyond Spellbrook there's a long, sweeping bend in the river and an even deeper sweep of river which runs behind it in a wooded copse. The towpath follows the navigable stretch, crossing either end of the deeper river bend by way of two small bridges, 200m apart. Between the two is **Tednambury Lock**.

▲ Canal boat on the Stort

Beyond the second of these bridges, the river sweeps round, running close by the railway, with marshy fields and reed beds to the left, fed by two small weirs that siphon water from the river. The path is quite narrow in places and you'll probably spend more time watching your feet than admiring the views, but look out for the abundant plant life, including blackberries and rosehips which line the way in summer.

Sawbridgeworth

3km

Just under 2km beyond Tednambury Lock the river passes under a low railway bridge and comes out on the northern outskirts of

Sawbridgeworth. At the last of the five locks – **Sawbridgeworth Lock** – cross over the access road (which leads off to the right to the lock houses) and continue straight on, along the left bank of the river, passing the backs of large houses, whose gardens run down to the far river bank. After a few hundred metres you come out on the road by some old malt houses; Sawbridgeworth's tiny **train station** lies a few hundred metres beyond them, to your left.

You can return to London from here, but it's worth having a look round the sprawling **antiques** shops in the old malt houses, where there's also a tiny **café**. Alternatively, walk up into the town centre, a few hundred metres up the hill to your right, to visit one of the many **pubs**. Head straight up The Forebury, the road at the bend to your right, which leads past a tiny green. Beyond the green, cross the road and take the leafy tarred path to the left past the flint-faced thirteenth-century church, Great St Mary's. Exit the churchyard through the gates and go straight up the lane. You emerge opposite the *Market House Hotel*; go straight ahead and turn right on London Road to reach the real-ale friendly *Gate* pub.

The Gate (Mon–Thurs 11.30am–2.30pm & 3.30–11pm, Fri & Sat 11.30am–11pm; ☎ 01279/722313) is a friendly family-run pub with a great range of beer – they even brew their own.

UTTLESFORD

Newport to Saffron Walden via Audley End

Distance and difficulty 13km; moderate.
Duration 3hr 20min.
Trains Liverpool Street to Newport (hourly; 1hr); return from Audley
End to Liverpool Street (every 30min; 1 hr).
Map OS Landranger 167 and 154: *Chelmsford* and *Cambridge &
Newmarket*; OS Explorer 195: *Braintree & Saffron Walden*.

This walk takes you through the gently rolling countryside of
northwest Essex, or **Uttlesford** as this well-to-do area prefers
to be known. Starting at **Newport**, with its wonderful half-
timbered medieval cottages, the route heads north for 8km to
the wealthy medieval market town of **Saffron Walden**, then
loops round the **Audley End Estate**, centred on the sprawling
Jacobean mansion of **Audley End**, before heading to Audley End
station in the village of **Wendens Ambo**. There's a good **pub** in
Saffron Walden, as well as a tearoom and restaurant in the Audley
End Estate. Both Newport and Audley End stations are on the
London to Cambridge railway line.

Getting started
1km

The walk begins at **Newport station**, at the eastern edge of
Newport village, though it's well worth making the short detour
into the attractive village centre to have a look at its characterful
mix of medieval cottages and elegant Georgian houses. To start
the walk, cross the footbridge from the northbound platform and
exit the station via the path at the foot of the bridge, which leads
into a small lane. Turn left here and, after a few metres, ascend
the wooden steps onto the field to the right, following the public
footpath sign. Climb to the brow of the hill and, at the top, head
through the gap in the hedgerow. Keeping the hedgerow to your
left, walk round the edge of the farmland, past a new house and on
towards **a large barn**.

Debden Water to Rosy Grove
1.5km

Before you reach the barn, the path veers left; head downhill,
between a hedge and a wire fence, to meet the Debden Road.
Cross this and follow the waymarked path opposite and just to the
right, downhill between hedgerows. This leads through a small

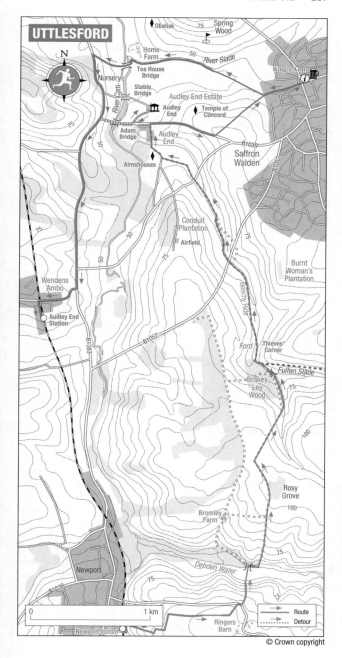

UTTLESFORD

Spring Wood
Obelisk
River Slade
75
Home Farm
50
King's Arms
Tea House Bridge
Nursery
Stable Bridge
Audley End Estate
River Cam
Audley End
Temple of Concord
75
Adam Bridge
Audley End
B1039
Saffron Walden
Almshouses
50
B1052
Conduit Plantation
Airfield
75
Burnt Woman's Plantation
75
Wendens Ambo
50
Beechy Ride
75
Audley End Station
B1383
B1052
Ford
Thieves Corner
Fulfen Slade
Brakey Ley Wood
75
100
Rosy Grove
100
Bromley Farm
75
Newport
Debden Water
75
B1038
0   1 km
Ringers Barn
Newport Station

Route
Detour

© Crown copyright

copse, across a field and down to **Debden Water**, at the foot of a wooded hillside.

Cross the wooden footbridge over Debden Water and turn right on the path through the woodland to reach a stile 50m ahead, which leads out into a field. Turn left and head up the hill, continuing straight on up the edge of the next field; a row of trees here marks the boundary of the field to your left. Keep heading up towards **Rosy Grove**, a clump of trees at the brow of the hill. Immediately before Rosy Grove, turn left, go over a drainage ditch in the hedge to your left and continue uphill, keeping the grove and ditch to your right.

Brakey Ley Wood and Thieves' Corner

1.5km

A hundred metres from Rosy Grove you come to a T-junction with a farm track; turn right onto the track to recross the ditch between the fields, then go sharp left to carry on straight downhill, keeping the ditch to your left, to reach the next thicket of trees. Go into the thicket and cross another small footbridge over a deep brook. Continue straight on, keeping the drainage ditch to your left, and head on along the edge of farmland past **Brakey Ley Wood**. At the end of this field, cross a third bridge, this one over tiny **Fulfen Slade**, and carry on, keeping this brook and the trees to your left. At the end of the next field you ascend to a T-junction with a field track.

This unremarkable spot is known by the romantic appellation **Thieves' Corner**, one of many evocative place names hereabouts – at **Burnt Woman's Plantation**, the attractive wooded hillside to the north, women were once executed for charges of witchcraft.

Thieves' Corner to Audley End

2.5km

Turn left at the T-junction at Thieves' Corner and carry on until you reach the Newport Road (B1052), a little under a kilometre ahead.

Cross to the opposite side of the Newport Road, heading gently downhill past a small private **airfield**. At a bend in the foot of the track, 500m from the road, Beechy Ride recrosses Fulfen Slade and merges with a lane, running right to left from the main road, above. From here, carry on for 750m to reach quiet **Wenden Road**. Cross this and continue down the track to Abbey Farm opposite (the private road signs apply only to cars).

The track leads past Abbey Farm and some attractive red-brick Jacobean almshouses, now used as a conference centre, before bearing right and heading up between the whitewashed Georgian cottages of **Audley End** village. This one-street settlement was a planned community, part of the Audley End Estate, and has changed little since it was built in the eighteenth century. After 200m the street reaches a T-junction with **Audley End Road**. Here, the chimney tops of **Audley End house** peep above the red-brick wall that flanks the road, marking the boundary of the estate. The main entrance, **Lion Gate**, is 100m to your left down Audley End Road. From here, the walk heads up to Saffron Walden, which lies a kilometre to your right, before making a circuit of the estate and returning to the main entrance of the house and grounds.

Saffron Walden

1.5km

Cross Audley End Road and turn right, following the pavement that runs alongside the estate's red-brick boundary wall to the brow of the hill. Some 600m from the junction with Audley End village, and just before the junction with Wenden Road, turn left through a gate into **Audley End Estate** (this is a public right of way and open at all times, irrespective of whether the house and grounds are open or shut).

Follow the track downhill through an avenue of trees towards the crenellated gatehouse at the bottom of the slope. You can't see anything of the stately house at this point, though if you look over to your left you can see two components of Capability Brown's grand design for the estate grounds (see p.290): the obelisk above Audley Park and, further west, the circular temple nestling on a wooded hillside. At the bottom of the track, 600m beyond Audley End Road, head out of the gate and into **Saffron Walden** via Abbey Lane, passing red-brick Victorian almshouses to your left before coming to a crossroads after 400m. From here, head straight on up George Street and then left onto Market Street, which takes you to the market place at the centre of this historic medieval town.

Set at the heart of rich farmland, there has been a wealthy market town here since Saxon times, when the area became a major supplier of wheat and barley, as well as the country's only producer of the **saffron crocus**, the tiny autumn flower used to dye wool that gave the town its name. There was a thriving weaving industry here, the sheep from the nearby Walden Abbey providing the wool, as well as a maltings industry (thanks to all that home-grown barley), until well into the nineteenth century. The main income, however, came from the locally produced saffron dye and traders came from all over the country to purchase it. Maybe because Saffron Walden never had to rely on one industry, the Industrial Revolution seemed to pass it by, allowing the town to retain its medieval character, with elegant Georgian and Victorian additions.

The medieval **Market Place** is still the commercial heart of Saffron Walden. The **town hall** is the square's most distinctive building, though the original eighteenth-century building is lost behind an overblown mock-Tudor gabled porch that was added in the late nineteenth century. The narrow lanes that radiate out from here are lined with half-timbered houses, filled with antique and secondhand bookshops. Just to the north of the square, up Market Hill, is the welcoming *King's Arms*, which serves typical pub grub.

The *King's Arms* (Mon–Sat 11am–midnight, Sun noon–midnight; ☏01799/522768) is a historic town-centre pub, with real fires and real ale.

Audley End Estate

3km

From Saffron Walden, the walk heads back into the **Audley End Estate**; go back down George Street and Abbey Lane to return to the crenellated gatehouse at the edge of the estate. Take the path to the right of the one you came down earlier – not the one that leads through an avenue of trees, but the lesser track just to its right that runs straight through a field. At the far side of the field, cross over a small brook and head along the edge of a wood to arrive at the southern edge of Audley End's grounds, the boundary of which is

Audley End

The estate is home to the country's largest Jacobean mansion, **Audley End**, built on the site of the twelfth-century Walden Abbey. Following the Dissolution, the estate passed into the hands of Lord Chancellor Audley, later Baron Audley of Walden. It was his grandson, Thomas Howard, later the Earl of Suffolk, who commissioned the rebuilding of the mansion in 1603, which he named in honour of his grandfather.

The present-day house is actually only a fraction of its original size – modernizing architect **Vanbrugh** was also responsible for demolishing the eastern range and large parts of the south and north ranges in the late eighteenth century to save the then owners money on the upkeep of the vast building. At the same time that Vanbrugh was revamping the house, the grounds were extensively landscaped by **Capability Brown**, with several strategically placed **Robert Adam** structures used to create vistas in Brown's trademark style. Adam's designs here include the Circular Temple, on the hillside to the west of the house, the three-arched Adam Bridge over the Cam and the Palladian Tea House Bridge.

marked by the tiny **River Slade** to your right, beyond which lies a golf course. To your left, the marshy edges of Audley End Park run across to a gentle rise, on top of which is the Corinthian **Temple of Concord**, built in 1791 to celebrate George III's recovery from madness – prematurely, as it turned out. The massive north facade of the house, topped by turrets and copper domes, stands majestically to its right.

Follow the course of the River Slade for 500m to reach a bridge over the river by **Home Farm**. By the bridge, take the path that leads through a small gap in the fence and follows the left bank of the river by the estate wall. In a few minutes, you come out on the main road into Home Farm; turn left and almost immediately you'll cross the River Cam (into which the Slade runs) at the curve in the road. Have a peek over the estate wall at the bend here: you're standing just behind Robert Adam's Palladian **Tea House Bridge**, with views along the landscaped water gardens to a picturesque weir.

When you reach London Road, 500m from the Cam, turn left and head downhill; there are glimpses to your left of the estate **nursery** and, at the original main entrance, the splendid **Jacobean stables**. Here, a ha-ha separates the estate from the roadside, and there are superb views of the crenellated main facade of the house. This western range remains pretty much as it would have been when the house was first built – an expanse of mullioned windows, gables, turrets and chimneys, faced with Ketton stone.

If you want to visit the house, turn left just to the south of it onto Audley End Road, crossing the elegant three-arched **Adam Bridge** over the Cam to reach the main visitors' entrance, just south of Audley End village. Inside, highlights include the massive, wood-panelled Great Hall and Adam's elegant neoclassical drawing rooms.

....

Audley End House is open Easter–Sept Wed–Fri & Sun 11am–5pm, Sat 11am–3.30pm; Oct Sat & Sun 11am–4pm; £10.50 (EH).

....

To the station

2km

From the house, continue down London Road for 2km, turning right at the road sign for **Wendens Ambo** village and **Audley End train station**. Take the first turning left in Wendens Ambo to get to the station itself.

ALONG THE CAM

Cambridge to Grantchester

Distance and difficulty 12.5km; easy.
Duration 3hr 10min.
Trains King's Cross or Liverpool Street to Cambridge (every 30min from each station; 45min–1hr); return from Cambridge to King's Cross or Liverpool Street (every 30min to both stations; 45min–1hr).
Map OS Landranger 154: *Cambridge & Newmarket*; OS Explorer 209: *Cambridge*.

This walk heads south from **Cambridge** along the bank of the **River Cam** to the picture-postcard village of **Grantchester**, little more than a high street with a church, a green and rustic thatched cottages. Grantchester has long been a popular day-trip from the city, and it's still *de rigueur* for local undergraduates to pack a picnic, rent a punt and spend a lazy summer's day on the river here. *The Orchard House Tearooms*, right on the river and with its own moorings, is an idyllic spot for **lunch** or afternoon tea. There are also several good **pubs** in the village, all offering bar meals. The return leg of the walk heads north into Cambridge via **The Backs**, the lawns behind the city's colleges from where there are superlative views of the colleges. Past the Backs, the route returns via leafy backstreets to the city's train station.

Getting started

1km

From **Cambridge station**, head straight up Station Road, turn right at the T-junction onto Hills Road, cross over to the far side at the pedestrian crossing and take the first turning left onto quiet, leafy Bateman Street. At the far end of Bateman Street, cross busy Trumpington Road at the pedestrian crossing and then head left down it for 100m, past Belvoir Terrace, to reach the edge of a meadow. Turn right here at the sign to Newnham and follow a tarred path off to the right.

Coe Fen and Paradise Nature Reserve

1.5km

Follow the path round the back of Belvoir Terrace. After a few hundred metres you'll reach a pair of metal footbridges marking the southern reaches of **Coe Fen**, a marshy area on the banks of the River Cam. Too soft to be of use for building, the land was historically used as free grazing land for local people and cows,

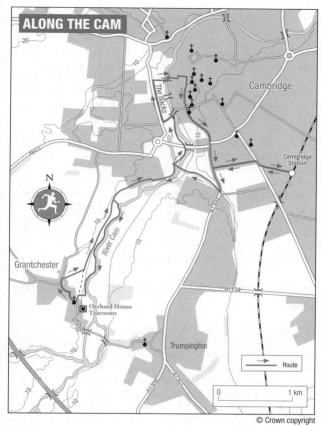

© Crown copyright

sheep and even horses are still left here to keep the grass trim and to encourage wild flowers to grow.

Cross both footbridges and bear immediately left down the far side of the riverbank (by a small car park) and through a kissing gate into the **Paradise Nature Reserve**. Like Coe Fen, this area is managed according to traditional methods; native wildflowers found here include the rare butterbur, a broad-leafed plant with pale-pink conical spikes that flowers in early spring; the leaves were once used for wrapping butter (hence the name) and, reputedly, for curing the plague.

Follow the riverside path for several hundred metres as it skirts the southern reaches of the city, with meadowland stretching away on the far bank, to emerge onto a quiet cul-de-sac. Bear left into **Grantchester Meadows**, a quiet, well-to-do suburban street that heads off left to the meadows after which it's named.

Grantchester Meadows

2km

The end of the street marks the edge of the city, beyond which grass meadows open up. To your left is **Skater's Meadow**, a riot of wild flowers in the spring, while ahead stretches the tarred path you take to Grantchester. At the far end of the university playing fields, pass through a metal gate and head left down a grassy track, over a small boardwalk and down to the riverbank.

You now follow the west bank of the river as it meanders through **Grantchester Meadows**. Like Skater's Meadow, this is still managed grazing land and visitors are asked to keep to the grassy path along the riverbank or the tarred path on the rise. You'll cross five small wooden bridges before reaching the edge of Grantchester itself. Here the path widens to a small meadow, with a metal gate ahead and the chimneys of a house visible to the right; turn to the right and head up the slope until you regain the tarred path, then go left and head through the narrow alley, passing the beer garden of the *Green Man* pub, to come out at the southern end of Grantchester's High Street.

The Orchard House Tearooms and Grantchester village

0.5km

Just to your left here, on the edge of the village, are **The Orchard House Tearooms**, the essential riverside stop for college undergraduates since they opened in 1897. Like Grantchester itself, the tearooms were made famous a generation later by Rupert Brooke's poem, *The Old Vicarage, Grantchester*, which the Cambridge graduate wrote in a fit of nostalgia while in Berlin in May 1912. Brooke had taken rooms at *The Orchard House* and then the Old Vicarage (the latter is now owned by disgraced ex-Tory MP, Jeffrey Archer) and his chums – amongst them E.M. Forster and Virginia Woolf – used to punt upriver to visit him, taking tea there and thus establishing a tradition that is still going strong today.

To reach the tearooms, turn left from the end of the public foot-path and head downhill to the bend 100m further on. The entrance is clearly marked here.

....

The *Orchard House Tearooms* (March–May & Sept–Nov 9.30am–5.30pm; June–Aug 9.30am–7pm; Dec–Feb 9.30am–4.30pm; ☎01223/845788) are open daily, serving morning coffee, lunches and afternoon teas, which you can take either alfresco in the spacious orchard itself, scattered with deckchairs, or inside in the original Victorian pavilion.

....

To get into **Grantchester** village, turn right and head up past the Perpendicular Church of St Andrew and St Mary — worth a peek inside for its fine chancel — and past the modern Vicarage (the Old Vicarage is tucked away down a private lane further up the road) to reach the small village green, edged by a couple of pubs.

Back to Cambridge
3.5km

Just beyond the green is the *Rupert Brooke* pub — filled with Brooke memorabilia and its clock set permanently at ten to three. A few metres beyond the pub, a public footpath sign marks the start of the **return route** to Cambridge. Turn right onto this path and follow it diagonally downhill until it joins a tarred path heading north towards Cambridge, with the city's skyline visible through the trees ahead. Continue along this path as it follows the high ground above **Grantchester Meadows**, offering quite different views to those from the grassy path along the Cam that you followed previously, even though it's only a little higher up. The horizon opens out and the river itself can barely be seen between the trees and hedgerows below.

After 1.5km you arrive back at **Skater's Meadow**. Retrace your steps along Grantchester Meadows Road and through Paradise Nature Reserve, past the car park and over the first metal bridge. Here, take the second path on the left (the one that heads diagonally over to the banks of the Cam), then turn left and follow the bank, concreted at this point, along the eastern edge of **Coe Fen** and up to a busy road, the Fen Causeway. Take the underpass under the road, a few metres to the left, and turn left on the tarred path on the opposite side, where you can just see the back of the Fitzwilliam Museum and, beyond it, Peterhouse College, peeping through the trees to your right; Coe Fen spreads out to the left.

After a few hundred metres, the city streets begin to close in on the right. Cross the footbridge opposite the Mill pub onto **Mill Lane** then turn left along the alley — Laundress Lane — behind the *Anchor* pub. At the end of the alley, turn left onto Silver Street, cross back to the west bank of the river via **Silver Street Bridge** and go over the road at the pedestrian crossing just beyond. The wooden bridge just north of Silver Street Bridge is the so-called **Mathematical Bridge**, a copy of the eighteenth-century original and so called because, it is claimed, it would remain standing even if all its nuts and bolts were removed.

From the Backs to the station
4km

Just beyond the pedestrian crossing, the grassy stretch of land that marks the start of the path to **The Backs** begins. The Backs comprise

▲ Punting on the Cam

a stretch of grazed lands, carpeted with daffodils and crocuses in spring, which run down to the Cam behind the oldest and most spectacular of the city's colleges, providing unforgettable views of the diverse college buildings. Turn right and follow the red-earth path round and then onto a rough white-concrete and stone track, where the sublime sight of **King's College Chapel** (entry £2) comes into view. Founded by Henry VI in the fifteenth century, the chapel is one of the country's finest examples of the Perpendicular style, the ornate late-Gothic buttressing and intricate tracery of its exterior offering a foretaste of the delicate fan-vaulting and exquisite stained glass inside. Next up is **Clare College**, founded in 1325 and thus the city's second oldest college. Beyond Clare College lies **Trinity College**, the city's largest, which was founded by Henry VIII in 1546. Trinity has more famous alumni than any other college – from poets and writers such as Byron and Dryden, to the spies Anthony Blunt and Guy Burgess, and scientists and philosophers such as Isaac Newton and Bertrand Russell.

Most of the colleges are open to visitors at limited times and for a small entrance fee (around £2).

Beyond the gates to Clare College, turn right along pedestrianized Garret Hostel Lane, over the Cam and onto Trinity Lane. Here, bear left then right and, at Trinity Street, right again to head down **King's Parade**, the narrow medieval street that runs past the front of these colleges. Originally the city's high street, King's Parade was half cleared to make way for (and renamed in honour of) its most famous college, King's. The screen that flanks the road is neo-Gothic, masking much of the older buildings from the view.

Continue past King's and St Catherine's colleges and onto **Trumpington Street**, a continuation of King's Parade, which runs past the front of Peterhouse and the grandiose **Fitzwilliam Museum** (Tues–Sat 10am–5pm, Sun 2–5pm; free), a superbly overblown Neoclassical edifice. The museum was opened in the late nineteenth century to house the private collection of Viscount Fitzwilliam, but has also ended up exhibiting a wonderfully eclectic range of other donations – everything from Egyptian sarcophogi to pieces by Hockney and Henry Moore. Continue along the same road for 1.5km to reach the pedestrian crossing that leads over to the far side of Trumpington Road, just north of Bateman Street. Retrace your steps along **Bateman Street**, across Hill Road via the pedestrian crossing at the far end and left onto Station Road for the **train station**.

THE FENS

Waterbeach to Ely

Distance and difficulty 21km; strenuous.
Duration 5hr 15min.
Trains King's Cross to Waterbeach (hourly; 55min); return from Ely to King's Cross (hourly; 1hr).
Map OS Landranger 154 and 143: *Cambridge & Newmarket* and *Ely & Wisbech*; OS Explorer 226 and 228: *Cambridge* and *March & Ely*.

Heading north from **Waterbeach** along the **Fen Rivers Way**, this walk is easy to follow and strenuous only in so much as it is long. There's a unique appeal to the route with huge skies and vast, perfectly flat landscapes stretching out to the horizon: if you really want open space, this is the place for you. On a clear day you can see for miles, with the odd tractor tracing a line on the vast acreages of farmland, bereft of hedgerows and planted with rapeseed and corn. The walk ends at **Ely**, whose cathedral dominates the flat surrounding farmland from its modest hilltop perch. There's a pub on the route but it's not great, so it's best to pack a **picnic** and round things off with Earl Grey and scones in Ely's award-winning **tearoom**.

Getting started

0.5km

From platform 1 of **Waterbeach station**, take the path from the station car park that runs parallel to the right-hand side of the road for 500m, before reaching the river. Turn left up onto the road and cross the bridge, turning left and following signs for the **Fen Rivers Way** to Ely. Almost immediately, the wide skies and flat fenlands open up before you. Bottisham Fen lies to the east, Swaffham Fen and North Fen stretch ahead.

To Upware

8km

Follow the track along the riverbank, passing the clipped lawns of the **Cambridge Sailing Club**, with its fancy pleasure boats and wooden summerhouses. Continue past a lock (Bottisham Sluice) and the bridge over **Bottisham Lode**, one of many man-made tributaries of the Cam that lead across to villages on firmer ground further east; this one goes down to the less than imaginatively named The Lode. Beyond the bridge, go along the grassy track that follows the meandering river for 1.5km before heading up to a road by some private moorings.

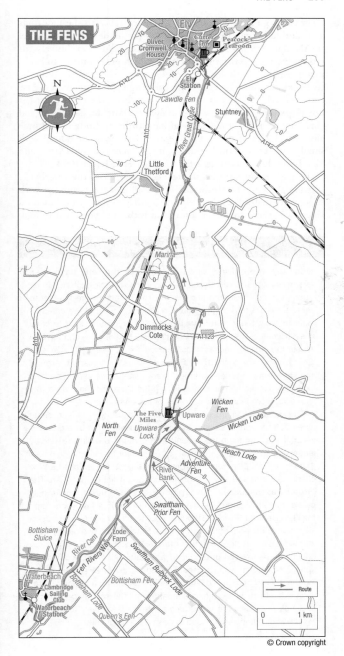

THE FENS

N

Ely

Oliver Cromwell's
House

Cutter
Inn

Peacock's
Tearoom

A142

Ely
Station

Cawdle Fen

Stuntney

River Great Ouse

A142

Little
Thetford

Marina

Dimmocks
Cote

A1123

Wicken
Fen

The Five
Miles

Upware

Wicken Lode

Upware
Lock

Reach Lode

North
Fen

River
Bank

Adventure
Fen

Swaffham
Prior Fen

Bottisham
Sluice

River Cam

Fen Rivers Way

Lode
Farm

Swaffham Bulbeck Lode

Waterbeach

Bottisham Lode

Bottisham Fen

Cambridge
Sailing
Club

Waterbeach
Station

Queen's Fen

Route

0   1 km

© Crown copyright

Turn left, go through the gate by the entrance to the moorings and continue along the Fen Rivers Way past Lode Farm. Unusually for the fens – whose rich, peaty soil is used almost exclusively for crop-growing – this farm has cattle, which graze on the embankments here. You may have to negotiate your way past them on the riverbank, or you might see them parading up and down on the far bank – the land being as valuable as it is here, the cows don't get much space to graze on. Carry straight on past the farmhouse and yard, and over the bridge at **Swaffham Bulbeck Lode** to continue along the banks of the Cam. The next 3km or so are dotted with small clutches of farm buildings, lost in acres of tilled land, and 1km beyond the moorings is the tiny hamlet of **River Bank**.

The path eventually begins to veer away from the riverbank, skirting the edge of **wetlands** – flooded meadows studded with willow trees. Just south of Upware village, you come out on a lane where there are information boards that tell you what to look

Taming the fens

Originally a reed-filled, boggy wilderness, **the fens** have been ever-more aggressively dyked and drained over the centuries in an attempt to use their land and waters. The Romans were the first to try to tame the fens, digging out Car Dyke just west of Waterbeach, both to drain the land for farming and to serve as a canal to carry grain from here to their garrison in Lincoln, 112km away. In medieval times, the wealthy monasteries diverted the course of the Ouse to Ely to make use of the river and waterways for transport. Around the same time, a series of "lodes" were dug – these served both as drainage ditches and as canals linking the Cam, the main waterway in the southern fens, to villages east of the river.

The most significant change to the landscape, however, came when Dutch engineer **Cornelius Vermuyden** was hired by a group of wealthy speculators in the seventeenth century to drain the marshy landscape so that its rich soil could be used for farming.

Vermuyden's plan was to bypass the Great Ouse, creating a new channel to carry the area's floodwaters straight out to the Wash. The project was introduced in two phases: the first cutting, confusingly called the Old Bedford River, was made in 1637; a few years later, the New Bedford River (or Hundred Foot Drain) was cut, just under a kilometre to the right of the first cutting. Between the two, Vermuyden created a plain, which absorbed the river's floodwaters in winter and could then be used as grazing land when the waters drained away in spring. Although it was successful in taming the fenlands and allowing the area to be farmed, Vermuyden's engineering had one unforeseen side effect: as the drains dried the land, the spongy peat began to shrink back until the entire area fell below sea level. To this day, hundreds of pumps are needed to keep the fens drained.

out for here: the area is home to a rich variety of wetland birds, including the redshank and wigeon. Turn left along the lane and across the bridge by **Upware Lock** over Reach Lode.

To continue along the Fen Rivers Way, head down the lane through **Upware** village (ignoring public footpath signs to your left and right) to a junction where you turn left down Old School Lane; a few metres further on head over the wooden footbridge to your right. You'll see a modern pub to the left of the footbridge – *The Five Miles* – handy for a drink, but nothing to write home about.

Upware to Ely
11km

Follow the track north past a marina and along the left-hand side of a couple of fields. You come to a T-junction with a track – turn right for 100m and then left up the long unsigned drove road. This leads in a little under a kilometre to the busy A1123 (Dimmock's Cote Road). Carry straight on along the track on the opposite side to a T-junction with a nature sanctuary ahead of you. Turn left on the permissive path and follow the tarred road up to the bend, then continue straight on along the grassy track between the trees. Some 200m from here the track bends round to the right, flanking the steep embankment of the River Cam for a few hundred metres before reaching the edge of a field. The path leads up onto the bank, over a stile and along a track above the river. From here, the impressive sight of Ely Cathedral dominates the skyline, making it easy to see how the cathedral – set (like the town around it) on a small island of clay a few metres above the marshy fens – has been dubbed "the Ship of the Fens".

Continue along the grassy top of the riverbank and past a marina on the far side some 500m further on, just beyond which the Cam and Great Ouse rivers merge. Follow the river, now called the **River Great Ouse**. It's a further 2km north along the riverside track from Lode End Bridge to the A142 (Soham Road) into Ely. To head home from here, turn left and follow Soham Road down and under the railway bridge and take the first left for the **station**.

Ely
1.5km

Set on a low hill in the midst of endless, pancake-flat fenland, the medieval town of **Ely** still feels like a tiny island in a sea of marsh – its name is a contraction of "Island of the Eels", referring to the plentiful eels that once lived in the waters around it. The town stands above the left bank of the River Great Ouse, with an attractive willow-fringed marina huddled on the riverbank itself.

Follow the Fen Rivers Way from the opposite side of the A142, down the path towards **Ely Marina**, a few hundred metres further on. Pleasure boats trawl the river here, and the odd narrow boat adds a splash of colour. Beyond the marina, Ely waterfront opens up before you. Ahead is the *Cutter Inn*, superbly located and serving great food. Carry on by the river a little further to reach the enticing *Peacocks Tearoom* by the pedestrian bridge, with tables in the abundant garden of a handsome old house.

The *Cutter Inn* (Mon–Sat 11am–11pm, Sun noon–10.30pm; ℡01353/662713) dishes up delicious fishcakes, pies, burgers and so on in its attached restaurant, while *Peacocks Tearoom* (Wed–Sun 10.30am–4.30pm; ℡01353/661100) serves light lunches and sandwiches as well as succulent home-made cakes and set afternoon *teas*.

Before the pub, at the point where the river bends round to the right, turn off and head up **Victoria Street**, a quiet side street lined with tiny cottages. At the top of the street, turn right onto Broad Street. A hundred metres or so along, take a left by a black tourist signpost up through **Cherry Hill Park** towards the cathedral.

Almost immediately after you enter the park, the view opens up to your right across meadows to **Ely Cathedral,** its highly decorated west tower and Octagon an unmistakable feature of the skyline. To your left, the apparent landscaping is actually the remains of a Norman motte and bailey castle. Continue up the path and exit the cathedral close through the medieval Walpole Gate. Turn right and head up **The Gallery**, the medieval heart of the city, which leads after 250m to the main (west) door of the cathedral. Best viewed from the green opposite, the western front owes its lopsided appearance to the lack of one of its transepts, which collapsed in the eighteenth century.

Ely Cathedral is open summer daily 7am–7pm; winter Mon–Sat 7.30am–6pm, Sun 7.30am–5pm; £5.50, with Octagonal Tower £9.

This wasn't the only piece of the cathedral to have fallen down. The original Norman crossing tower collapsed in the fourteenth century, taking part of the chancel out with it, which is how the cathedral came to have its unusual **Octagon**, the building's architectural highlight. Outside, the delicate tracery of the eight-sided stone structure – topped at each corner by crocketed pinnacles – is surmounted by a smaller, octagonal timber lantern. This is impressive enough, but the interior is even finer, creating a kaleidoscopic effect with its magnificent fan-vaulted ceiling arching up towards the lantern, decorated in gold, green and red floral patterns.

To get to the **station**, retrace your steps through Cherry Hill Park and along the edge of the marina to the A142. Turn right along the road and go below the underpass, turning left into the station.

Explore

SE London's Green Chain

FOR YOUR HEART, MIND, BODY AND SOUL

The official Green Chain Walk Route Pack contains 10 laminated route cards, with colour maps of the network of footpaths and places of interest along the walk.

To obtain your copy, please send a cheque for £3.50 (P&P included) made payable to

"Greenwich Council" with your name and address details to:

SE London Green Chain (RG) PO Box 22119 London SE18 6WY

For more information visit
www.greenchain.com
Green Chain Information Line
020 8921 5028

Discover Lee Valley Regional Park

At twice the size of London's Royal Parks, with 26 miles of riverside trails, nature reserves, country parks, heritage sites and urban oases, there's no better place to challenge yourself.

Covering part of Hertfordshire, Essex and London the Regional Park is home to outstanding wildlife and fantastic sporting facilities.

To help you enjoy the Regional Park we've created various useful guides, including our Get Active booklet which

has 40 routes designed to suit individual interests and abilities and celebrates the diversity and beauty of this fantastic green lung. Why not come and discover where the 50 mile, Lea Valley Walk runs through the Regional Park or where the Capital Ring Walk visits us?

Whether it's walking, cycling, running or just relaxing – the Regional Park is just waiting to be discovered.

For more information or to request a free guide:

0845 677 0600
info@leevalleypark.org.uk
www.leevalleypark.org.uk

small print &

Index

A Rough Guide to Rough Guides

In 1981, Mark Ellingham, a recent graduate in English from Bristol University, was travelling in Greece on a tiny budget and couldn't find the right guidebook. With a group of friends he wrote his own guide, combining a contemporary, journalistic style with a practical approach to travellers' needs. That first Rough Guide was a student scheme that became a publishing phenomenon. Today, Rough Guides include recommendations from shoestring to luxury and cover hundreds of destinations around the globe, including almost every country in the Americas and Europe, more than half of Africa and most of Asia and Australasia. Millions of readers relish Rough Guides' wit and inquisitiveness as much as their enthusiastic, critical approach and value-for-money ethos. The guides' ever-growing team of authors and photographers is spread all over the world.

In the early 1990s, Rough Guides branched out of travel, with the publication of Rough Guides to World Music, Classical Music and the Internet. All three have become benchmark titles in their fields, spearheading the publication of a range of more than 350 titles under the Rough Guide name, including phrasebooks, waterproof maps, music guides from Opera to Heavy Metal, reference works as diverse as Conspiracy Theories and Shakespeare, and popular culture books from iPods to Poker. Rough Guides also produce a series of more than 120 World Music CDs in partnership with World Music Network.

Visit www.roughguides.com to see our latest publications.

Rough Guide travel images are available for commercial licensing at www.roughguidespictures.com

Publishing information

This second edition published January 2009 by Rough Guides Ltd, 80 Strand, London WC2R 0RL. 345 Hudson St, 4th Floor, New York, NY 10014, USA.

Distributed by the Penguin Group
Penguin Books Ltd, 80 Strand, London WC2R 0RL
Penguin Group (USA), 375 Hudson Street, NY 10014, USA
14 Local Shopping Centre, Panchsheel Park, New Delhi 110017, India
Penguin Group (Australia), 250 Camberwell Road, Camberwell, Victoria 3124, Australia
Penguin Group (Canada), 195 Harry Walker Parkway N, Newmarket, ON L3Y 7B3, Canada
Penguin Group (NZ), 67 Apollo Drive, Mairangi Bay, Auckland 1310, New Zealand
Typeset in Bembo and Helvetica to an original design by Henry Iles.
Cover concept by Peter Dyer.

Printed and bound in Singapore by SNP Security Printing Pte Ltd

© Rough Guides

No part of this book may be reproduced in any form without permission from the publisher except for the quotation of brief passages in reviews.
312pp includes index

A catalogue record for this book is available from the British Library

ISBN 978-1-85828-154-4

The publishers and authors have done their best to ensure the accuracy and currency of all the information in Walks in London & Southeast England, however, they can accept no responsibility for any loss, injury, or inconvenience sustained by any traveller as a result of information or advice contained in the guide.

1   3   5   7   9   8   6   4   2

Help us update

We've gone to a lot of effort to ensure that the second edition of Walks in London & Southeast England is accurate and up-to-date. However, things change – opening hours are notoriously fickle, restaurants and rooms raise prices or lower standards. If you feel we've got it wrong or left something out, we'd like to know, and if you can remember the address, the price, the phone number, so much the better.

Please send your comments with the subject line "Walks in London & Southeast England Update" to ✉mail@roughguides.com. We'll credit all contributions and send a copy of the next edition (or any other Rough Guide if you prefer) for the very best emails.
Have your questions answered and tell others about your trip at ✆community.roughguides.com

Rough Guide credits

Text editor: Emma Gibbs
Layout: Daniel May and Pradeep Thapliyal
Cartography: Rajesh Mishra
Picture editor: Mark Thomas

Proofreader: Anne Burgot
Production: Rebecca Short
Cover design: Chloë Roberts

The author

Helena Smith comes from Scotland and lives in Hackney, north London. She combines her career as a freelance portrait and travel photographer (⊛helenasmith.co.uk) with writing, editing, and lots and lots of walking.

Acknowledgements

Many thanks to the team at Rough Guides, especially to editor Emma Gibbs for her thoughtful approach and judicious comments, and to Katie Lloyd-Jones for editing the maps.

A hug for Markie, Dan, Angela, Matthew & Lee, Nicky & Alice, Laura, Jason, Phil, Danni, Sean and Bernadette who walked with me, and to Claire Saunders for a bed in Lewes. And a grateful salute to my walk testers for their care and diligence:

Clifton Wilkinson, Sally Schafer, Janine Eberle, Dave Guest & Laura, Natasha Foges, Ed Aves, Chloë Roberts, Di Jarvis, Emma Gibbs (again) and Helen Phillips. Continued gratitude to Gavin Thomas, who edited the book first time around – bahoot bahoot dhanya-waad…

This book is for my family: Grahame, Angela, Matthew and Dan Smith.

Photo credits

All images © Rough Guides except the following:

p.1 The garden of England © Chris Parker/Axiom
p.2 Three walkers on a gate in Sussex
    © Ian Cumming/Axiom
p.4 Footpath sign © Helena Smith
p.5 South Downs © Getty
p.6 Walkers in Silchester © Helena Smith
p.7 Hampton Court Palace © Axiom
p.8 Beer pumps © Alamy
p.8 Inquisitive Cow © Axiom
p.9 Gas Tower on Regents Canal © Helena Smith
p.10 New Forest ponies © Helena Smith
p.11 Fishbourne mosaics © Linda Kennedy
p.12 Afternoon Tea © Rough Guides
p.12 Autumn in Surrey © Peter K Lloyd/Alamy
p.22 Green Man, Parkland way © Helena Smith
p.27 Kenwood House, Hampstead Heath © Axiom
p.68 Epping Forest © Gary Roebuck/Alamy
p.79 Watts Gallery © Helena Smith

p.96 Canterbury Cathedral © Mark Thomas
p.111 Knole House © Mike Booth/Alamy
p.123 Bayham Abbey © Helena Smith
p.133 River Arun view © Helena Smith
p.148 South Downs Way © Travel Ink/Alamy
p.176 Battle Abbey © Krys Bailey/Alamy
p.181 Bosham © Helena Smith
p.189 Ridgeway © Helena Smith
p.215 Windsor Castle and Park © Alamy
p.224 Sign in Silchester © Helena Smith
p.248 Chiltern Hills © Alamy
p.252 Blenheim Palace © David Newton/Alamy
p.265 St Albans, Tim Draper/Rough Guides
p.275 Woburn © Helena Smith
p.284 Canal Boat on the River Stort
    © G Owston/Alamy
p.296 The Cam, Tim Draper/Rough Guides

Maps

'Reproduced by permission of Ordnance Survey on behalf of HMSO.
© Crown Copyright (2009). All rights reserved.
Ordnance Survey Licence number 100020918.'

Selected images from our guidebooks are available for licensing from:
ROUGHGUIDESPICTURES.COM

Index

Maps are marked in colour

1066 Country Walk......... 168

A

accommodation 11
  in Alfriston 153
  in Chilham................... 92
  on The Ridgeway 191
Adam, Robert 290
afternoon tea................... 12
Albury Nowers............... 244
Aldbury 249
Alexandra Palace 24
Alfred the Great 132, 188
Alfriston......................... 153
Alperton 42
Amberley........................ 129
Amersham Old Town 232
Amersham-on-the-Hill..... 231
amphitheatre 227
Amwell........................... 264
Appspond....................... 272
Apsley Guise.................. 273
architecture 7
Arun Valley 133
Arun, the....................... 129
Arundel 134
Arundel Castle 134
Arundel Cathedral 134
Arundel Park.................. 131
Ashburnham 173
Ashridge Estate 247
Audley End 289
Austen, Jane 74
Aylesbury Ring............... 240

B

Balcombe Hill 236
Barnardo, Dr Thomas 53
Bartley Mill 122
Basted 108
bathing ponds,
  Hampstead 26
Battle 175
Battle Abbey 176
Bayeaux Tapestry........... 182
Bayham Abbey............... 124
Beachy Head 157
Beaker Folk 152
Beaulieu Heath 210
Becket, Thomas.............. 97
Bethnal Green................. 51
birds 133
Birling Gap 157

Bishop's Stortford 281
Bladon 250
Blenheim Palace 254
Bloomsbury Group 145
Blowing Stone................ 190
Boer War monument 237
Boreham Street 173
Borough Green 107
Bosham......................... 180
Bottisham Lode.............. 298
Boudicca 269
Boughton Aluph 91
Boughton Lees 90
Box Hill......................... 73
Bramley......................... 228
Bridgewater Canal 248
Bridgewater Monument.... 248
Broadway Market........... 57
Brockenhurst 210
Brooke, Rupert.............. 294
Brown, Capability 252, 289
Brownbread Street......... 173
Browning's Pool 18
Burpham 132
Bushy Park.................... 36
Butler's Retreat............... 64

C

Caesar, Julius 263
Calleva.......................... 227
Cambridge..................... 292
Camden 17
canal boat trips.............. 18
Canbury Gardens............ 35
Canterbury 95
Canterbury Cathedral 96
Canterbury Tales, The ... 88, 95
Canute 182
Capital Ring................ 30, 40
Cathedral of St Alban 267
Catsfield 175
Catuvellauni, The 263
Chalfont St Giles............ 234
Charing 89
Charleston Manor 156
Charleston Farmhouse 145
Chartham Hatch.............. 94
Chase Wood 113
Chaucer, Geoffrey 88
Chelsfield 46
Chequers....................... 238
Chichester Harbour 178
Chiddingstone................ 102
Chilham......................... 91
Chiltern Way 222

Chilterns, The 229
Chinese, Limehouse......... 54
Chingford Plain............... 63
churches
  All Saints,
    Boughton Aluph 91
  All Saints,
    Herstmonceux............ 171
  All Saints, Little Kimble.... 240
  Arundel Cathedral 134
  Canterbury Cathedral 96
  Cathedral of St Alban 267
  Church of St John the
    Baptist, Boldre 209
  Ely Cathedral 302
  Holy Trinity Church,
    Bosham................... 182
  St Andrews, Alfriston 154
  St Helen's,
    Wheathampstead 261
  St James', Shere 83
  St John the Baptist,
    Penshurst.................. 105
  St Laurence's, Combe 255
  St Leonard's,
    South Stoke............... 131
  St Mary the Virgin,
    Battle 177
  St Mary the Virgin,
    Clapham................... 137
  St Mary the Virgin,
    Hambleden 221
  St Mary the Virgin,
    Silchester 221
  St Mary, Chiddingstone ... 103
  St Mary's, Streatley 194
  St Nicholas,
    Brockenhurst 210
  St Nicholas, Pevensey 170
  St Peter's, Firle 146
  St Peter's, Rodmell........ 152
  St Thomas, Goring 194
  St Thomas, Winchelsea ... 166
Churchill, Winston ... 203, 250
Cinq Ports 165
Cissbury Ring 139
Clapham........................ 137
Clapham Wood 138
Clare College................. 296
Clergy House, Alfriston 155
Cliff End 164
Coe Fen 292
Combe 253
Combe Gibbet............... 197
Compton 78
Coombe Hill 236
Court Hill Centre 191
Crouch End 21
Cuckmere Haven 157
Cuckmere River 156
Cuckoo Wood 46, 50

Cudham 49
Cudham Circular
   Walk...................... 47, 50
Cumberland Lodge.......... 215
Cymbeline's Mount 241

D

Darwin, Charles 48
Davenport Wood 223
Debden Water................. 287
Debussy, Claude 157
deer 276
Defoe, Daniel 74
Devil's Dyke................... 262
Didcot Power Station....... 193
Dido Belle....................... 28
Down House.................... 49
Downe 48
Dragon's Hill 190
driving................................ 6
druids 102, 203

E

East Dean...................... 157
East End........................ 256
East Ilsley 193
Eastbourne 158
Ecclesbourne Glen 163
Eden Valley.................... 103
Eel Pie Island.................. 34
Eliot, T.S. 97
Ely 301
Ely Cathedral 302
Epping Forest 63
Eridge Green 116
Eridge Park.................... 116
Eridge Rocks 113
Essex 280

F

Fairlight.......................... 164
Fairlight Glen 163
farm shop........................ 90
Fen Rivers Way 298
fens, draining................. 300
Findon........................... 138
Firle 144
Firle Place 144
Firle Plantation.............. 146
Fishbourne 178
Fishbourne Palace 179
Fitzwilliam Museum 297
forest retreats,
   Epping........................ 66
Foxhill 187

Frant............................. 113
funicular, Hastings........... 163

G

Glynde........................... 144
Gomshall........................ 82
Gorhambury House 270
Gorhambury Manor 271
Gorhambury Park........... 270
Goring 194
Goring-by-Sea 135
Grand Union Canal........... 42
Grant, Duncan 145
Grantchester.................. 295
Grantchester
   Meadows.................. 294
green man legend........... 22
Greensand Way 110
Grim's Ditch 245
Groombridge.................. 117
Groombridge Place 117
Guildford 76
Guildford Cathedral 81

H

Hackney 56
Hackney Marsh................ 59
Ham House 33
Ham Lands 24
Hambleden 221
Hamilton, Arthur............. 238
Hammerton's Ferry 33
Hampstead Heath 25
Hampton Court Palace 35
Hampton Court Park......... 35
Hanborough................... 250
Harbledown..................... 95
Harpenden..................... 259
Harrison's Rocks............. 116
Hastings 161
Hastings Country
   Park 161
Hawksmoor, Nicholas 254
Henley........................... 219
Henley Regatta 219
Hensington Gate,
   Blenheim.................. 252
Herstmonceux 171
Herstmonceux Castle 172
Hertford Union Canal........ 59
Hertfordshire 258
Hertfordshire Way ... 249, 262
High Beach...................... 66
High Rocks 118
High Weald.................... 112
Highdown Hill 136
Highgate.......................... 21
Highgate Wood 23

hill forts................136, 139,
   143, 163, 187, 189, 191,
   197, 247, 283
Hill Hoath 103
Homefield Wood............. 223
Hook Green 125
Horsenden Hill 44

I

Icknield Way 247
Ightham Common 109
Ightham Mote 109
immigration, Limehouse 54
Incombe Hill 246
Inkpen........................... 197
Isabella Plantation.......... 39
Ivinghoe Beacon 246
Ivy Hatch 109

J

Jevington 156
Jevington Jigg 158
Julius Caesar................. 263

K

Keats, John 29, 74
Kenwood House.............. 27
King's College................ 296
King's Wood 91
Kingston Bridge 35
Kintbury 195
Knole Park..................... 111

L

Lea, River 259
Lewes 141, 147
Limehouse Basin 54
Litlington 156
Little Bayham 123
Little Kimble 240
Little Venice 18
London Fields 57
London Zoo 17
Long Man,
   Wilmington 156
Long Walk 215
Loseley Park.................... 80
Loughton Brook............... 67
Loughton Camp.............. 67
Lutyens, Sir Edwin
   Landseer 83
Lymington 206

M

maps 9
Marble Hill House.............. 33
Marlow............................. 223
Mathematical Bridge 295
Meredith, George 74
Mickleham......................... 72
Mickleham Downs 73
Mile End Park.................... 53
Mill End............................ 221
Milton, John 234
Milton's Cottage.............. 234
Monk's House.................. 150
Mortimer 224
mosaics, Roman 256
Mount Caburn 142
Muswell Hill 24

N

Nelson.............................. 75
network railcards 8
New Forest...................... 206
Newport 286
Nomansland 263
Normanton Down
  Barrows...................... 204
North Downs, The 69
North Downs Way 77,
  85, 89
North Leigh Roman
  Villa............................ 256
North Wessex Downs 195

O

oast houses 104
Old Sarum 201
Old Wives Lees 92
Olympics 61
Omega Workshop 146
Oppidim 262
Ordnance Survey 10

P

Pantiles 118
Paradise Fields 45
Paradise Nature
  Reserve 293
parakeets 40
Parkland Walk................... 20
Parliament Hill 25
Parsonage Wood............. 231
Peake, Mervyn................ 132
Pembroke Lodge.............. 41

Penshurst........................ 105
Penshurst Place.............. 105
Perivale Wood 45
Perry Court Farm Shop...... 90
Petersham Nurseries........ 38
Pett Level 164
Pevensey 168
Pevensey Castle 170
Pevensey Levels 170, 171
Pilgrims' Way................... 86
Pilley 208
Pitstone Hill 245
Pitstone Windmill 245
Pitt, William
Potters Crouch............... 272
Prospect of Whitby.......... 55
public transport 6
pubs 8

Q

Queen Elizabeth's Hunting
  Lodge........................... 64
Queen's Wood 23

R

Ragged School Museum ... 53
railcards 8
red kites......................... 222
Regent's Canal 15, 51, 57
Regent's Canal, building of 15
Regent's Park 17
Richmond......................... 31
Richmond Bridge 31
Richmond Hill 41
Richmond Park............... 37
Rickney 171
Ridgeway, The 185, 249
River Lea........................ 259
River Lee Navigation 59
River Stort 281
Rodden Downs 194
Roman remains 11
Romans..........168, 179, 190,
  194, 226–227, 256, 269
rotten borough
Royal Military Canal 164
Roydon Wood 209
Rushy Mead Nature
  Reserve 283

S

Saffron Walden 289
Salisbury 199
Salisbury Plain 201
Savill Garden 217

Sawbridgeworth.............. 284
Scutchamer Knob 193
Segsbury Castle 191
senior railcards 8
Seven Sisters................. 157
Sevenoaks..................... 111
Shere 83
Sidney, Sir Philip 105
Silchester 226
Silent Pool 85
smuggling 158, 165
solstice 203
South Downs
  Way................... 146, 152
South Downs, The........... 127
South Stoke................... 131
Southease 146, 152
Spa Valley Railway 117
St Albans....................... 265
St John's Wood................ 15
St Michael's................... 268
Steven's Crouch............. 175
Stonehenge 199, 204
Stort, River 281
Streatley........................ 194
summer solstice 203
Sussex Border Path......... 122
swimming................ 26, 164

T

tea................................. 12
Teddington Lock 34
Thames Towpath............31,
  55, 219
Thieves' Corner 288
trains 8
Tring 243
Trinity College 296
Triumphal Gate,
  Blenheim................... 252
Tunbridge Wells 112, 118

U

Uffington Castle 189
Upper Woodford............. 202

V

Vale of Aylesbury 241, 245
Vale of the White Horse... 188
Valley Gardens............... 217
Vanbrugh, John 252, 290
Verlamion 270
Vermuyden, Cornelius 300
Verulamium Museum 269
Verulamium Park 268

Victoria Park...................... 58
Virginia Water 217

Wadhurst........................ 119
Walbury.......................... 283
Walbury Hill 197
Walthamstow.................... 60
Walthamstow Market 61
Walthamstow Marsh 60
Warner houses 60
Warningcamp Hill............. 133
Warren Glen 163
Waterbeach.................... 298
Watling Street................. 270

Watts Chapel.................... 79
Watts Gallery 78
Watts, George Frederic...... 78
Watts, Mary...................... 78
Waylands' Smithy 187
Weald, The 99
Weller's Town 104
Wendens Ambo 291
Wendover....................... 236
Wesley, John 166
Westdean Forest............. 156
Westhumble 71
Wheathampstead............. 261
White Horse, Uffington 189
Whitehill Wood............... 114
wildlife 10
William the Conqueror..... 170
Winchelsea...................... 166

Winchelsea, history of 165
windmill, Pitstone............. 245
Windsor Castle 216
Windsor Great Park......... 213
Woburn 277
Woburn Abbey 276
Woburn Safari Park......... 275
Wood's Green 125
Woolf, Virginia......... 145, 150
Worthing 140

Yeltsin, Boris................... 239
young persons railcard........ 8

We're covered. Are you

Travel insurance could be the most important thing you pack!

Rough Guides has teamed up with Columbus to offer readers comprehensive coverage at fantastic value.

Visit our website at **www.roughguides.com/insurance** or call:

COLUMBUS
Travel Insurance

ROUGH GUIDES

- ⓣ UK: 0800 083 9507
- ⓣ Spain: 900 997 149
- ⓣ Australia: 1300 669 999
- ⓣ New Zealand: 0800 55 99 11
- ⓣ Worldwide: +44 870 890 2843
- ⓣ USA, call toll free on: 1 800 749 4922

Please quote our ref: *Rough Guides books*

Cover for over 46 different nationalities and available in 4 different languages.